Writings on Music

Writings on Music
1965–2000

STEVE REICH

Edited with an Introduction
by Paul Hillier

OXFORD
UNIVERSITY PRESS

OXFORD

UNIVERSITY PRESS

Oxford   New York
Auckland   Bangkok   Buenos Aires   Cape Town   Chennai
Dar es Salaam   Delhi   Hong Kong   Istanbul   Karachi   Kolkata
Kuala Lumpur   Madrid   Melbourne   Mexico City   Mumbai   Nairobi
São Paulo   Shanghai   Taipei   Tokyo   Toronto

Copyright © 2002 by Oxford University Press, Inc.

First published in 2002 by Oxford University Press, Inc.
198 Madison Avenue, New York, New York 10016

www.oup.com

First issued as an Oxford University Press paperback, 2004.

Oxford is a registered trademark of Oxford University Press.

Library of Congress Cataloging-in-Publication Data

Reich, Steve, 1936–
[Essays, Selections]
Writings on music, 1965–2000 / Steve Reich ; edited with an introduction by Paul Hillier.
p.   cm.
Includes bibliographical references and index.
ISBN 0-19-511171-0; ISBN 0-19-515115-1 (pbk.)
1. Music—20th century—History and criticism. I. Hillier, Paul. II. Title.
ML60 .R352 2002
789'.9'04—dc21   2001037477

1 3 5 7 9 8 6 4 2

Printed in the United States of America
on acid-free paper

a spouse . . .
associated in a common activity . . .
on the same side in a game or sport . . .
companion in a dance

This book is dedicated to Beryl Korot,
my partner in all senses of the word.

In the introduction to my earlier *Writings about Music* in 1974 I wrote, "You want to hear music that moves you, and if you don't, then you're not really very curious to find out how it was put together." I would stress that again today. Movements, be they serial, aleatoric or minimal, pass away rather quickly, and what we are left with is a small number of musical compositions that musicians want to play and audiences want to hear. I also wrote in 1974, "Books by composers, including this one, are probably of most interest to those already interested in the composer's music." I believe this is still true.

One of the essays from that early book was "Music as a Gradual Process." It seems a lot of younger musicians have read this. I was recently in residence at Dartmouth College, and after playing a tape of my recent (1999) *Triple Quartet* for a composition class, one of the students asked how that piece was an example of music as a gradual process. I told him it was most certainly *not* an example of a gradual process. I explained to him, as I have to several others over the years, that from as early as 1973, if not earlier, I have tried to expand and develop my musical vocabulary. I think anyone who listens first to say, *Piano Phase* (1967) and, then to, perhaps, *Tehillim* (1981) might wonder if the same composer wrote both pieces. My essay written in 1968 was an excellent description of the way I wrote music *up to 1968*. It was a piece of music theory describing, as all music theory does, the past. As Walter Piston says in the introduction to his *Harmony* textbook: "theory must follow practice . . . theory is not a set of directions for composing music . . . It tells not how music will be written in the future, but how music has been written in the past."[1] There were theories, when I was a music student in the late 1950s and early '60s, coming from Boulez and others in Europe, and from Cage and others in America, that purported to tell one how they should compose and think about music. These theories were dutifully put into

---

1. Walter Piston—*Harmony*, W.W. Norton & Co. New York, 1978, Introduction to the First Edition (1941) p. xix.

practice by some for a while, but have now thankfully taken their places in the history of music theory. "Music as a Gradual Process" was not a manifesto for my, or anyone else's, musical future. Following manifestos seems profoundly uninteresting. By contrast, if you find a composer's music of interest, you may find the thinking he has done about that music of interest as well. You also may find it of interest to read how that thinking has developed over the years.

This collection of almost everything I have written since 1965 is arranged chronologically. This was Paul Hillier's idea and I believe it has proved to be a sound one. Whenever we diverged from it, the general train of thought became less clear. Readers can, of course, read whatever interests them, and in any order. Some of the essays are partly technical, most are not.

Paul Hillier is, of course, one of our finest singers and conductors of early music. It was my good fortune to have him take an interest in my music several years ago when he sometimes added *Clapping Music* to his performances of Dufay, Machaut, and others. He saw, quite correctly, some of the formal concerns that are common to my canonic practices and those of medieval and Renaissance music. We finally began corresponding, and in the early 1990s he moved to America and we discussed the idea of working together. This led to his conducting all the premiere performances of my first video opera collaboration with Beryl Korot, *The Cave*. He then had the idea of my setting a text for early music voices which led to *Proverb*, a piece dedicated to him. Finally, it was his idea to edit this collection of my writings. He has contributed not only the chronological ordering of materials, but careful editing of every essay as well as brief 'connective tissue' between essays. Beyond that, he has been a pleasure to work with and a constant source of good advice about every aspect of this book.

Paul brought this book to Maribeth Payne at Oxford University Press and I would like to thank her for setting the wheels in motion for its publication. Her assistant, Maureen Buja, was helpful with getting permissions for photos. Shortly after that, Maribeth left Oxford to take over music books at Norton and her assistant Maureen left also. Ellen Welch took over and was very helpful working with designers for the cover as well as editing text for the bookflaps. I want to particularly thank production editor Robert Milks and copyeditor Laura Lawrie, who did all the closely detailed work necessary to clarify just about everything in this book. It was a pleasure working with them.

I would also like to thank many people who, over the years, have been a source of inspiration, clarification and support. First, to all the members of my ensemble, and particularly to Russell Hartenberger, James Preiss, Bob Becker, Garry Kvistad, Nurit Tilles, Edmund Niemann, Tim Ferchen, Gary Schall, Jay Clayton, Leslie Scott and Virgil Blackwell many of whom were there in the early '70s and continue to this very day. More recently, I have also relied on Thad Wheeler, Frank Cassara, Cheryl Bensman Rowe, Marion Beckenstein, Phillip Bush, Elizabeth Lim Dutton, Todd Reynolds, Lois Martin, Scott Rawls, Jeanne Le Blanc, Steven Ehrenberg, Jeffrey Johnson, James Bassi and the wonderful British vocal group Synergy, founded by Micaela Haslam.

I have been fortunate to have worked with Bob Hurwitz at Nonesuch Records ever since 1984. In an industry not known for its interest in music except as a means for making money, Bob has managed to keep focused on the music he loves and, because his tastes are so wide-ranging, he has managed to keep Nonesuch profitable as well. Together with David Bither, Peter Clancy, Karina Beznicki, Debbie Ferraro and Melanie Zessos they, together with my producer and long time friend Judith Sherman as well as our engineer John Kilgore have made recording, and everything associated with it, a pleasure.

My music publisher, Boosey and Hawkes, have consistently helped to facilitate performances of my music all over the world. While this is the purpose of any music publisher, anyone connected with the field knows that it is the rare publisher indeed who makes this a reality. I would like to thank Tony Fell, David Drew, Janis Susskind, Sylvia Goldstein, Linda Golding, David Huntley (in memoriam) Holly Mentzer, and Jenny Bilfield who, together with all their colleagues and staff, continue to work so effectively on behalf of my music.

My ensemble has performed throughout the world with the help of Andrew Rosner at Allied Artists in London. It has been my pleasure to have worked with him since the early 1970s and he continues to oversee all our activites in Europe. More recently, we have been fortunate to work with Elizabeth Sobol at IMG Artists in New York to represent us in all areas of the world outside of Europe. Still more recently, Howard Stokar has been managing all my individual activites in America.

I would like to acknowledge and thank my teachers William Austin (in memoriam), Hall Overton (in memoriam), Vincent Persichetti (in memorium) and Luciano Berio.

In addition I would like to express my gratitude to photographer, patron and friend Betty Freeman and to many others including, Michael Tilson Thomas, Renée Levine, Sydney (in memoriam) & Frances Lewis, Ellis Freedman, James Kendrick, Ed Townsend, Harvey Lichtenstein, Karen Hopkins, Joe Melillo, Michael Nyman, Wolfgang Becker, Bill Colleran, A.M. Jones (in memoriam) and K. Robert Schwarz (in memoriam).

Finally I thank my wife, Beryl Korot and our son, Ezra. They have made it all possible.

Author's Introduction to *Writings about Music* (1974)

Books by composers, including this one, are probably of most interest to those already interested in the composer's music.

Some of the essays in this book discuss the rhythmic structure of my music since rhythmic structure has a kind of universality that lends itself very naturally to analysis and explanation. Other aspects of the music, like pitch and timbre, while clearly of equal importance, are not mentioned as often because they are more subjective and, perhaps, less suited to explanations and analysis.

The choice of pitch and timbre in my music has always been intuitive. Even the choice of rhythmic structure or system is finally intuitive. In fact, although there is always a system working itself out in my music, there would be no interest in the music if it were merely systematic. You want to hear music that moves you, and if you don't, then you're not really very curious to find out how it was put together. The truth is, musical intuition is at the rock bottom level of everything I've ever done.

Some of the essays, like *Gahu, a Dance of the Ewe Tribe in Ghana* and *The Phase Shifting Pulse Gate—Four Organs; An end to Electronics,* are partly technical. The others are generally not.

I would like to thank Kaspar Koenig[1] for suggesting I put together this collection in the first place. He and Ilka Schellenberg read all the material, offered useful suggestions, and then worked out the details of layout while I was in Halifax, and later in New York, during the summer and fall of 1973.

Steve Reich 3/74

1. Editor of *The Nova Scotia Series—Source Materials of the Contemporary Arts,* in which Reich's book appeared. Other books in the same series documented work by Ludwig Wittgenstein, Claes Oldenburg, and dancer Simone Forti.

This collection of writings by Steve Reich contains all the original essays and program notes from his earlier *Writings about Music* (Halifax, Nova Scotia, 1974), together with a great deal more material (including some interviews) from the intervening quarter-century. Some editorial changes have been made to reduce the instances of repetition and to clarify or indeed correct a few minor points. All of these alterations have been discussed with the composer and the resulting text in all details has been given his final approval. Nevertheless, the reader will find that certain ideas and turns of phrase do recur from time to time, and although the texts have been edited with this partly in mind, I have preferred to err on the side of inclusivity. If too much is taken out, smoothed over, or rationalized, then the distinctive tone of the composer's voice would be distorted.

It becomes clear, as we listen to his music or read his words, that Reich is one of those composers who moves steadily and logically from one work to the next. He holds certain views, is preoccupied with certain concepts and processes, which form the background of his life's work. What impresses is not the glittering variety of disparate moods and discoveries but rather the consistency of an unfolding aesthetic development that yields its own kind of variation and ultimately coheres and stands as a very forthright artistic statement. What also becomes clearer with time is the importance of his Jewish heritage, both as an ancient culture from which his life takes meaning and substance, and as a prism for viewing ongoing events.

In my introduction, I have given a short account of Reich's early life, which leads into the period of his first mature works and at that point is overtaken by the writings themselves. In the course of preparing this book, several people who read the manuscript asked that we extend the biographical account to cover the rest of his life. We have chosen not to do so, because in essence Reich's life since then has been the story of his works and the international tours with his ensemble (and others) to perform them. No doubt some account of that activity could be given, but it was felt to be neither necessary nor appropriate here. Instead, we have assembled a final contribution drawn from a series of conversations in which we discuss his thoughts on composing, younger composers, and *Three Tales* (as we go to press still very much a work in progress).

It has been both a pleasure and an honor to work on this collection of writings and I am grateful to many people for their help and encouragement. Among them I should like particularly to mention Lena-Liis Kiesel, Beryl Korot, Ingram Marshall, and Dean Suzuki.

I have also drawn on two earlier collections of Reich's writings, one published in French: *Ecrits et Entretiens sur la Musique,* ed. Christian Bourgois (Paris, 1981), and one in Italian: *Reich,* ed. Enzo Restagno (Turin, 1994).

My biggest debt, of course, is to Steve Reich himself: for his patience with my tendency to work *adagio* (I don't think this word appears in any of his scores), for his concise and always generous response to my suggestions, and for the opportunity to get to know his music, which I already loved, in greater depth and perspective.

CONTENTS

Writings on Music

Music

In the music of Steve Reich, we encounter one of the most radical renewals of musical language in recent times. Beginning in the mid-1960s with an austerely reductive minimalism, Reich gradually built up a richly nuanced yet instantly recognizable sound, which has influenced a number of contemporary and younger composers without being directly imitated. Although the core of this sound was well established by the mid-1970s, it has continued to evolve and is still in the process of change and development.

But Reich is no revolutionary. His own influences lie all around us and are easily identified—Bartok, Stravinsky, Weill, postwar jazz (especially John Coltrane), African drumming, the Balinese gamelan, Perotin. Like many successful American composers, Reich has built a language that fuses the heightened discourse of serious music with strong elements of the vernacular. His particular strength lies in having done so in a style that is uniquely and recognizably his own. Reich's works constitute a steady evolution of style and technique, and take their own rightful place in the history of modern music, although at no point do they offer that shock to the system, that affront to normality, which we habitually associate with the new when it is "avant-garde"—except, that is, for a brief period of time in the late 1960s and early 1970s.

In works such as *It's Gonna Rain* (1965) and *Come Out* (1966), *Piano Phase* and *Violin Phase* (1967), and *Four Organs* (1970), with their rigorous focus on

All quotes in this introduction, unless otherwise acknowledged, are taken from Restagno, 1994, an English typescript of the original interviews (with Enzo Restagno in New York, January 1994) having been given to me for this purpose by the composer. Here and elsewhere in the book small modifications and corrections to previously published material have been made, in consultation with the composer, without further acknowledgment.

process per se, unalleviated by harmonic variation of any kind, and unsoftened by any change of register or timbre, Reich contributed his most radical contribution to the nonmetaphorical, nonallusive style of art that dominated the 1960s and '70s—and was every bit as "avant-garde" as anything that had preceded it. It is also a fair guess that with these abrupt gestures he would have left his mark on music history even had he stopped composing there and then—although it is the later, more developed and better known works, from *Drumming* (1971) on, that give that mark its full significance.

At that point, Reich was one of a number of composers moving in a broadly similar direction—one characterized at the time (often negatively) as a reaction against the prevailing complexities of total serialism. In place of atonality, constant variation, and rhythmic asymmetry, these composers proposed a steady-state tonality, a fixed rhythmic pulse, and unremitting focus on a single, slowly unfolding pattern that anyone could follow who had a mind to do so.

By the mid-1970s, this direction had earned the epithet "minimalist" (borrowed from art critics and never returned), although the composers most deeply involved were already beginning to produce works of such size and stature that both the label and the dismissiveness with which it was so often applied begin to look mean-spirited and, worse, misguided. A year such as 1976 seems to set the tone: Steve Reich produced his second major work,[1] *Music for 18 Musicians,* and his erstwhile colleague Philip Glass finished *Einstein on the Beach* (in close collaboration with the stage director Robert Wilson); in Europe, meanwhile, Louis Andriessen completed the composition of *De Staat,* Arvo Pärt had created the first pieces in his new tintinnabuli style, and Henryk Górecki composed his Symphony no. 3—*The Symphony of Sorrowful Songs.* The differences between these various composers are as significant ultimately as any similarities, and yet the force with which they cast a simultaneous breath of fresh air across the musical world is unmistakable. Each of them, perhaps surprisingly, is rooted in tradition—but tradition as a sense of the past that embraces the ancient and medieval worlds more readily than the Europe of the Age of Enlightenment, and that follows in the paths of Stravinsky and Bartók rather than Schönberg and Berg among the moderns.

The underlying process in all of Reich's earlier music is the simultaneous repetition in two or more voices of a pattern with self-regulating changes. Normally this consists of a melodic/rhythmic pattern, which at any given moment appears fixed and static but full of energy. Through various techniques a process of gradual change is established, which the ear soon recognizes as the work itself in progress. The unfolding of this process constitutes the work's fulfillment.

Above all, it becomes clear that the changes that we hear emerge from the process itself, are a consequence of that process, and are not arbitrarily imposed from without. Reich's special brilliance lies in making apparently simple melodic/

---

1. The first being *Drumming.*

rhythmic states yield surprising aural ambiguities, so that our sense of a phrase's identity—its beginning and end, or the precise location of its downbeat or principal accents—may suddenly shift as new light is shed on it from within.

This sense of shifting views of the same basic object informs Reich's use of harmony, too, which has evolved directly out of the polyphonic techniques he applies to melodic and rhythmic ideas. All in all, his musical language has been formed in a manner strikingly similar to any one of his earlier works—that is to say, as a gradual process—and, as a result, is profoundly integrated.

The musical process that most closely corresponds to the idea of different views of the same object—which not only permits it but encourages it—is, of course, canon. This, more than any other single device, dominates Reich's musical processes. Whether as strict imitation or in derivative forms (such as voice-exchange or isorhythm), canonic devices permeate the texture of almost every one of Reich's works.[2] This feature links him to composers as far back as Perotin, Machaut, Dufay, Josquin, and, of course, Bach. But the earliest technique used by Reich—phasing—arose directly from his experiments with multiple tape loops, and could hardly have been imagined until the invention of tape and the new opportunities it afforded for manipulating sound.

As Reich has said, phasing is essentially a form of canon using irrational numbers. In his early tapeworks and first instrumental works, a complete pattern is presented at the outset by two players (or tape machines). This is then juxtaposed against itself, as one player moves slightly ahead and therefore out of phase with the other. At first, only minute segments of time separate the two parts, creating the illusion of an acoustic echo. As the disparity between the two parts grows, the aural effect becomes more complex, and eventually this resolves into a clear imitative pattern, once the two parts have achieved a rational degree of separation of one beat or more.

The interlocking of two models of the same pattern at different points produces additionally a series of resultant patterns, which also change as the relationship between the constituent parts changes. In the early works, these resultant patterns, which give the music much of its rich surface texture, are essentially unforeseen and nothing is done with them—they are simply allowed to play out until the next change comes into effect. In later works, such material is specifically emphasized and Reich eventually uses this as a way to generate new melodic entities. This owes much to his earlier manner of working, and yet is open to a more freewheeling, intuitive style of composition.

Another basic rhythmic ingredient in Reich's musical language, in addition to phasing (which he stopped using in 1972), is the use of rhythmic construction—the substitution of beats for rests until a complete pattern is revealed, and then the superimposition of the same process beginning at a different point in the

2. Except *Four Organs*, which uses augmentation—a technique that then remains a basic element of Reich's compositional style.

pattern, or at the same point but on a different beat. *Drumming* is the first work that displays this technique—par excellence—and Reich discusses it in his essay on that work.

Further refinements of these basic ideas continue to produce fresh results throughout Reich's oeuvre; looking back, it seems that each new detail of technique has evolved quite naturally out of the previous work. And if it seems we can find external influences—African drumming, gamelan, medieval organum, Bartók's use of arch form, Janáček's interest in speech melody—in each case Reich reached toward them only after the seed of that particular idea had already been planted in his music, and seems to use them both as confirmation of a direction in which he was already moving and as a springboard for further compositional activity of his own. The development in *Octet* (1979) of melodic construction influenced by Jewish cantillation techniques, for example, is in fact prefigured in earlier works by the use of resultant patterns from phasing to generate short melodic passages.

In the last decade, Reich has turned full circle, scooping up ideas from his earliest works—especially the use of taped speech—and moving into yet another new area of activity that combines familiar concepts but also offers something completely new and unique. He has always preferred the objective "facts to be resolved"[3] to the subjective play of emotion. His choices of topic reflect an interest in social issues, rather than individual drama. His preference is for a documentary account of things rather than fiction. And his approach to a piece of information—historical document, fragment of speech—is to take several looks at it from different points of view. Finally, in *Different Trains* (1988), in *The Cave* (1993), in *City Life* (1995), and now in *Three Tales* (1998–2002), he fuses together two of the strongest elements of his vision: canon and speech-melody—the one essentially repetitive, unified, strictly and even abstractly musical; the other fortuitous, multifarious, corporeal.

Early Life

Although he is thought of as a quintessentially American composer, Steve Reich traces both sides of his family back to central Europe. His paternal grandfather, Ignaz Reich, was born in or near Cracow and emigrated to New York around 1890. There he met his future wife, Anne, who came from a village near Budapest. "I know my grandfather spoke German, Yiddish, Polish, and English. But when I knew him, he only spoke English, and never talked about Europe, only of America, as many immigrants did. They wanted to talk about the new country, and everything else was forgotten."

His mother's family, Sillman, came from Germany and had moved to America considerably earlier, settling in Detroit. During the early 1930s, they moved to Los

---

3. Quoted from "The Desert Music—Text" (no. 27), see p. 126.

Angeles. "Grandfather Mort ran a jewelry store on Hollywood Boulevard, but he was also a piano player and a frustrated vaudevillian, and he encouraged his children to go into show business." Reich's mother, June Carroll, became a singer on Broadway and was also a lyricist. Her greatest successes were the songs "Love Is a Simple Thing" and "Penny Candy," which she sang in the 1952 musical review *New Faces*, produced by her brother Leonard; the show also featured Eartha Kitt.

Reich's father, Leonard, the youngest child of five, studied law and became an attorney. The composer does not know when or how his parents met, but they were married in 1935. He was born in New York City in 1936, but his parents' marriage was soon over. They arranged for divided custody, six months with each of them. As his mother had decided to move back to Los Angeles, this meant that from the age of two until five (school age) he was obliged to cross the country by train twice a year accompanied by his governess, Virginia Mitchell. Not surprisingly, these journeys (four days with a change at Chicago) at such a young age left a lasting impression—as *Different Trains*, the most autobiographical of his works, bears witness.

Primarily, however, throughout his boyhood and youth Reich lived with his father in New York City on the Upper West Side; Virginia remained as governess until he was 10. In 1950, they moved to Larchmont, a suburb just north of the city: "It was '50s America like the Kodak advertisements in Life magazine. . . . I think my father probably thought it was a much healthier environment in which to raise a teenager, but whereas in New York I had been somewhat athletic, in Larchmont I became very reclusive because I had no friends. I had to make new ones and one of them was pianist. We got interested in jazz and I began playing the drums. So I became a composer partly because I had lost all my social contacts when we left New York and went to this place where I knew nobody and investigated my own life."

In fact, Reich had started playing the piano several years earlier, at first just experimenting with fourths and fifths, "playing what I called cowboy songs," then from the age of eight or nine taking lessons: "My father seemed to feel I should. He didn't think it would lead to any trouble—'trouble' meaning that I would be like my mother."

At the age of 14, he had his first exposure to contemporary music, baroque music, and jazz—thanks to a friend's recordings of Stravinsky's *Rite of Spring*, Bach's Fifth Brandenburg Concerto, and 1950s bebop jazz—and also began reading philosophy (Plato's *Republic*). At the same time, he began studying percussion with Roland Kohloff (who later became principal timpanist with the New York Philharmonic). He frequently went into Manhattan to jazz clubs like Birdland, where he heard players such as Bud Powell, Miles Davis, and Kenny Clarke. "Birdland was dark and smoky and romantic—everything that Larchmont was not. Kenny Clarke produced a buoyant, floating sense of time which I think you can hear me trying to imitate in the '70s pieces like *Drumming* and *Music for 18 Musicians*. I also remember hearing Stravinsky conduct in Carnegie Hall around the same time."

In 1953, at the age of 16, Reich entered Cornell University where he majored in philosophy. "My father paid my tuition, while I earned money for food by playing in jazz and dance bands on the weekends." The Austrian philosopher Ludwig Wittgenstein had recently been to Cornell, and made a lasting impression on the philosophy department, particularly through his later work (published in *Philosophical Investigations*). The influence of Wittgenstein's aphoristic style can quite clearly be discerned in Reich's own writings.

Reich also pursued music studies at Cornell. His principal music teacher there was William Austin, who provided encouragement to be a composer at the point when Reich had to decide between a career in music or going to Harvard graduate school to study philosophy. He already knew that music was what he wanted to do but was nervous about making the decision. Against his father's wishes, he returned to New York and began private studies for two years (1957–59) with Hall Overton, a composer and jazz musician who had studied composition with Vincent Persichetti and was also a good friend of Thelonius Monk. They worked on Bartók's *Mikrokosmos,* studying the application of modal counterpoint, which provided Reich with a useful model for working tonally, yet outside the tonic-dominant matrix of the classical tradition, and for exploring the basics of canonic technique. "You learn your modes, learn about canons, and play them. It was very clear teaching: skills.

"The milieu around Overton was very lively. Thelonius Monk was there; Jimmy Raney and Jim Hall, the two jazz guitarists; Mal Waldron, the piano player. All these people were coming in and out of the studio and you'd see them. Downstairs from Overton, there was the famous American photographer, Eugene Smith, who made the photographs during the Spanish Civil War for *Life* magazine. I visited him once and he was absolutely insane, fantastic; his entire studio, every wall, was photographs. Into the photographs were stuck more photographs. He wanted to hear my little string quartet pieces—I think I was visiting Overton after I'd been at Juilliard for a while. I was thrilled to play these, not for another student-composer, but for a real artist. So the ambience around Overton was very positive. Later he was asked to go to Juilliard and he accepted. I remember seeing him then and it was as if his shoulders had begun to sag—the weight of the academy was on his shoulders, and he died shortly thereafter. He was a heavy smoker and a bit of a drinker. A wonderful man, and a very gifted teacher."

In the spring of 1959, Reich entered Juilliard. Here he studied with Persichetti and made analyses of works by Bartok (especially the fourth and fifth Quartets and their arch forms), Schönberg (*Five Pieces for Orchestra* Op. 16 and *Six Little Piano Pieces* Op. 19), and Webern (*Five Pieces for String Quartet* Op. 5)—works that go to the brink of tonality but do not pass beyond it. Studying with someone, however, was not the most important aspect of being at Juilliard. "The most important thing was that I'd write a piece almost every other month and immediately have it played. And this is the good thing about a conservatory. Everybody is a musician. I learned most of my craft there by writing music, having it played, correcting mistakes, taking suggestions from players."

The final piece Reich composed during his Juilliard years was *Music for String Orchestra* (completed in May 1961), a short serial work with strong tonal tendencies in which the row was simply repeated in its original position, without inversions, retrogrades, or transposition. "Basically what I did was regroup [the row]. The first four notes are a chord. The next time around, the first three notes are a melodic fragment. The fourth note then joins the next three. This was actually a kind of thinking that could happen right now, so writing in the twelve-tone style actually was the beginning, in a sense, of the kind of thinking that I continued in my own music. The repetition of the row is not significant enough to say that's the beginning of repetition. But, in fact, that's how I dealt with it and the rhythmic regrouping is, in fact, something that I could see doing now with a limited gamut of tones."[4]

Of the general New York scene at the time, Reich recalls: "I was aware of the painters in particular. I was sometimes down at the Cedar Bar where de Kooning and Feldman were. I was certainly aware of what John Cage was doing (and went to the famous Cage retrospective at Town Hall in 1958), and Boulez, Stockhausen, and Berio. Around that time, Stockhausen gave a lecture at Columbia University and they thought the devil had come to town. In those days, Elliott Carter was still regarded by some Juilliard faculty as part of the lunatic fringe, but I was interested in Carter's use of metric modulation."

By 1961, Reich felt the need to leave New York and moved out to northern California: "Like most people who go to California, I was getting away from something—my family, primarily. I wasn't clear at first whether I would go to UC Berkeley or Mills College (Oakland), but Mills seemed the more interesting place because of Berio.[5]

"Studying with Berio at that time was extremely exciting. Serialism was just then becoming known in this country, and he was a primary member of the team. So being able to analyze Webern with him was very appropriate. . . . At night I used to go the Jazz Workshop where John Coltrane was playing—modal jazz,[6] with a lot of notes and very few changes of harmony. This was the most interesting music for me at that time—by day I was learning about what I did not want to do, but by night I was learning about something that I did want somehow to work into my life. Student composers at that time were writing enormously complicated pieces, but as Mills didn't have an orchestra, they weren't played. You had the feeling that no one was hearing it in their head; no one was playing it on an instrument; it was just paper music. And then at night you see Coltrane playing—he just gets up and plays. So it was at that point that I decided I must play in my own pieces—whatever my limitations, I must become a part of the ensemble. So when I wrote some terrible 12-tone jazz pieces at Mills, the good thing

4. SR interview with Dean Suzuki, May 1984.
5. Berio was a visiting professor at Mills for the academic year 1961–62.
6. The development of modal jazz is discussed in Strickland, 1993, pp. 149–51.

about them was that I put together my own ensemble to play them. It included John Chowning [the computer musician, but trained as a drummer] and Jon Gibson [saxophonist now with Philip Glass], plus trumpet and bass players, and myself playing piano."

His master's thesis was the composition *Three Pieces for Jazz Quintet*—trumpet, alto saxophone, piano, bass, and drums—(completed in 1963). "It was basically 12-tone jazz, the worst thing I've ever written. . . . The idea that you can take the 12-tone system and bring the rhythmic and gestural world of jazz to it is absurd."

Among the works Reich showed Berio was *Music for String Orchestra* written the previous year back in New York. Berio's response was: "If you want to write tonal music, why don't you?"—Reich assured him that he would.

The record library at Mills had old 78s of African music that "I now began listening to with great interest. In 1962 Berio took our class down to Ojai where Gunther Schuller gave a lecture about the history of early jazz. He mentioned a book, *Studies in African Music*, by A. M. Jones. Back in Berkeley I found a copy in the music library and took it home. It was like looking at the blueprint for something completely unknown. Here was a music with repeating patterns (similar to the tape loop material I was beginning to fool around with), which were superimposed so that the downbeats did not coincide."[7]

While still at Mills, however, he began to make new contacts—notably with R. G. Davis, who had formed the San Francisco Mime Troupe. This was a politically committed street theater group[8] that worked out of an old church in San Francisco's Mission District, and for whom, in January 1963, he wrote music to accompany a film. "My first use of tape came when I was making a film track for Robert Nelson, called *The Plastic Haircut*.[9] I took a recording called 'Greatest Moments in Sport,' which was a collage of the voices of Babe Ruth, Jack Dempsey, and other famous American athletes from the past, and to make it more complex I overlaid them on top of themselves, and I got into making tape loops. I began listening to what happens rhythmically when you make shorter and shorter loops—and this was right at about the time when I discovered A. M. Jones's book on African music. I was fascinated with the relationship between what I was hearing in the tape loops and the African use of independent repetition of simultaneous patterns." The spoken materials are clearly audible at the beginning, but as the fragments begin to overlap with greater and greater rapidity, the sounds eventually merge into noise—a precursor of Reich's later tape pieces, although without their more controlled structure and more systematic use of repetition.

During his time at Mills, Reich had had a graduate assistantship and supplemented this modest income by teaching rock 'n' roll to ghetto children in Hunt-

7. See also "Non-Western Music and the Western Composer" (no. 37), p. 147.
8. Neither purely given to mime nor always in the street.
9. See also "First Interview with Michael Nyman" (no. 6), p. 52.

er's Point. After leaving the college, Reich avoided lingering in academia. "I was married at the time and had to make a living, so I took part-time jobs, including driving a taxi and later working in the Post Office."

His association with the San Francisco Mime Troupe continued, and in the fall of 1963 he composed the incidental music for their production of Alfred Jarry's surrealist masterpiece *King Ubu*. The music was scored for clarinet, strummed violin, and kazoo (played through a PG&E traffic cone megaphone). The show's designer was the artist William Wiley, who later designed the LP cover for Reich's first solo disc in the Columbia Masterworks Series.

Reich now formed a new music improvisation group, which included the trumpeter Phil Lesh (later bass player with The Grateful Dead), saxophonist Jon Gibson, keyboard player Tom Constanten (who also later joined The Grateful Dead), violinist George Rey (also a philosopher), and cellist Gwen Watson. For this group, he composed *Pitch Charts*, "using graphic notation derived from Berio's *Tempi Concertati*, but providing a semblance of tonality in that it remained within given pitch groups for periods between cues. The series of boxes that served as markers in the score went so far as to specify the notes to be played, but not so far as to specify the rhythm or manner of their playing."[10] When one player played a note of the next cell, all the performers are to move to the new cell. This piece was first performed at the Community Music School in San Francisco's Mission District and repeated the following year at a San Francisco Mime Troupe concert.

In February 1964, he composed *Music for Two or More Pianos or Piano & Tape* (ex. I-1), in which the influences of Morton Feldman mingled with those of jazz pianist Bill Evans: "It was a series of nine chords in a cycle so that you can play the chord several times, like Morty's 'floating in the air' sound. And a second and third piano would answer all of the chord, or part of the chord, breaking it up freely. And the effect was note upon note in different free rhythms, and timbre upon timbre." The modular structure of this work prefigures Reich's later style, now strongly in the making, and the loosely tonal foundation of the harmonies seems characteristic of his later chordal patterns.

"It was influenced by a hearing of Stockhausen's *Refrain* (1959), which was itself influenced by Feldman's *Four Pianos* (1957). It was also very much influenced by jazz structure (a sequence of chords which form a cycle which can be repeated for as many 'choruses' as you like). It was particularly influenced by the sound of Bill Evans."[11]

Reich continued to experiment with tape: "When I had the job as a taxi driver, I used to put a microphone up where the dome light is inside the cab, and so I could bug the cab. In this way, I gathered a large amount of material out of which

---

10. Strickland, 1993, p. 185.
11. SR, letter to Dean Suzuki, May 1982.

MUSIC for TWO or MORE PIANOS

or
PIANO + TAPE

The nine chords should all be played + in conventional order, as notated. The entire series may be repeated as many times as performers feel appropriate. Chords may be arpeggiated or broken in any way. Performers may remain with any chord for as long as desired, but as soon as any performer moves from one chord to the next, all performers should move on similarly, as soon as possible. Thus, at any given time, all performers will be simultaniously dealing with the same chord. The resulting possibilities of repetition + imitation of single notes, intervals, chords, + melodic fragments may thus be explored in a relatively free rhythmic context.

In addition this piece may be performed by one or more pianos and tape. In this case recordings of the chord series must be made prior to performance by the performer(s) involved. If possible, recordings should be made of the actual piano(s) to be used in performance.

Steve Reich
2/64

Example Intro-1 (*these two pages*). Scores of *Music for Two or More Pianos or Piano and Tape*. COPYRIGHT © 1987 BY HENDON MUSIC, INC., A BOOSEY & HAWKES COMPANY. REPRINTED BY PERMISSION.

I made a short collage piece called *Livelihood.*" As Dean Suzuki describes it: "About 10 hours of [taped material] were distilled into a three-minute, fast-cut, musique concrète collage. . . . Textual cognition is of primary importance, thus the voices are clearly heard and understood. Each section of the work repeats words, phrases, or sounds (names of specific destinations, the car door slamming

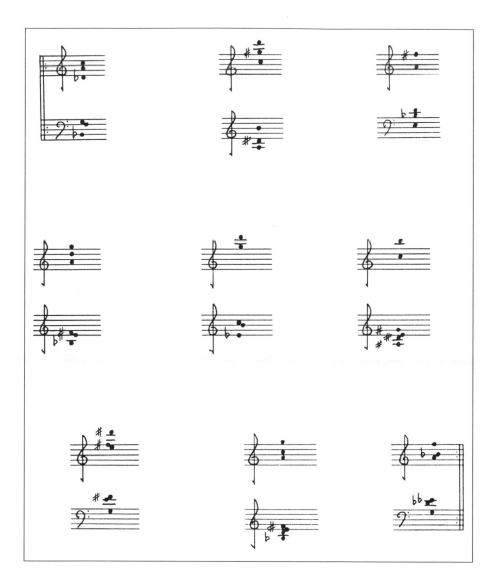

shut, sirens, words of thanks), though they are spoken by different persons and recorded at different times, thus not literal repetitions. Traffic noises and other sounds tend to function as an accompaniment to the voices."[12]

Reich was now working on the fringes of San Francisco's alternative theater and art scene and, as was earlier the case in New York (and would be so again), the art world continued to hold at least as much fascination for him as the music

12. Dean Suzuki, "Minimal Music: Its Evolution as Seen in the Works of Philip Glass, Steve Reich, Terry Riley, and LaMonte Young and Its Relation to the Visual Arts," unpublished doctoral dissertation, University of Southern California, Los Angeles, 1991, p. 445.

world. But another, purely musical current was swimming toward him—the music of Terry Riley and LaMonte Young, which would instigate the style known as "minimalism." Much has already been written about the genesis of this style, and the question of influences and chronologies has been well documented (most recently in Potter, 2000). LaMonte Young, generally acknowleged as the first minimalist, had been a graduate student at UC Berkeley in the late 1950s, where he had produced a number of conceptual pieces that rivaled John Cage in their radical displacement of what constituted a piece of music. But Young's most influential work lay in the exploration and use of held tones of massively long duration: most famously from this period the String Trio completed in 1958.

The significance of Young's early work may have been acknowledged in print but can scarcely be said, even now, to have become part of most musicians' actual experience. Its importance lies in the altered perception of time it propagates, which is one of the fundamental characteristics of minimal music—based not just on longevity but on slow, almost static harmonic change, a sense of rotation or circular development, rather than the linearity of more conventional Western music, and a nonfunctional use of harmony (tonal or otherwise).

Terry Riley, who knew Young in the late 1950s, later collaborated with him on numerous projects while both were living in New York. They were both active to varying degrees on the fringes of Fluxus, and they later both studied Indian raga singing under Pandit Pran Nath. Riley's decisive contribution to what would soon be called minimalism was the use of repetitive modules or clusters of melodic figures, and diatonic tonality.

In the early fall of 1964, Reich's group was performing at the San Francisco Mime Troupe (the program included various improvisations and *Pitch Charts*). Terry Riley was in the audience, having just returned from Europe, and the two composers later got to know each other and discuss each other's music. As Riley recalls: "I showed him *In C*, which I was working on, and he was really enthusiastic for the project."[13] Reich helped form the ensemble rehearsing *In C* (the work which was to become the signature piece of minimalist music). *In C* was premiered in November 1964 at the San Francisco Tape Center,[14] and there can be no doubt that the experience of meeting Riley and becoming involved in this particular work at this particular time had a radical effect on the development of Reich's own music, helping to crystallize his own work at an especially fortuitous moment. During rehearsals of *In C*, Reich contributed the idea of adding a pulse to help keep the musicians together, and the work's modular structure and free juxtaposition of multiple downbeats must have blended well with his own inclinations at the time.

Meanwhile, a filmmaker friend had told Reich about an extraordinary black preacher, Brother Walter, who could be heard every Sunday in San Francisco's

---

13. Quoted in Strickland, 1991, p. 114.
14. Founded in 1961 by Ramón Sender and Morton Subotnick. It was located first on Jones Street, then for four years at Divisadero Street, where there was a hall that could seat 150. It later moved to Mills College under the direction of Pauline Oliveros, who also composed for the S. F. Mime Troupe.

Union Square. He suggested Reich go down and record the preacher, as there was some talk of making a film about him. Reich had already invested in a portable tape machine and a shotgun microphone (then a new thing), and the idea intrigued him enough to go and make the recording, although at the time he had no clear idea of what he might do with the material. It was only a couple of months later that he became interested in manipulating the tape and experimenting with loops. By January 1965, he had composed a whole piece based entirely on the recording of Brother Walter's impassioned sermon, and focusing in on the words "It's gonna rain." The first section of this work[15] was presented at a San Francisco Tape Center concert the same month, together with *Music for Two or More Pianos or Piano and Tape* and *Livelihood*.

Later in 1965, he composed music to accompany a 10-minute film, *Oh Dem Watermelons* by Robert Nelson. Reich used the ending of Stephen Foster's *Massa's in de Cold Cold Ground* and a fragment of his *Oh Dem Watermelons* as part of the Mime Troupe's "minstrel show," a satire on the racial stereotypes implicit both in Foster's music and the original minstrel shows.

Two descriptions of this piece have been published. R. G. Davis, the troupe's director, writes: "Bob Nelson, Landau and I, with members of the troupe, conceived, wrote and played in a movie about the life and death of a watermelon or 30 ways of doing in or getting done in by a symbol. The film, 'Oh, Dem Watermelons,' won award after award for its rapid-fire hysterical insight. In the production, the live sound was made by the cast, who chanted a Steve Reich repetitive round, as the audience viewed the film. 'Watermelon, wa-ter-mel-on-WATERMELON, etc.' The repetition of sound increased as the film came to a close, and the watermelon started chasing people up streets and up steps."[16]

Actor Peter Coyote, who was part of the Mime Troupe at the time, describes it thus: "Near the end of the first act, a 10-minute film played in which a watermelon is kicked, stabbed, hacked, run over, disemboweled, and dropped from high windows. It eventually reassembles its parts and drives away its tormentors. The soundtrack, written by avant-garde composer Steve Reich . . . was performed live by the company. Three tiers of minstrels seated stage right of the screen sang . . . a four-note round. . . . The effect was hypnotic, deconstructing the word *watermelon* into a shimmer of rhythms."[17]

This appears to have been Reich's last association with the Mime Troupe.[18] By 1965, the hippie scene so closely identified with San Francisco was beginning to warm up, but for Reich this was the world of a slightly younger generation and something for which he had little sympathy. "I was not happy in San Francisco. I

---

15. He thought the second part might be considered too oppressive.

16. R. G. Davis, *The San Francisco Mime Troupe: The First Ten Years* p. 62.

17. Peter Coyote, *Sleeping Where I Fall*, p. 43.

18. In a list of Mime Troupe productions (R. G. Davis, 1975) Reich is credited as composer on six occasions:

December 1962–January 1963   *Plastic Haircut,* film by Robert Nelson, Bill Wiley, Robert Hudson, R. G. Davis, Judy Rosenberg; sound by Steve Reich.

felt I could not do there what I needed to do. There was also a very restricted performance situation at the time—basically, the people I was in touch with were about all there was going to be—there wasn't the pool of freelance musicians that you find in New York City. And when Phil Lesh started with the Grateful Dead I wasn't about to follow him in that direction. It seemed a good time to move on."

In September 1965, Reich moved back to New York City and began looking for somewhere to live. He found a place on Duane Street in Tribeca and has been living in the same neighborhood ever since.

Reich continued to work with Jon Gibson (who also had moved from California to New York) and reestablished contact with Art Murphy, a composer and pianist friend from Juilliard. In 1966, he composed *Reed Phase* and also a new tapework again using recorded speech (*Come Out*). These were followed in 1967 by *Piano Phase, Melodica, Violin Phase, My Name Is,* and a conceptual piece, *Slow Motion Sound.* During 1968, Reich summed up what he had learned so far in the essay *Music as a Gradual Process,* a collection of aphoristic observations and ideas that still constitutes his single most influential written statement.

Throughout the late '60s, Reich was an active participant in New York's avant garde, a term that embraced not only different art disciplines but also a number of artists who were active in more than one field, even if later their reputations were consolidated in just one. Experimental film and dance were especially fertile areas of interactive creativity, and among those involved were people such as Michael Snow, Bruce Nauman, Meredith Monk, Richard Serra, Robert Morris, Sol LeWitt, and Laura Dean.

During 1967, Reich gave three concerts at the Park Place Gallery, the second of which was attended by Philip Glass. Glass and Reich had known each other at Juilliard but had not been close. Now they struck up a friendship and began to work together. More concerts followed, typically at Art Museum venues such as the Whitney, the Guggenheim, and the Walker Art Center in Minneapolis, as well as informally in the lofts of New York's downtown art world. Eventually the first European tour was arranged—just three concerts in 1971. It was shortly after this tour that Reich and Glass parted company and their group divided up between them. The reason for the split between these two most successful composers of the minimalist school concerns the question of influence. Just as Reich has acknowledged the influence of Riley's music, so he believes that Glass should similarly acknowledge the influence of Reich's music. In his book on the minimalists, Schwarz writes, "And so began one of the great rivalries in contemporary music. Reich claims that Glass has deliberately obscured the degree to which his

---

August 15–September 2, 1963   San Francisco Mime Troupe presents *Ruzzante's Maneuvers,* by Milton Savage at Capp St. Studio after premiere fiasco at the San Francisco Museum of Art; produced and directed by R. G. Davis . . . music by Steven Reich and William Spencer.

December 11–29, 1963   *Ubu King* by Alfred Jarry; directed by R. G. Davis . . . sets, props and costumes by William Wiley; music composed by Steve Reich; film by Robert Nelson.

February 27, 1964   *Event III (Coffee Break);* projections by Elias Romero; sound by Steve Reich and Phil Lesh; movement by R. G. Davis and Fumi Spencer.

new minimalist language was indebted to Reich," and concludes, "Ultimately, however, the proof lies in the music. And its chronology would seem to support Reich's point of view." In support of this view, Reich has a manuscript of an early Glass piece called *Two Pages for Steve Reich*—which was subsequently published without the dedication.[19]

Until about 1972, Reich still found it necessary to support himself by means other than composing: "Phil Glass and I had a moving company—'Chelsea Light Moving'—and I was a part-time social worker too. I taught an electronic music class at the New School and also at the School for Visual Arts, both for a couple of years in the late '60s."[20] He also found work as a tape editor for recordings and as a freelance sound engineer in the film industry, both of which provided useful professional experience in areas that would be directly related to his work as a composer. It was only in 1972, after the success of *Drumming* and with further invitations to tour in Europe, that Reich began to support himself entirely from composing and performing his own music.

In 1974, Reich met Beryl Korot, who would become his wife in 1976. He also turned toward his roots in Judaism. Korot, born in New York in 1945, was an artist interested in the use of video (including the use of multichannel installations) to create documentary works with social content, but she also worked at weaving—one of the most ancient of technologies—and created works that fused the influences of these two very different media (including the invention of a personal system of abstract calligraphy).

Reich now started to learn biblical Hebrew, and this in turn led him to discover the subject of Jewish cantillation, in which he became so interested that he also took a brief course of study with a New York cantor. In 1977, he and Beryl traveled to Israel to record chanting of the first five verses of Genesis by cantors representing different Middle Eastern sephardic traditions. This short two-week trip would have an influence on his subsequent technical development as a composer. Eventually he and his wife would also collaborate artistically on projects that, with hindsight, we can see forming at this time—further trips to Israel, the recording of cantors, the use of video, would all be fused together in *The Cave*.

Reich has remained a New Yorker, but he and his family (their son, Ezra, was born in 1978) now divide their time between an apartment in New York City and a house in Vermont. Reich's work as a composer centered around the ensemble that bears his name throughout his earlier years. By now, the vast majority of per-

July 24, 1964–March 1965   *Tartuffe,* adapted from Moliere's play by Richard Sassoon; directed by R. G. Davis and Nina Serrano Landau . . . music by Steve Reich.

June 17, 1965   Bill Graham presents the S.F. Mime Troupe in *A Minstrel Show* or *Civil Rights in a Cracker Barrel;* written by Saul Landau and R. G. Davis from original, traditional, and improvised material; directed by R. G. Davis; movie (*O Dem Watermelons*) filmed and edited by Robert Nelson; music by Steve Reich.

19. This is discussed further in no. 65; see pp. 234–35. See also Schwartz, 1996, pp. 118–23, and Alburger, 1997, pp. 13–15.

20. Conversation with the editor, 1998.

formances of his work are by other ensembles throughout the world. Nevertheless he is proud to have maintained an active role as a touring musician, and still tours frequently (mostly in Europe) as part of the process of earning his livelihood. The group he tours with are mostly old friends—some have been with Reich for over 20 years. Their role in administering to the creation of Reich's earlier works is significant (as some of the writings in this book will testify). Of course, Reich would anyway have composed as he composes, and other ensembles have performed his music with great distinction, but it is they who have given him invaluable support as a kind of living workshop and provided him with consistently expert performances.

Finally, based on personal observation and experience, here are a few comments about the performance of Reich's music.

Reich has composed for ensembles of very different sizes, although most typically for groups ranging from six to about a dozen or so players and singers. These smaller formations function as chamber ensembles. Some of the larger works, of course, require a conductor, although basically only to coordinate things and give cues. A conventional maestro is not needed for expression or interpretation, and indeed such an approach would simply be out of place. In this respect, the conductor becomes more like the director in baroque music (often the lead continuo player). In both kinds of music very often there is no separate conductor: instead, one of the players may function as a leader, like the master drummer in African music.

In rehearsal, apart from the mastering of individual technicalities that simply require adequate private practice, a few basic procedures seem to be necessary. The interlocking rhythms need to be practiced both together and separately, and at first below performance tempo. Although the music may strike the listener as being full of short notes, it is important to give full written length to all the notes. Many of the works require amplification, and a skilled and musically sensitive sound engineer is needed to create a clear and well-balanced ensemble sound and to monitor it carefully throughout the performance. (On tour, when not needed on stage, Reich usually shares the role of sound engineer with his technician.) Singers will need to learn how to work with a microphone; although jazz singers usually have plenty of microphone experience, more classically trained singers (including those with early music experience) do not. Reich's music may often make listeners want to dance or at least move along with it, but the players in Reich's ensemble do not betray any such impulse—they stand alert with only their hands moving, while their bodies are very centered and without tension. While this is probably part of the training of any good percussion player, it is also a useful goal for anyone who performs fast music with complex rhythmical patterns.

Reich's music has always made considerable demands on its performers. There is no call or indeed opportunity for outward display or other personal kinds of audience "communication." It is the music that makes contact with the audience. The players may provide an interesting spectacle, but they are—have to be—absorbed in what they are doing. There is virtuosity, but it is turned inward, onto the music itself.

Much of the material in sections 1, 2, 4, 5, 7, 8, 9, 10, and 11 was originally written as program notes for concerts and recordings during the late 1960s. Reich then reworked the material as he was preparing it for his 1974 *Writings*. In consultation with the composer, some of this material has been slightly altered for this book. Additional sources are noted below.

It's Gonna Rain (1965)

Late in 1964, I recorded a tape in Union Square in San Francisco of a black preacher, Brother Walter, preaching about the Flood. I was extremely impressed with the melodic quality of his speech, which seemed to be on the verge of singing. Early in 1965, I began making tape loops of his voice, which made the musical quality of his speech emerge even more strongly. This is not to say that the meaning of his words on the loop, "it's gonna rain," were forgotten or obliterated. The incessant repetition intensified their meaning and their melody at one and the same time.

By using recorded speech as a source of electronic or tape music, speech-melody and meaning are presented as they naturally occur. It is quite different from setting words to music where one has to fit a number of syllables to a number of notes, and decide what their melodic relation will be. In speech, questions of how many notes to a syllable, or what their melody will be, do not arise; the speech just comes out. Instead of setting words to music, I simply chose the exact segments of recorded speech I was intuitively drawn to as musical material. My original interest in electronic music was the possibility of working with recorded speech.

During the early '60s, I was interested in the poetry of William Carlos Williams, Charles Olsen, and Robert Creeley, and tried, from time to time, to set their poems to music, always without success. The failure was due to the fact that this poetry is rooted in American speech rhythms, and to "set" poems like this to music with a fixed meter is to destroy that speech quality. (Later, in 1984, I was to succeed at last with Williams in *The Desert Music* by using flexible, constantly changing meters.) Using actual recordings of speech for tape pieces was my solution, at that time, to the problem of how to make vocal music.

I remember it seemed disappointing that tape music, or musique concrète as it was called, usually presented sounds that could not easily be recognized, when what seemed interesting to me was that a tape recorder recorded real sounds like speech, as a motion picture camera records real images. If one could present that speech without altering its pitch or timbre, one would keep the original emotional power that speech has while intensifying its melody *and* meaning through repetition and rhythm.

Constant repetition through tape loops produces just such a rhythmic intensification. The idea of using constant repetition partially grew out of working with tape loops since 1963, but mainly through helping Terry Riley put together the first performance, in 1964, of his *In C*, where many different repeating patterns were combined simultaneously. My problem was then to find some *new* way of working with repetition as a musical technique. My first thought was to play one loop *against itself* in some particular relationship, since some of my previous pieces had dealt with two or more identical instruments playing the same notes against each other. In the process of trying to line up two identical tape loops in unison in some particular relationship, I discovered that the most interesting music of all was made by simply lining the loops up in unison, and letting them slowly shift out of phase with each other. As I listened to this gradual phase shifting process, I began to realize that it was an extraordinary form of musical structure. This process struck me as a way of going through a number of relationships between two identities without ever having any transitions. It was a seamless, uninterrupted musical process.

In retrospect, I understand the process of gradually shifting phase relationships between two or more identical repeating patterns as an extension of the idea of infinite canon or round. Two or more identical melodies are played with one starting after the other, as in traditional rounds, but in the phase shifting process the melodies are usually much shorter repeating patterns, and the time interval between one melodic pattern and its imitation(s), instead of being fixed, is variable. Nevertheless, that this new process bears a close family resemblance to the thirteenth century musical idea of round* seems to give it some depth. Good new ideas generally turn out to be old.

The first part of the tape piece *It's Gonna Rain,* completed in January 1965, is a literal embodiment of this process. Two loops are lined up in unison and then gradually move completely out of phase with each other, and then back into unison. The experience of that musical process is, above all else, impersonal; *it* just goes *its* way. Another aspect is its precision; there is nothing left to chance whatsoever. Once the process has been set up it inexorably works itself out.

I discovered the phasing process by accident. I had two identical loops of Brother Walter saying "It's gonna rain," and I was playing with two inexpensive tape

---

*Or rota [ed.].

recorders—one jack of my stereo headphones plugged into machine A, the other into machine B. I had intended to make a specific relationship: "It's gonna" on one loop against "rain" on the other. Instead, the two machines happened to be lined up in unison and one of them gradually started to get ahead of the other. The sensation I had in my head was that the sound moved over to my left ear, down to my left shoulder, down my left arm, down my leg, out across the floor to the left, and finally began to reverberate and shake and become the sound I was looking for—"It's gonna/It's gonna rain/rain"—and then it started going the other way and came back together in the center of my head. When I heard that, I realized it was more interesting than any one particular relationship, because it was the process (of gradually passing through all the canonic relationships) making an entire piece, and not just a moment in time.

Black Pentecostal preaching hovers between speaking and singing. The phasing process intensifies this—taking one little phrase, the vowel pitches, and the consonantal noises that go with them. As I recorded Brother Walter, a pigeon took off near the microphone, and it sounds like a beating drum. So you've got a kind of drum beat, a low rumble from the traffic going in Union Square, and then Brother Walter's words—all of this going against itself at a constantly varying time rate. As you listen to the result, you seem to hear all kinds of words and sounds that you've heard before, and a lot of psychoacoustic fragments that your brain organizes in different ways, and this will vary from person to person. All music to some degree invites people to bring their own emotional life to it. My early pieces do that in an extreme form, but paradoxically they do so through a very rigid process, and it's precisely the impersonality of that process that invites this very engaged psychological reaction.

I recorded Brother Walter in 1964; this was in San Francisco shortly after the Cuban missile crisis, and I thought we might be going up in so much radioactive smoke. With that hovering in the background and this preacher laying it down about the Flood and Noah, it really had a lot of resonance. So I wanted people to hear the words; I didn't wanted to disguise them (as tends to happen in musique concrète). Personally, at that time, I was going through a divorce, and the piece is expressive of an extremely dark mood. The second part of the work took Brother Walter's words about people knocking on the door of the ark—"but it was sealed by the hand of G-d"—and the sentence *doesn't* reconstruct and come back together. It goes further and further out of phase until it is reduced to noise. The emotional feeling is that you're going through the cataclysm, you're experiencing what it's like to have everything dissolve.

Using the voice of individual speakers is not like setting a text—it's setting a human being. A human being is personified by his or her voice. If you record me, my cadences, the way I speak are just as much me as any photograph of me. When other people listen to that they feel a persona present. When that persona begins to spread and multiply and come apart, as it does in *It's Gonna Rain*, there's a very strong identification of a human being going through this uncommon magic.

Come Out (1966)

Late in 1965, I moved back to New York, and in 1966 composed two more tape pieces, *Come Out* and *Melodica*. *Come Out* was essentially a refinement of *Its Gonna Rain* both in choice of speech source, and in the exact working out of the phase shifting process.

Come Out was originally part of a benefit concert presented at Town Hall in New York City for the retrial, with lawyers of their own choosing, of the six boys arrested for murder during the Harlem riots of 1964. The voice is that of Daniel Hamm, now acquitted and then 19, describing a beating he took in Harlem's 28th precinct police station. The police were about to take the boys out to be "cleaned up" and were only taking those that were visibly bleeding. Since Hamm had no actual open bleeding, he proceeded to open a bruise on his leg so that he would be taken to hospital. "I had to like open the bruise up and let some of the bruise blood come out to show them."

Come Out is composed of a single loop recorded on both channels. First the loop is in unison with itself. As it begins to go out of phase, a slowly increasing reverberation is heard. This gradually passes into a canon or round for two voices, then four voices and finally eight.

Melodica (1966)

Melodica (see ex. 1-1) is interesting in two respects. First, it has almost exactly the same rhythmic structure as *Come Out*. The two pieces listened to one after the other are an example of how one rhythmic process can be realized in different sounds to produce different pieces of music. Second, I dreamed the melodic pattern, woke up on May 22, 1966, and realized the piece with the melodica (a toy instrument) and tape loops in one day.

Piano Phase (1967)

Shortly after *Melodica* was completed, I began to think about writing some live music. *Melodica*, which turned out to be the last purely tape piece I made, was composed of musical pitches (as opposed to speech) manipulated with tape loops. It felt like a transition from tape music to instrumental music. Unfortunately, it seemed to me at the time impossible for two human beings to perform that gradual phase shifting process, since the process was discovered with, and was indigenous to, machines. On the other hand, I could think of nothing else to do with live musicians that would be as interesting as the phasing process. Finally, late in 1966, I recorded a short repeating melodic pattern played on the piano, made a tape loop of that pattern, and then tried to play against the loop myself, exactly as if I were a second tape recorder. I found, to my surprise, that while I lacked the perfection of the machine, I could give a fair approximation of it while

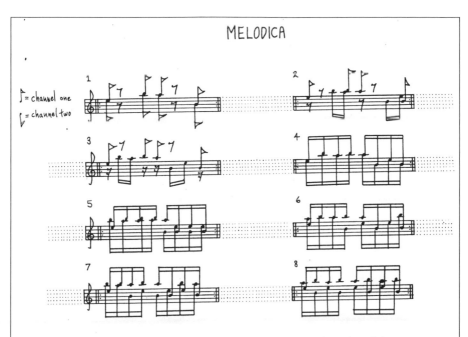

The music exists on magnetic tape. The only source recorded is a loop of the composer playing the original figure (at 1 above) on the Melodica. This loop is first recorded on channel one and is then recorded on channel two in unison with the first channel as shown at 1 above. The dotted lines indicate the gradual shift of phase as channel two begins to slowly move ahead of channel one. Thus at 2 above channel two has moved a sixteenth ahead of the first channel, and at 3, an eighth ahead. Between 3 and 4 there occurs the only splice in the tape as the combination of channels one and two (as they appear at 3) is looped and recorded on both channels. To begin with (at 4 above) both channels are in unison and thus there is no rhythmic change heard between 3 and 4. Then, as before, channel two begins to gradually move ahead and out of phase with channel one. By 5 it is a sixteenth ahead, at 6 an eighth ahead, at 7 a dotted eighth, and finally at 8 a quarter ahead. This last relationship is held steadily for more than 2½ minutes to permit the listener to examine the sound in detail without any phase shift to occupy his attention.

Melodica was conceived and realized in one day, May 22, 1966.

Steve Reich

Example 1-1. Score of *Melodica*. COPYRIGHT © 1986 BY HENDON MUSIC, INC., A BOOSEY & HAWKES COMPANY. REPRINTED BY PERMISSION.

enjoying a new and extremely satisfying way of playing that was both completely worked out beforehand, and yet free of actually reading notation, allowing me to become totally absorbed in listening while playing.

In the next few months, Arthur Murphy, a musician friend, and I, both working in our homes, experimented with the performance of this phase shifting process using piano and tape loops. Early in 1967, we finally had the opportunity to play together on two pianos and found, to our delight, that we could perform this process without mechanical aid of any kind.

While this piece, *Piano Phase,* was later completely written out in musical notation with dotted lines between one bar and the next to indicate the gradual phase shifting, it was not necessary for us to read this notation while we played, nor is it necessary for any other musicians who play the piece. The musical material in *Piano Phase* (see ex. 1-2) is simply a number of repeating melodic patterns that may be learned and memorized in several minutes. The score then shows that two musicians begin in unison playing the same pattern over and over again and that while one of them stays put, the other gradually increases tempo so as to slowly move one beat ahead of the other.

This process is repeated until both players are back in unison, at which point the pattern is changed and the phasing process begins again. The piece is divided into three sections marked off by changes of notes and pattern length. The first is twelve beats in B minor, the second eight beats forming an apparent E dominant chord, and the last is four beats in A (probably major but lacking a stated third degree).

To perform the piece, one learns the musical material and puts the score aside because it is no longer necessary, it would only be a distraction. What you have to do to play the piece is to listen carefully in order to hear if you've moved one beat ahead, or if you've moved two by mistake, or if you've tried to move ahead but have instead drifted back to where you started. Both players listen closely and try to perform the musical process over and over again until they can do it well. Everything is worked out, there is no improvisation whatever, but the psychology of performance, what really happens when you play, is total involvement with the sound: total sensuous-intellectual involvement.

Looking back on the tape pieces that preceded *Piano Phase,* I see that they were, on the one hand, realizations of an idea that was indigenous to machines, and, on the other hand, the gateway to some instrumental music that I would never have come to by listening to any other Western, or for that matter non-Western, music. The question may then arise as to what it is like to imitate a machine while playing live music. I believe there are human activities that might be called "imitating machines," but that are, in reality, simply controlling your mind and body very carefully as in yoga breathing exercises. This kind of activity turns out to be very useful physically and psychologically, as it focuses the mind to a fine point.

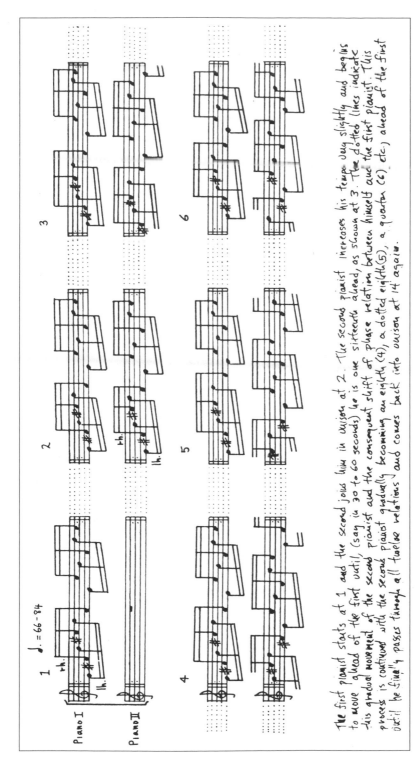

The first pianist starts at 1 and the second joins him in unison at 2. The second pianist increases his tempo very slightly and begins to move ahead of the first until, (say in 30 to 60 seconds) he is one sixteenth ahead, as shown at 3. The dotted lines indicate this gradual movement of the second pianist and the consequent shift of phase relation between himself and the first pianist. This process is continued with the second pianist gradually becoming an eighth (4), a dotted eighth (5), a quarter (6) etc.) ahead of the first until he "lines" q passes through all twelve relations and comes back into unison at 14 again.

Example 1-2. *Piano Phase*, bars 1–6.

Violin Phase (1967)

In October 1967, I completed *Violin Phase* for either violin and three channels of tape, or, preferably, four violins. This piece was basically an expansion and refinement of *Piano Phase* in two ways. First, there were four voices moving against each other instead of only two, as in *Piano Phase;* second, and perhaps more important, I became clearly aware of the many melodic patterns resulting from the combination of two or more identical instruments playing the same repeating pattern one or more beats out of phase with each other.

As one listens to the repetition of the several violins, one may hear first the lower tones forming one or several patterns, then the higher notes are noticed forming another, then the notes in the middle may attach themselves to the lower tones to form still another. All these patterns are really there; they are created by the interlocking of two, three, or four violins all playing the same repeating pattern out of phase with each other. Since it is the attention of the listener that will largely determine which particular resulting pattern he or she will hear at any one moment, these patterns can be understood as psychoacoustic by-products of the repetition and phase-shifting. When I say there is more in my music than what I put there, I primarily mean these resulting patterns.

Some of these resulting patterns are more noticeable than others, or become noticeable once they are pointed out. This pointing-out process is accomplished musically by doubling one of these preexistent patterns with the same instrument (see ex. 1-3). The pattern is played very softly, and then gradually the volume is increased so that it slowly rises to the surface of the music and then, by lowering the volume, gradually sinks back into the overall texture while remaining audible. The listener thus becomes aware of one pattern in the music that may open his ear to another, and another, all sounding simultaneously in the ongoing overall texture.

Slow Motion Sound (1967)

Slow Motion Sound (see ex. 1-4) has remained a concept on paper because it was technologically impossible to realize. The basic idea was to take a tape loop, probably of speech, and ever so gradually slow it down to enormous length *without lowering its pitch*. In effect, it would have been like the true synchronous soundtrack to a film loop gradually presented in slower and slower motion.[1]

Slow Motion Sound—score first published in Interfunktionen, number 9, Heubach Verlag, Cologne, 1972. Score with explanatory notes first published in Soundings, number 7–8, Davis, California, Winter 1973–74.

1. Now, some 30 years later, it is possible. See discussion of *Three Tales* in "Steve Reich in Conversation with Paul Hillier," (no. 65), p. 239.

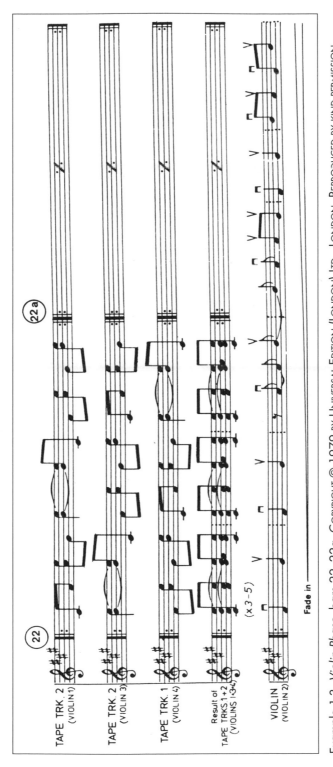

Example 1-3. *Violin Phase*, bars 22–22a. Copyright © 1979 by Universal Edition (London) Ltd., London. Reproduced by kind permission.

SLOW MOTION SOUND

Very gradually slow down a recorded sound to many times its
original length without changing its frequency or spectrum
at all.

Steve Reich   9/67

Example 1-4. *Slow Motion Sound.* © 1967 by Steve Reich.

The roots of this idea date from 1963 when I first became interested in experimental films, and began looking at film as analog to tape. Extreme slow motion
seemed particularly interesting, since it allowed one to see minute details that
were normally impossible to observe. The real moving image was left intact with
only its tempo slowed down.

Experiments with rotating head tape recorders, digital analysis and synthesis
of speech, and vocorders all proved unable to produce the gradual yet enormous

elongation, to factors of 64 or more times original length, together with high-fidelity speech reproduction, which were both necessary for musical results.

The possibility of a live performer trying to speak incredibly slowly did not interest me since it would be impossible, in that way, to produce the same results as normal speech, recorded, then slowed down.

I was able to experiment with a tape loop of a little African girl learning English by rote from an African lady school teacher in Ghana. The teacher said, "My shoes are new," and the little girl repeated, "My shoes are new." The musical interest lay in the speech melody that was clearly e', c♯', a, b, both when the teacher spoke and when the little girl responded. Since African languages are generally tonal (see no. 56, "Music and Language"), and learning the correct speech melody is as necessary for understanding as is the correct word, this was simply carried over into the teaching of English. The loop was slowed down on a vocorder at the Massachusetts Instititute of Technology to approximately 10 times its original length, in gradual steps, without lowering its pitch. Although the quality of speech reproduction on the vocorder was extremely poor, it was still possible to hear how "My," instead of merely being a simple pitch, is in reality a complex glissando slowly rising from about c♯' up to e', then dissolving into the noise band of "sh," to emerge gradually into the c♯' of "oe," back into the noise of "s," and so on.

Slowing down the motion in musical terms is *augmentation;* the lengthening of duration of notes previously played in shorter note values. Although *Slow Motion Sound* was never completed as a tape piece, the idea of augmentation finally realized itself in my music as *Four Organs* of 1970, and then again in *Music for Mallet Instruments, Voices and Organs* of 1973.

Although by now I have lost my taste for working with complex technology, I believe a genuinely interesting tape piece could still be made from a loop of speech, gradually slowed down further and further, while its pitch and timbre remain constant.

My Name Is (1967)

My Name Is exists as a verbal score only; it was never published. It was done in '67 against a context of what was then called live electronic music—Cage, Stockhausen, and so on,—and the idea was, instead of playing tapes in a dark hall, we'd twist dials in a lighted hall. So someone from the group stands at the door as people are coming into the hall and says: "Will you please say my name is—and then your first name." So you record: "My name is X." "My name is Y." And then you take your tape backstage during the first half of the concert, and while the concert is going on you're in the back editing out five, six, seven names

---

This piece is also discussed in "Videotape and a Composer" (no. 17a, p. 83). The following brief description is taken from a conversation with the editor in 1999.

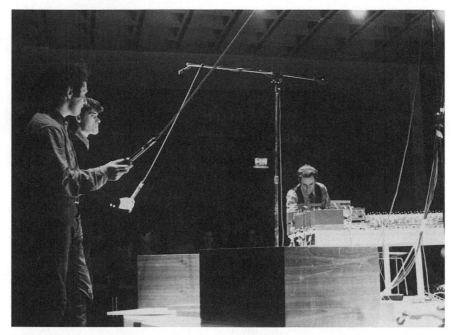

Figure 1-1. *Pendulum Music* performed at the Whitney Museum of American Art in 1969 by, left to right: Richard Serra, James Tenney, Steve Reich, Bruce Nauman, and Michael Snow. PHOTO BY RICHARD LANDRY.

that you think are particularly interesting melodically and making three identical tape loops of each of those names. After the intermission, we had three little monophonic tape recorders that had built in speakers (low-fi, which was well suited to the piece), which would be sitting on the table and you would come out and you would spindle up one X, and then two Xs, then three Xs, and it would run so the phase relationships were whatever they were. And then after a minute or less of that you would fade out one X and fade in one Y, so you'd have two Xs and one Y, and then two Ys and one X, and then three Ys—and so on until you got all the way up to the last name. Musically, you'd be accepting whatever the phase relationships were. Psychologically, the result was interesting because usually people said their name in a very offhand way, because it was a funny thing to do when you walked into the hall. They'd been through the first half of the concert and now they were sitting quietly ready for the second half, and so their perception of the whole thing was reflecting on themselves and how they were no longer in that state of mind. And also hearing your name in that way tends to get to people—it's sort of like doing a sketch of people at the door and it was very suited to doing at concerts where pieces like *Pendulum Music* might also be performed.

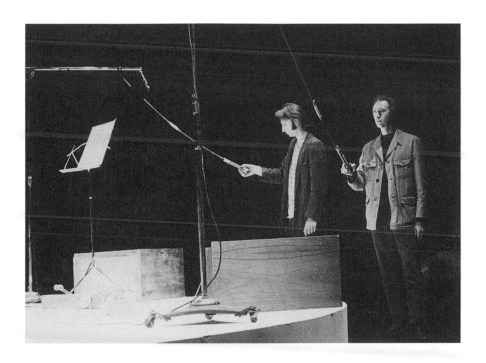

Pendulum Music (1968)

Five years after working together on Ubu Roi, *Reich and Wiley collaborated again in the multimedia piece* Over Evident Falls *at the University of Colorado in August 1968.* Pendulum Music *originated there, Reich says, when he had soaked in the atmosphere to the point that he began to twirl a microphone cord like a lasso in Wiley's Boulder studio and discovered the effect of its feedback as it crossed the path of a speaker [see fig. 1-1]. It was incorporated into the performance accompanying a snowfall (of Ivory Snow flakes) in black light; the second part featured a tape piece called* My Name Is, *in which Reich played multiples of various taped voices providing that information, while Wiley passed cards with some of the resulting nonsense syllables or contextually interesting words across the black-lighted stage on a clothesline [see ex. 1-5]. From Strickland, 1963 (p. 191).*

Pendulum Music—Anti-Illusion: Procedures/Materials, *Marcia Tucker and James Monte, Whitney Museum of American Art, New York, 1969. See also "Second Interview with Michael Nyman" (no. 19), p. 95.*

PENDULUM MUSIC

FOR MICROPHONES, AMPLIFIERS, SPEAKERS AND PERFORMERS

2, 3, 4 or more microphones are suspended from the ceiling by their cables so that they all hang the same distance from the floor and are all free to swing with a pendular motion. Each microphone's cable is plugged into an amplifier which is connected to a speaker. Each microphone hangs a few inches directly above or next to it's speaker.

The performance begins with performers taking each mike, pulling it back like a swing, and then in unison releasing all of them together. Performers then carefully turn up each amplifier just to the point where feedback occurs when a mike swings directly over or next to it's speaker. Thus, a series of feedback pulses are heard which will either be all in unison or not depending on the gradually changing phase relations of the different mike pendulums.

Performers then sit down to watch and listen to the process along with the audience.

The piece is ended sometime after all mikes have come to rest and are feeding back a continuous tone by performers pulling out the power cords of the amplifiers.

Steve Reich 8/68

Example 1-5. *Pendulum Music.* COPYRIGHT © 1980 BY UNIVERSAL EDITION (LONDON) LTD., LONDON. REPRODUCED BY KIND PERMISSION.

Q.: You have been friendly with other artists who work with film, sculpture, geometric structures, conceptual art—people like Michael Snow, Bruce Nauman, William Wiley, Richard Serra, and Sol LeWitt. What do you consider your relationship to them to be?

REICH: In the summer of 1968, I began thinking about what I had done musically, primarily about the phase pieces. I began to see them as processes as opposed to compositions. I saw that my methods did not involve moving from one note to the next, in terms of each note in the piece representing the composer's taste working itself out bit by bit. My music was more of an impersonal process. John Cage discovered that he could take his intentions out of a piece of music and open up a field for many interesting things to happen, and in that sense I agree with him. But where he was willing to keep his musical sensibility out of his own music, I was not. What I wanted to do was to come up with a piece of music that I loved intensely, that was completely personal, exactly what I wanted in every detail, but that was arrived at by impersonal means. I compose the material, decide the process it's going to be run through—but once these initial choices have been made, it runs by itself.

Q.: Do you associate this with Richard Serra or Michael Snow, or Sol Le Witt's thinking?

REICH: The analogy I saw with Serra's sculpture, his propped lead sheets and pole pieces (that were, among other things, demonstrations of physical facts about the nature of lead), was that his works and mine are both more about materials and process than they are about psychology. In Snow's films, there is usually some continuous process at work, either a repetitive or continuous camera movement, which inexorably goes along its way, often with very slow changes. What I learned from Michael Snow that I hadn't thought of, was about the gradations of symmetry which, in musical terms, would be the difference between the pulses of a metronome, the pulses of the human heart, and waves landing on the shore. What is close with Sol [LeWitt] is the spirit in which he will set up an idea and work it through rigorously. He has concentrated on a very direct and complete working out of a given concept.

Adapted with minor changes from Wasserman, 1972 (p. 48).

2b MUSIC AS A GRADUAL PROCESS (1968)

Music as a Gradual Process — first published in the catalogue to the exhibition *Anti-Illusion: Procedures/Materials*, Marcia Tucker and James Monte, Whitney Museum of American Art, New York, 1969.

This oft-quoted and oft-translated set of observations and aphoristic statements remains the core exposition of Reich's aesthetic ideals as a young composer beginning to establish a reputation. It was written in New Mexico during the summer of 1968 — "trying to clarify for myself what I was doing" — at the suggestion of Richard Serra's wife, sculptor Nancy Graves. James Tenney visited and read the manuscript during its preparation.

I do not mean the process of composition but rather pieces of music that are, literally, processes.

The distinctive thing about musical processes is that they determine all the note-to-note (sound-to-sound) details and the overall form simultaneously. (Think of a round or infinite canon.)

I am interested in perceptible processes. I want to be able to hear the process happening throughout the sounding music.

To facilitate closely detailed listening a musical process should happen extremely gradually.

Performing and listening to a gradual musical process resembles:
  pulling back a swing, releasing it, and observing it gradually come to rest;
  turning over an hour glass and watching the sand slowly run through to
    the bottom;
  placing your feet in the sand by the ocean's edge and watching, feeling,
    and listening to the waves gradually bury them.

Although I may have the pleasure of discovering musical processes and composing the musical material to run through them, once the process is set up and loaded it runs by itself.

Material may suggest what sort of process it should be run through (content suggests form), and processes may suggest what sort of material should be run through them (form suggests content). If the shoe fits, wear it.

As to whether a musical process is realized through live human performance or through some electromechanical means is not finally the main issue. One of the most beautiful concerts I ever heard consisted of four composers playing their tapes in a dark hall. (A tape is interesting when it's an interesting tape.)

It is quite natural to think about musical processes if one is frequently working with electromechanical sound equipment. All music turns out to be ethnic music.

Musical processes can give one a direct contact with the impersonal and also a kind of complete control, and one doesn't always think of the impersonal and complete control as going together. By "a kind" of complete control, I mean that by running this material through this process I completely control all that results, but also that I accept all that results without changes.

John Cage has used processes and has certainly accepted their results, but the processes he used were compositional ones that could not be heard when the piece was performed. The process of using the *I Ching* or imperfections in a sheet of paper to determine musical parameters can't be heard when listening to music composed that way. The compositional processes and the sounding music have no audible connection. Similarly, in serial music, the series itself is seldom audible. (This is a basic difference between serial—basically European—music, and serial—basically American—art, where the perceived series is usually the focal point of the work.)

What I'm interested in is a compositional process and a sounding music that are one and the same thing.

James Tenney said in conversation, "Then the composer isn't privy to anything." I don't know any secrets of structure that you can't hear. We all listen to the process together since it's quite audible, and one of the reasons it's quite audible is because it's happening extremely gradually.

The use of hidden structural devices in music never appealed to me. Even when all the cards are on the table and everyone hears what is gradually happening in a musical process, there are still enough mysteries to satisfy all. These mysteries are the impersonal, unintended, psychoacoustic by-products of the intended process. These might include submelodies heard within repeated melodic patterns, stereophonic effects due to listener location, slight irregularities in performance, harmonics, difference tones, and so on.

Listening to an extremely gradual musical process opens my ears to *it*, but *it* always extends farther than I can hear, and that makes it interesting to listen to that musical process again. That area of every gradual (completely controlled) musical process, where one hears the details of the sound moving out away from intentions, occuring for their own acoustic reasons, is *it*.

I begin to perceive these minute details when I can sustain close attention and a gradual process invites my sustained attention. By "gradual" I mean extremely gradual; a process happening so slowly and gradually that listening to it resembles watching a minute hand on a watch—you can perceive it moving after you stay with it a little while.

Several currently popular modal musics like Indian classical and drug-oriented rock and roll may make us aware of minute sound details because in being modal (constant key center, hypnotically droning and repetitious) they naturally focus on these details rather than on key modulation, counterpoint, and other peculiarly Western devices. Nevertheless, these modal musics remain more or less strict frameworks for improvisation. They are not processes.

The distinctive thing about musical processes is that they determine all the note-to-note details and the overall form simultaneously. One can't improvise in a musical process—the concepts are mutually exclusive.

While performing and listening to gradual musical processes, one can participate in a particular liberating and impersonal kind of ritual. Focusing in on the musical process makes possible that shift of attention away from *he* and *she* and *you* and *me* outward toward *it*.

---

3 WAVELENGTH BY MICHAEL SNOW (1968)

Written in 1968 as a spontaneous reaction to the film and not published until it was included in the catalogue for a retrospective exhibition of Michael Snow's work: *Presence and Absence—Films of Michael Snow*, edited by Jim Shedden (Art Gallery of Ontario, Toronto, 1995). See also Snow, 1994.

Wavelength—as in Length of Sound or Light Wave; Wave as in the Sea

Begins with girl having bookcase moved into loft room. Sync sound. Documentary level. Sounds of the street and traffic. People leave—the room by itself. What does a room feel when no one is there? Does the tree fall in the forest if no one sees it? The camera (no one?) sees it. Two girls enter (one coming back? from where?). And turn on a transistor radio—*Strawberry Fields*—traffic and they turn it off before tune is over and they leave. And then we get a new sound (no sound?) of the 60-cycle hum of the amplifier slowly beating against an oscillator tone that then, slowly, very slowly, begins to rise creating faster and faster beats and finally intervals and in short we're in a realm of pure sound and then the images change color and there are filters used all on the same shot out the windows and different film stock and so we've moved out of documentary reality into the reality of film itself—not film about something and so we've moved into the filmmaker's head. There are suggestions of strobe effect of the image, "you could strobe" but he doesn't have to, you complete it in your head. A fast moving red light blur from right to left—was it a special film trick or a tail light from a car out the window (is it night time?). More and more variations of exposure, film stock, focus, and filters all on the one shot (perhaps sometimes a little closer than others) of those four windows with the space between with pictures on the wall, a desk, and a yellow chair. Completely taken up with the filmic variations possible on one image and—a man enters just as the rising oscillator tone reaches the octave above the 60-cycle tonic hum and sync sound mixed in on top of the oscillator, and the man falls to the floor in a heap. We all laugh—it is a long movie. Comic relief and right on the octave to boot. But then the sync sound stops after he's on the floor and we're back with the oscillator and the 60-cycle hum and the four windows with the space between with the pictures on the wall and the desk and yellow chair and the oscillator didn't stop at the octave (why should it?) but is rising slowly, very slowly, into the second octave and we're beginning to zoom slowly, very, very slowly in closer to the windows—or is it between the windows. And there are more filters and film stocks and variations on the same image that does, yes, get still closer and slowly, closer and are we going to zoom out the window and "into the world" or, and it looks like we are, aiming at the space between the windows where pictures are on the wall and then after the fourth or fifth octave has been passed by the oscillator on its inexorable rise—a girl comes in and sync sound is again mixed over the oscillator and we're back in "documentary reality" again (keeping all the balls in the air) and she makes a telephone call. "Richard will you come over? There's a man on my floor and he's dead." Then out of sync sound and back to the rising oscillator. A little play with superimposing the image (on a different film stock) of the girl over herself making the phone call, one could make a movie of that but he doesn't have to, you complete it in your head. Then back to the oscillator, the filters, slowly zooming in now more and more just between the two windows and what about the dead man? Now it's getting closer to the picture with the four thumbtacks, one in each corner, the rectangular picture of—could it be the sea? It's slowly getting still closer and, slowly, at last, it is a picture of THE SEA, a picture of the sea and it fills the whole screen. A picture of a picture of the sea in black and white, and what about the dead man? We could go further into the picture of the sea, but he doesn't have to, you complete it in your head.

4 THE PHASE SHIFTING PULSE GATE—FOUR ORGANS—PHASE PATTERNS— AN END TO ELECTRONICS (1968-70)

"An End to Electronics—Pulse Music, the Phase Shifting Pulse Gate, and Four Organs, 1968–1970"—appeared originally in *Source Magazine*, no. 10, edited by Alvin Lucier, Composer/Performer Edition, Davis, California, Fall 1972.

Each drum is capable of producing two sounds differing in pitch, one from each end of the drum. Each player creates a different rhythmic pattern through irregular alternation of left hand with right hand; the drums, however, are interdependent and their patterns dovetail into each other to create an unbroken succession of tones.

Anklung Gamelans in Bali, *Colin McPhee, 1937*

Hocket. In medieval music, a peculiar technique of composition characterized by the quick alternation of two voice parts with single notes or short groups of notes, one part having a rest where the other has notes.

The Harvard Brief Dictionary of Music, *1961*

On Lincoln's birthday in 1968, I had the idea that if a number of single tones were all pulsing at the same tempo but with gradually shifting phase relations, a great number of musical patterns would result. If the tones were all in phase (struck at the same instant), a pulsing chord would be heard. If the tones were slowly shifted just a bit out of phase, a sort of rippling broken chord would be heard that would gradually change into a melodic pattern, then another, and so on. If the process of phase shifting were gradual enough, then minute rhythmic differences would become clearly audible. A given musical pattern would then be heard to change into another with no alteration of pitch, timbre, or loudness, and one would become involved in a music that worked exclusively with gradual changes in time.

In terms of performance, this meant that each performer could play two notes (one hand, one note), pause, play two notes, pause, and so on. Depending on when performers played and paused (their phase relation), various interlocking melodic patterns would occur. This would be in contrast to the Western and generally non-Western practice of creating melodies that one person can play or sing by himself, but would resemble the interlocking figuration of the Balinese Gamelan and the hocketing procedures in medieval music. Performing such interlocking music would not be too hard to do, but to play, pause, and also very gradually shift one's phase relationship to the other players would be almost impossible. Clearly an electronic device was needed that would be both an instrument in itself, and also a sort of phase variable metronome enabling several performers to play together.

Later, in February 1968, I visited Larry Owens, an electronic engineer at the Bell Laboratories in Holmdel, New Jersey, and, after several months, the block diagrams and descriptions shown in figure 4–1 resulted.

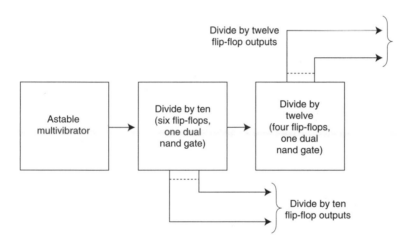

Component digital clock

Each of the 12 channels must concern itself with periodically gating an analog signal for a programmable length of time, and then must be capable of being programmed to shift phase position so that this gating occurs at any one of 120 subdivisions of the constant time period.

The digital clock, common to all channels, is shown above. The constant time period for all channels is determined by the period of the astable multivibrator divided by the counting ratio of 120. The period of the astable multivibrator can be varied over a specified range. The constant time period is thus divided into 120 equal intervals, or counts, any one of which may be selected by simple digital logic (fig. 4–2).

Figure 4-1. Technical description of phase shifting pulse gate.

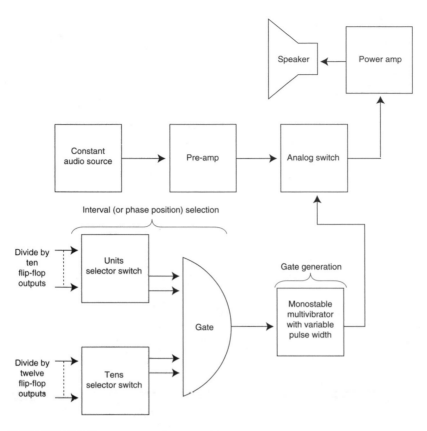

Per-channel equipment

The per-channel equipment shown above must select one of the 120 intervals or counts (phase positions) from the common clock, develop the gate, and gate the incoming analog signal. The choice of one of the 120 counts is made by two selector switches (one with 10 positions and the other with 12) in tandem. The digital outputs of these selector switches are logically combined to select the desired interval or phase position. The gate is then derived from the selected interval with a pulse width determined by the adjustable time constant of a monostable multivibrator. This gate waveform is then applied to an analog switch that, when gated, allows the analog signal to pass through it.

Figure 4-2. Diagram of phase shifting pulse gate.

From a more musical viewpoint, one could describe each channel as capable of dividing a repeating time period or "measure" into 120 equal parts or "120th-notes." Thus, if all channel selectors switches are set to one, and one channel is moved one unit ahead of the other, that pulse will be heard one "120th-note" before the others, or one "120th-note" out of phase. Since even at very slow tempos the rhythmic movement from one "120th note" to the next is barely perceptible, each channel becomes, on a perceptual level, continuously phase variable in relation to all the others.

Figure 4-3. Steve Reich with phase shifting pulse gate at Whitney Museum of American Art, 1969. PHOTO BY RICHARD LANDRY.

The device is purely rhythmic in nature and produces no sound of its own. Provision is made to patch in any 12 constant sounds one wishes. These sounds may be either acoustical via microphone (droning violins, voices, or one's finger constantly rotating on the moistened lip of a thin vibrating wine glass), or electronic (oscillators). When one of the gates opens, a short pulse, varying from one-fifteenth to one-half second in width, is passed through the gate, into a power amp, and out to a loudspeaker. When the gate is closed, there is no sound, or simply the acoustical sound of the instrument if an acoustical source is used.

More than a year after my first visit to Bell Labs, the Phase Shifting Pulse Gate was completed. I constructed it myself with a good deal of help from Larry Owens and David Flooke.

Musical Applications

In April 1969, I first performed Pulse Music on the Phase Shifting Pulse Gate at a concert at The New School in New York. On May 27, 1969, I gave the second performance of Pulse Music in a more elaborated form at the Whitney Museum of American Art. For that performance, eight oscillators were patched into the gate and tuned to the same natural minor scale as four log drums used earlier in that same concert. Although only eight different pitches were used, four of them were patched into two channels each, so that 12 oscillator tones were actually used. In bars 13 through 16 (see ex. 4–1), one can see this separation of the doubled tones into two separate phase positions. All the dotted lines between bars indicate

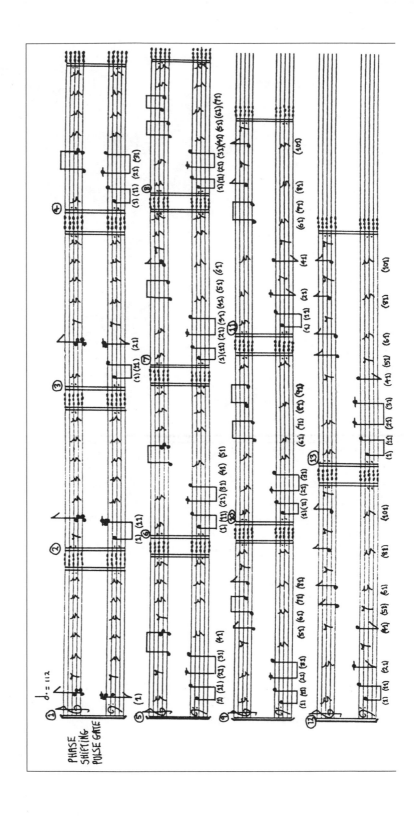

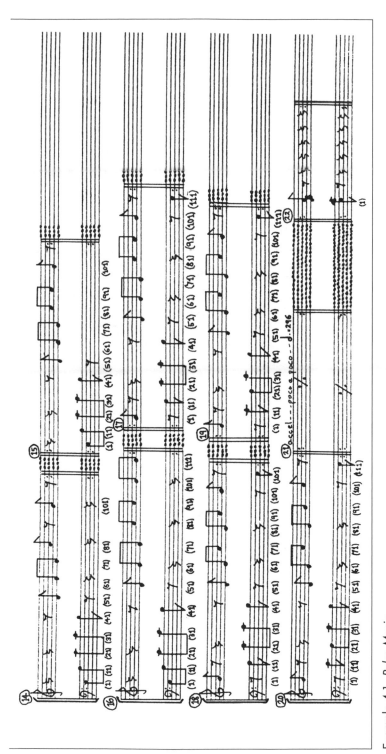

Example 4-1. *Pulse Music.*

the gradual 120th-note-by-120th-note phase shifting. The small numbers in parenthesis indicate the position of the rotary selector switches. If (1) is the first eighth-note in a measure of $\frac{12}{8}$ divided into 120 equal divisions, then (1 1) will be the second eighth-note, (21) the third, and so on. These numbers helped me correlate the musical notation with the actual movements of the rotary selector switches during performance. At bar 21, the final pattern is very gradually accelerated to more than twice its original tempo, creating a sound better described as a blur of color than as a series of discrete pulses. After bar 21, the long dotted lines indicate the final gradual phase shifting of this blur into a fast pulsing chord at bar 22.

Preceding the performance of Pulse Music at the Whitney Museum was the first and only performance of Four Log Drums, in which the gate functioned as a programming device for four performers each playing a two-note wooden log drum. The pulses from the gate were transmitted to each performer via headphone, and each performer played his log drum in exact synchronism with the pulses that I sent them from the gate. Since the earphones only somewhat softened the sounds going on in the room, the performers could and did listen to each other. It was found during rehearsals that although performers tried to follow their pulses exactly, they could only create the musically correct overall pattern when they listened to each other as well. It will be noted that not only are the pitches the same as in Pulse Music but the tempo as well. Pulse Music began directly and without pause from the end of bar 14 of Four Log Drums (see ex. 4–2).

Four Organs—An End to Electronics

After the performance at the Whitney Museum, I brought the Phase Shifting Pulse Gate back to my studio in its fiber case, and didn't immediately unpack it. The pressure of performing with a device that was essentially a prototype—and could easily have ceased functioning at any time—was one of the reasons. Another, and more serious, reason was that the "perfection" of rhythmic execution of the gate (or any electronic sequencer or rhythmic device) was stiff and unmusical. In any music that depends on a steady pulse, as my music does, it is actually tiny microvariations of that pulse created by human beings, playing instruments or singing, that gives life to the music. Last, the experience of performing by simply twisting dials instead of using my hands and body to actively create the music was not satisfying. All in all, I felt that the basic musical ideas underlying the gate were sound, but that they were not properly realized in an electronic device.

Three months later, in August 1969, I had the idea that if a group of tones were all pulsing together in a repeating chord, as at the beginning of Pulse Music, one tone at a time could gradually get longer and longer in duration until the gradual augmentation (lengthening) of durations produced a sort of slow motion music. This would simply be using the variable pulse width aspect of the gate

Figure 4-4. *Four Organs* being rehearsed at the Walker Art Center, Minneapolis, 1969, by, left to right: Arthur Murphy, Phillip Glass, Jon Gibson, Steve Chambers, and Steve Reich. PHOTO BY RICHARD LANDRY.

(which I hadn't used in the Whitney Museum version at all) exclusively, and to enormous proportions. The tones would simply begin in unison in a pulsing chord, and then gradually extend out like a sort of horizontal bar graph in time. Instead of loading my pulse width control with more and more capacitors, I thought about playing a repeated chord on an organ, and then holding one and then several of the notes down longer. Instead of the common digital clock, I thought of a musician playing a steady pulse with a rattle (maracas) that would enable the organists to count together as they held their notes down longer and longer (see fig. 4-4). Since I was unable to start work on this piece for several months, it took until January 1970 to see *Four Organs* for four electric organs and maracas completed. *Four Organs,* like *Piano Phase,* is an example of a piece of live instrumental music with a rhythmic structure (see ex. 4-3), the basic idea of which derives from an electronic device. This feedback of ideas from electromechanical devices and processes to instrumental music has brought me to think of electronic music as a kind of interlude filled with new ideas for the ongoing history of instrumental and vocal music.

It was my intention to resume work with the Phase Shifting Pulse Gate after I finished *Four Organs,* but the experience of composing and then rehearsing with my ensemble was so positive, after more than a year of preoccupation with electronics, that another piece for four organs, *Phase Patterns,* happened very spontaneously a month later in February 1970. In this piece, the four of us were literally drumming on our keybords in what is called a "paradiddle" pattern in Western rudimental drumming. This piece proved to be as positive an experience as *Four Organs* and led, together with other factors, to a trip to Africa to study drumming.

The Phase Shifting Pulse Gate is still in its fiber case on top of the closet in my bedroom. I haven't unpacked it yet.

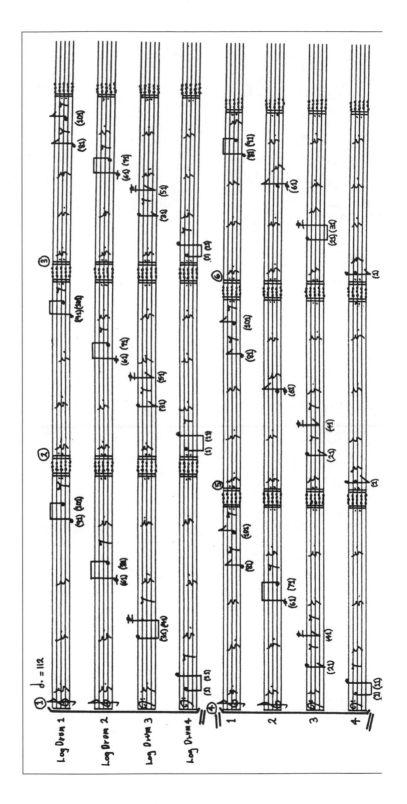

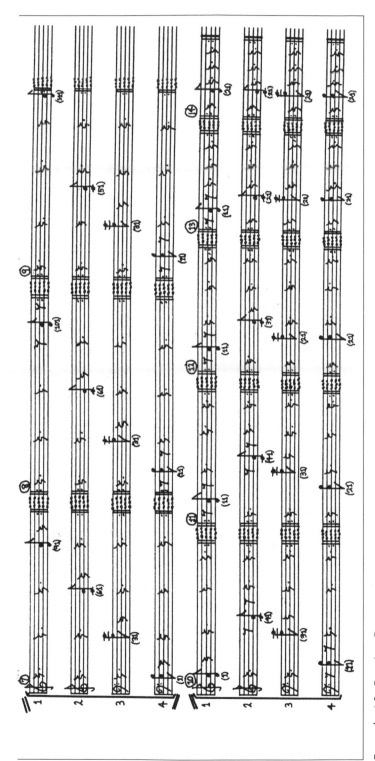

Example 4-2. Four Log Drums.

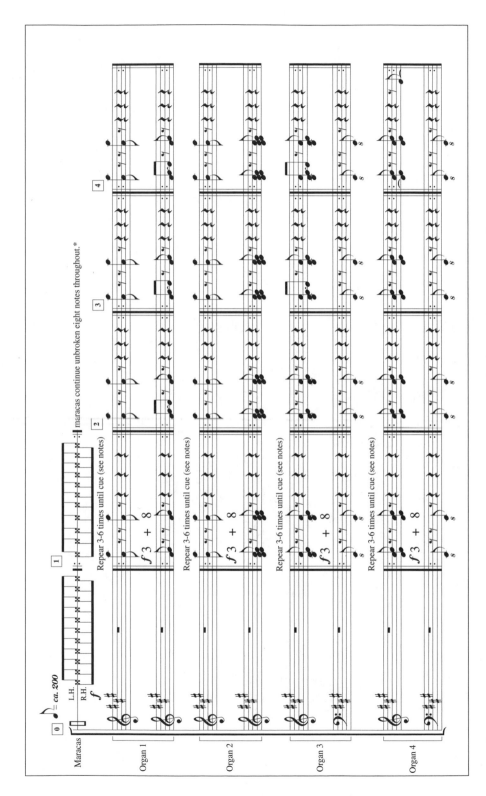

Example 4-3a. *Four Organs*, mm. 0–4. Copyright © 1980 by Universal Edition (London) Ltd., London. Reproduced by kind permission.

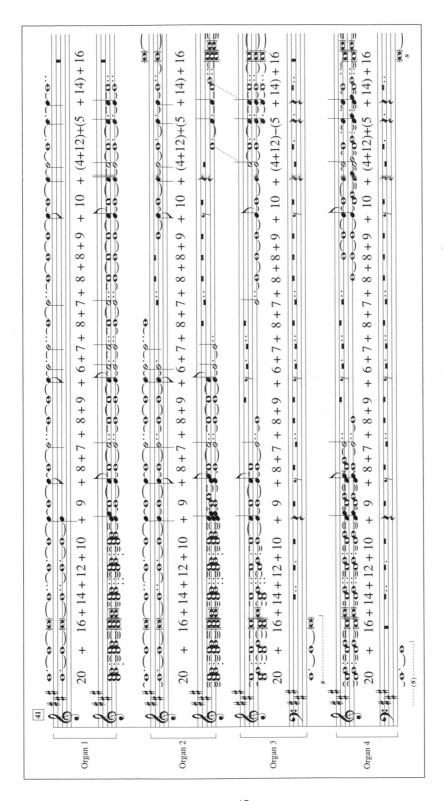

Example 4-3b. *Four Organs*, m. 41. Copyright © 1980 by Universal Edition (London) Ltd., London. Reproduced by kind permission.

Four Organs—Program Note

Four Organs is composed exclusively of the gradual augmentation (lengthening) of individual tones within a single (dominant 11th) chord. The tones within the chord gradually extend out like a sort of horizontal bar graph in time. As the chord stretches out, slowly resolving to the tonic A and then gradually changing back to the dominant E, a sort of slow-motion music is created. The maracas lay down a steady time grid of even eighth-notes throughout, enabling the performers to play together while mentally counting up to as much as 256 beats on a given cycle of sustained tones.

Four Organs is the only piece I am aware of that is composed exclusively of the gradual augmentation of individual tones within a single chord. From the beginning to the end there are no changes of pitch or timbre; all changes are rhythmic and simply consist of gradually increasing durations. This process of augmentation was suggested by the enormous elongation of individual tenor notes in *Organum* as composed by Perotin and others in the twelfth and thirteenth centuries in Paris at Notre Dame Cathedral. Tenor notes that in the original chant may have been equivalent to our quarter- or half-notes can take several pages of tied whole-notes when augmented by Perotin or Leonin.

Four Organs was composed in January 1970. It was first performed at the Guggenheim Museum in New York City by myself and members of my own ensemble later that same year. It also turned out to be one of my first pieces to be heard by a large concert-going public when Michael Tilson Thomas invited me to perform it with him and members of the Boston Symphony Orchestra in Boston in 1971 and at Carnegie Hall in 1973, where it provoked a riot.

Phase Patterns

Almost immediately after the completion of *Four Organs*, I composed another piece for four electric organs, *Phase Patterns*. In this piece, the performers are drumming on their keyboards. Each hand plays certain notes throughout the piece without change, only alternating up and down, left, right, left, left, right, left, right, right, which, in Western rudimental drumming, is called a paradiddle. The idea of drumming on the keyboard comes out of my limitations as a keyboard player, together with my studies of rudimental drumming as a teenager. Although the cause here is one of physical limitation, the effect is of a new approach to the keyboard. I now look at all keyboard instruments as extraordinary sets of tuned drums (see ex. 4-4).

Example 4-4. *Phase Patterns,* bar 11. COPYRIGHT ©
1980 BY UNIVERSAL EDITION (LONDON) LTD., LONDON.
REPRODUCED BY KIND PERMISSION.

SOME OPTIMISTIC PREDICTIONS (1970) ABOUT THE FUTURE OF MUSIC   5

These predictions (which 30 years later seem to have proven largely correct) were first printed as part of the program note to a concert at the Guggenheim Museum in May 1970, and then published in *Synthesis,* no. 2, Spring 1971 (Minneapolis: Scully-Cutter Publishing, 1971).

Electronic music as such will gradually die and be absorbed into the ongoing music of people singing and playing instruments.

Non-Western music in general and African, Indonesian, and Indian music in particular will serve as new structural models for Western musicians. Not as new models of sound. (That's the old exoticism trip.) Those of us who love the sounds will hopefully just go and learn how to play these musics.

Music schools will be resurrected through offering instruction in the practice and theory of all the world's music. Young composer/performers will form all sorts of new ensembles growing out of one or several of the world's musical traditions.

Serious dancers who now perform with pulseless music or with no music at all will be replaced by young musicians and dancers who will reunite rhythmic music and dance as a high art form.

The pulse and the concept of clear tonal center will reemerge as basic sources of new music.

---

6 FIRST INTERVIEW WITH MICHAEL NYMAN (1970)

> This interview was first published in *The Musical Times*, vol. cxii, 1971, pp. 229–31. It is reprinted here with the omission of biographical material, which is presented elsewhere in this book. The interview was recorded in May 1970 when Reich was in London en route to Africa. David Behrman, who had produced the recordings of Reich's tape pieces for CBS, had suggested that Reich contact Nyman in London. Nyman and Reich spent a week together and established a friendship, which resulted in Reich's return the following year to present two concerts of his works, one in London (at the Institute of Contemporary Arts) and one in Paris. While in Africa, Reich contracted malaria and had to return home earlier than planned. He flew via Rome, visiting the composer Frederic Rzewski, and his plane was then delayed at Bangor, Maine. Reich recalls that the passengers were eventually taken out for dinner, but with the combined effects of jetlag and incipient malaria, he was not in the best of spirits.

NYMAN: Is there a convenient descriptive label you like to attach to your music?

REICH: When the Columbia record was produced (with *Violin Phase* and *It's Gonna Rain*)[1] we talked about what would be the best title, and we came up with Live/Electric. Then I wrote a piece called *Pulse Music;* in a review someone said that I'd been playing pulse music elsewhere, and I realized that he had construed it as a generic term for my music. That's not bad, so I'm inclined to use it sometimes; at last it gives some indication of the nature of the music, more than "avant-garde," "experimental," or "modern," all of which are deadly.

NYMAN: You once said that you would prefer to have your works recorded commercially than on a subsidized basis, and to succeed "out there" as a composer because these are the terms on which music survives. How does this affect the way you choose (or are forced) to earn a living?

---

1. The LP Columbia MS 7256.

REICH: I can get by as a composer now, although I teach one day a week (at the New School in New York), but I'd like to drop that and try to make a living as a performer, which I am on the verge of doing. But for at least 10 years I did all kinds of things and I would certainly rather take my chances in the commercial world, as a person, than in an academic world. I think that if you have any close connection or involvement with a department—and this is a particularly American situation—then it's going to wipe you out. Being an A & R man for a record company or a location recordist for a movie (I've done a little bit of that) is one thing, whereas if you go off to a university thinking "This is the way I'll survive, I'll have a nice little scene going here and have a lot of time to compose," I don't think that works (that is, if you stay in one place for any length of time).

NYMAN: *Come Out* is the only piece of yours that is at all known over here. The phase relationships are fascinating; how did you do them? Presumably there was no tape editing at all?

REICH: I first made a loop of the phrase "Come out to show them," and recorded a whole reel of that on channel 1 of a second tape recorder. I then started recording the loop on channel 2; after lining up the two tracks, with my thumb on the supply reel of the recording machine, I very gradually held it back (I was literally slowing it down, but at such an imperceptible rate that you can't hear) until "Come out to show them" had separated into "come out-come out/show them-show them" (which is something like two eighth notes apart). Then I took that two-channel relationship, made a loop from it, fed it into channel 1 again, and held it back with my thumb until it was four eighth-notes away from the original sound and could be heard as a series of equal beats, quite distinct melodically. I then spliced together the two-voice tape with the four-voice tape—they fit exactly—and what you sense at that point is a slight timbral difference, due to all this addition, and then all of a sudden a movement in space. At that point I divided it again into eight voices, separated it by just a thirty-second-note, so that the whole thing began to shake, then I just faded it out again and put those two takes together. So there's absolutely no manipulation of the tape.

NYMAN: What was your first tape piece?

REICH: The first piece I did was for a movie called *The Plastic Haircut*. It was very heavily edited, a cross between animation and live film. Somebody said he heard a sportscaster trying to narrate the action. So I got hold of a record called "The Greatest Moments in Sport" (a kind of old talkie LP that I had heard as a child) and made a collage of it in the most primitive of all ways. I'd record a bit, stop the tape, move the needle, and then start taping again, so there was hardly any splicing. Formally it started very simply and turned into noise through overdubbing with loops, rather like a surrealist rondo with all kinds of elements recurring. The exciting thing was that the voices, used as sound, nevertheless have a residual meaning that was also very ambiguous—it could be sporting, or sexual, or political—and immediately seemed to me to be the solution to vocal music. So I went on this binge of working with tape, which came to a point about two and a half years later when I felt that I'd had enough.

NYMAN: Since *Come Out* you've been writing (and performing) only live music. How did you make the change from tape to instruments?

REICH: 1966 was a very depressing year. I began to feel like a mad scientist trapped in a lab; I had discovered the phasing process of *Come Out* and didn't want to turn my back on it, yet I didn't know how to do it live, and I was aching to do some instrumental music. The way out of the impasse came by just running a tape loop of a piano figure and playing the piano against it to see if in fact I could do it. I found that I could, not with the perfection of the tape recorder, but the imperfections seemed to me to be interesting and I sensed they might be interesting to listen to.

NYMAN: So through tape you arrived back at live music.

REICH: What tape did for me basically was on the one hand to realize certain musical ideas that at first just had to come out of machines, and on the other to make some instrumental music possible that I never would have got to by looking at any Western or non-Western music.

NYMAN: What about the mechanical aspect of your writing?

REICH: People imitating machines was always considered a sickly trip; I don't feel that way at all, emotionally. I think there's a human activity, "imitating machines," in the sense in which (say) playing the phase pieces can be construed; but it turns out to be psychologically very useful, and even pleasurable. So the attention that kind of mechanical playing asks for is something we could do with more of, and the "human expressive quality" that is assumed to be innately human is what we could with less of right now. That ties in with non-Western music—African drumming or the Balinese gamelan—which also have an impersonality to them as the participants accept a given situation and add their individual contributions in the details of the working out.

NYMAN: You work with an absolute minimum of musical material—five words in *Come Out* and a dominant seventh chord with the tonic sitting on the top in *Four Organs.*

REICH: *Four Organs* is not a phase piece at all: it consists of one chord growing in time. My preoccupation with gradual processes—which don't affect the timbre or dynamic of the sound, but only its rhythmic and durational values—means that you can begin to take an interest in things that in older music were just details. In baroque music, you might hear a few harmonics in a certain passage that stays within one chord, or you might begin to hear all kinds of details of the action of a keyboard instrument. These are merely incidental details, but by isolating them you can legitimately use them as your basic musical material.

NYMAN: So one has to learn to listen in a fundamentally different way.

REICH: Yes. You listen to developmental music, and you just can't stay with it, or you can't stay with it once you've seen the way you stay with something else. I'm interested in a process where you can get on at the beginning and literally rest on it, uninterrupted, right to the end. Focusing in on a musical process makes possible a shift of attention away from the *he* and *she* and *you* and *me*, outward toward *it*.[2]

NYMAN: What is your particular interest in African drumming?

REICH: I became interested in African music through A. M. Jones's book, and I recently found a group at Columbia University with a Ghanaian drummer from the tribe Jones had written about. One of my reasons for going to Ghana and studying drumming is, in the very simplest sense, to increase my musical abilities. I studied rudimentary Western drumming when I was 14 and interested in jazz, and this last piece, *Phase Patterns*, is literally drumming on the keyboard: Your left hand stays in one position and your right hand stays in one position and you alternate them in what's called a paradiddle pattern, which produces a very interesting musical texture because it sets up melodic things you could never arrive at if you just followed your melodic prejudices and your musical background.

NYMAN: You're not interested in taking over the sound of the music and incorporating it into your music?

REICH: What I don't want to do is to go and buy a bunch of exotic-looking drums and set up an Afrikanische Musik in New York City. In fact what I think is going to happen more and more is that composers will study non-Western music seriously so that it will have a natural and organic influence on their music.

GAHU—A DANCE OF THE EWE TRIBE IN GHANA (1971)   7

Written in 1971; "Gahu, A Dance of the Ewe tribe in Ghana"—*Source Magazine*, no. 10, edited by Alvin Lucier, Composer/Performer Edition, Davis, California, Fall 1972. During the second visit to London (1971), Reich also met A. M. Jones and showed him the transcriptions that appear in this essay.

During the summer of 1970, I went to Ghana to study drumming. With the help of a travel grant from the Special Projects division of the Institute of International Education, I traveled to Accra, the capital of Ghana, where I studied with a master drummer of the Ewe tribe who was in residence with the Ghana Dance Ensemble, the national dance company that rehearses daily in the Institute of African Studies at the University of Ghana.

---

2. Reich is here virtually quoting from his own 1968 essay "Music as a Gradual Process" (no. 2b); see p. 36.

I took daily lessons with Gideon Alorworye and recorded each lesson. Afterward I would return to my room, and, by playing and replaying the tape, sometimes at half or one-quarter speed, I was able to transcribe the bell, rattle, and drum patterns I had learned. The basis for learning each individual instrument was as follows: First I would learn the basic double bell (gong-gong) pattern, which is the unchanging timeline of the whole drumming. Then I would learn the rattle (axatse) pattern, which is quite similar to the gong-gong pattern and also continues without change throughout the entire performance. We would then proceed to the drums by my playing the gong-gong while my teacher played one of the drum patterns. We then exchanged instruments and I would try and play the drum pattern while he played the bell. I found that while I could pick up the drum patterns fairly rapidly by rote, I would forget them almost as rapidly. I couldn't really remember them until I could understand exactly what was going on rhythmically between the drum and the bell patterns. This process of understanding was greatly aided and accelerated by replaying the tapes of my lessons until I could finally write down with certainty the relationship between any given drum and the bell pattern. One drum after the other was learned and written down in relation to the bell until an entire ensemble was notated. This method was followed as the result of reading A. M. Jones's *Studies in African Music* (Oxford University Press, 1959). Dr. Jones has been able to make the first full scores of African music (as it happens, of the Ewe tribe) by using his own drum recorder, which consists of a moving roll of paper that is electrically marked each time a drummer touches one of his metal pencils to a metal plate. As Dr. Jones tapped out the bell pattern, an Ewe master drummer would tap out one of the drum parts, and both patterns would be recorded in accurate graph form on the moving paper. This was then transferred to conventional notation. My readings in Dr. Jones's book in 1963 first awoke my interest in African music, and that interest grew through listening to recordings, corresponding with Dr. Jones, and finally having two brief lessons with Alfred Ladzopko, another Ewe master drummer in New York who was working with Nicholas England at Columbia University. Finally, I decided it was important to go to Africa myself and learn some drumming by drumming.

Gahu is an extremely popular dance. It can be performed whenever and wherever the musicians and dancers feel like it. This is in contrast to the court dances Atsiagbeko of the Ewes and Fontenfrom of the Ashantis, both of which are only performed at the proper formal time and place. All Ghanaian dances are appropriate to particular situations, and Gahu is appropriate to a relaxed informal one.

Gahu is not a purely Ewe dance. My teacher told me that it originally came from the town of Gbadagri (ba-da-gree), which used to be situated in Nigeria between Lagos and the Dahomey border. The Ewes used to go on fishing trips with these people who were called Agunnas or Guans, and had their own language that was neither Yoruba nor Ewe. My teacher did not say how long ago this had been.

In Ghana, the name of a piece of music is also the name of the dance that is performed to that music. The two are inseparable. (I once attended an informal recording session outdoors in back of the Institute of African Studies where several musicians were playing directly in front of two microphones. Although they all were quite aware that only sound was being recorded, several people, nevertheless, started dancing the appropriate dance.) Gahu is a circle dance performed by men and woman. The basic step is simply alternating the feet in small steps forward (left, left, right, right) while swinging the arms gently to the opposite side of the body (right, right, left, left) all on the basic four quarter-notes of the bell pattern. There are many other variations I am not familiar with.

Often in the afternoon, preceding the evening's drumming, the Ewes perform Hatsyiatsya songs, which are sung to the accompaniment of four iron bells; two gong-gongs and two atokes. This accompaniment is a minature polyrhythmic drumming made of beautiful bell sounds. I became extremely fond of these sounds and asked Gideon to teach me the Hatsyiatsya patterns for Gahu (see ex. 7-1).

This represents a very approximate notation of the pitch of these bells. The high E♭ in the first atoke is actually a bit sharp, while the high C in the second atoke is a bit flat. The E♭ on the first gong-gong is very flat, and, depending on where you strike the bell, is sometimes a sort of minor second with D and E♭ combined. The second gong-gong is about a quarter-tone above the A in the notation. The absolute pitch of these kind of bells varies a good deal, although gong-gongs are usually roughly tuned to octaves or major sixths.

The basic pattern is played by the first atoke who, together with the second atoke, never changes his pattern throughout the piece. The second atoke is free to add two sixteenth-notes in place of his single eighth-note on any or all beats. The two gong-gongs each have a first pattern only two quarter-notes long, so that two of their patterns equals one atoke pattern. Both of them begin their patterns in different places, and neither of them begins on the first beat of the atoke pattern. This, in simplified miniature, is the essence of African rhythmic structure: several repeating patterns of the same or related lengths and each with its own separate downbeat. Pattern two for the gong-gongs is a simple alternation of double sixteenth-notes on their lower bells, which acts as a sort of changing pattern leading to their third pattern, which, for the first gong-gong, begins on the last eighth-note of the atoke pattern, while the second gong-gong begins on the third quarter-note of the atokes. There is no hard and fast rule as to when the gong-gongs will change from one pattern to the next, but they must do so together. Players are also free to reverse the order of high and low bells within a particular pattern. Since players are seated, the rests in the gong-gong patterns are created by bringing the large bell directly down on the thigh on each rest, thereby muting it. The atokes are muted on rests by touching the edge of the bell with the thumb of the hand holding it. My teacher mentioned that there were many other patterns, and also said that up to eight gong-gongs could play with the two atokes.

I have not transcribed the songs because, basically, I was not really attracted to them. The accompaniment was what I found to be unique, beautiful, and quite

Example 7-1. *Hatsyiatsya bell patterns.*

different from anything in Western music. Since I am a composer/performer and not a musicologist, I am passing along the information that I believe may be of particular interest to others in situations like my own. Those wishing to see other Hatsyiatsya songs transcribed more completely with accompaniment and melody are urged to look at A. M. Jones's *Studies in African Music.*

The instruments used in the full drumming of Gahu are: one or two gong-gongs, at least one rattle, although it is common for several people to double the easy rattle part in any Ghanaian drumming, and the following drums: kagan, the smallest; kidi, the second smallest; sogo, the next to the largest; and agboba, the master drum (see ex. 7-2). Those familiar with Ewe music should note that for Gahu, which as mentioned earlier, is a dance the Ewes imported from Nigeria, a special drum, agboba, is used in place of the customary Ewe master drum, atsimevu.

Unfortunately, because of illness, I was unable to stay in Ghana and complete the preceding transcription, so that only the basic repeating bell and rattle parts, together with the beginning pattern in the master drum with the appropriate response patterns in the supporting drums, appear here. The pitch of the drums, which is important although it varies a bit from performance to performance, is also not notated for lack of time. Those interested in the pitch of Ewe drums are again referred to Jones's work. With all these limitations this is, nevertheless, the first and at present the only transcription of both the Hatsyiatsya patterns and the basic drumming of Gahu.

The basic pattern of the whole dance appears in the gong-gong. It is exactly what the first atoke was playing in the Hatsyiatsya patterns. The first time the pattern is played, the performer may remind all the other musicians of his downbeat by playing it on his low bell. Thereafter, unless someone loses his place in relation to the bell pattern, the gong-gong player just "rides" his top bell only, ringing out over the whole ensemble. This $\frac{4}{4}$ pattern is a bit unusual for Ewe or West African music in general, where one most often finds the basic bell pattern to be in what we would call $\frac{12}{8}$, as in the transcription of Agbadza that follows. When I finally decided that this pattern had to be written as it appears on page 60, I wrote to A. M. Jones to ask for his reaction to what I considered to be an unusual pattern. He responded that it was, in fact, quite similar to the basic gong-gong pattern in the Ewe dance Sovu and was, therefore, quite correct. If a second gong-gong is played, it will play the same part as the second atoke in the Hatsyiatsya patterns for Gahu, that is, a simple pulse on each of the four quarter-notes of the first gong-gong part, with the option of playing two sixteenth-notes instead of one eighth-note on any or all of the pulses. The atoke itself is only used for Hatsyiatsya patterns, and is not used in the full drumming.

The rattle, axatse, is played in a sitting position, and is struck downward on the thigh and then upward against the open palm or closed fist of the other hand held above it. The down strokes (notes below the line) exactly double the gong-gong, while the upward movements (notes above the line) simply fill in the rests.

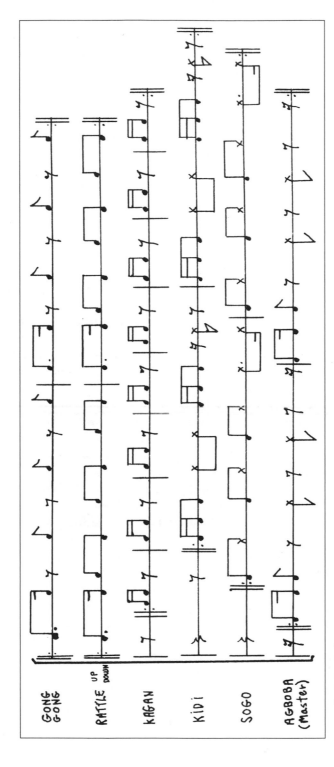

Example 7-2. *Gahu music.*

Ewe drums are played both with sticks and by hand. In Gahu, all the drums are played with sticks. The Xs in the drum notation indicate muted beats. In kidi and sogo, this is played by pressing one stick down on the drum head while gently striking the head with the other stick. Because of the added tension on the head, the pitch of a muted beat is higher, by about a fifth, than a regular beat. In the agboba, the muted beats are played by striking the stick rather sharply against the wooden side of the drum.

The kagan keeps up the same pattern throughout, and in this respect is closer to the gong-gong and rattle than it is to the other drums. This is generally kagan's role in all Ewe music, and not just in Gahu.

There are many different master drum patterns, and each has a different response pattern from kidi and sogo. I simply did not have time to learn more than this first one. While the master drum makes constant improvised variations on his pattern, which I realistically felt were completely beyond the scope of my short visit to learn and therefore transcribe, the other drums simply repeat their patterns without variation until the master changes. They make the appropriate change then to the proper response pattern, and repeat it without variation. In the patterns above, the master drum begins a sixteenth-note after the gong-gong, and sogo responds on the second quarter of the bell pattern, while kidi answers an eighth-note later. All instruments in this particular section have patterns the same length as the gong-gong, except for kagan, whose pattern is only one quarternote in duration.

Before I became interested in Gahu, my teacher started me off with Agbadza, perhaps the best known Ewe social dance. Although an excellent full transcription of Agbadza, complete with master drum improvisations, appears in Jones's *Studies in African Music,* I offer the following so that readers here may see how the master drum plays a changing signal, changes to a second pattern, and is responded to by the supporting drum. In Agbadza, the master drum is sogo, which is played with the hands, while kidi and kagan are both played with sticks. My transcription is not only simpler than Jones's, it also differs slightly in the master drum patterns and the kidi responses. This is due partly to the fact that there are many different patterns for Agbadza, and also to the fact that my teacher was about 10 years younger and from a different village than the master drummer Jones worked with. Patterns do apparently change in time, and there are also apparently regional differences in performance. Basic patterns, like that of the gong-gong, however, do not change (see ex. 7-3).

The gong-gong pattern in $\frac{12}{8}$ here is the most common in West Africa. Again, the player will start by playing the first beat on his low bell, but will then continue on his high bell only, unless some musician needs a reminder as to where the first beat of the gong-gong is. The rattle once again doubles the bell with his downstrokes while filling in rests with his upward motion. Here, however, he begins his pattern on the second quarter-note of the bell pattern. Kagan's pattern is somewhat similar to that in Gahu, and once again four kagan patterns equal one bell pattern. Like the bell and rattle, kagan continues without change for the en-

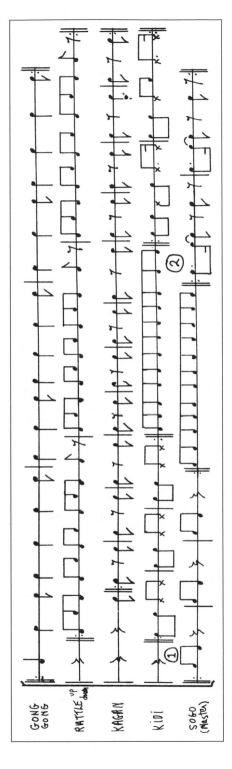

Example 7-3. Agbadza.

tire performance. The first sogo master pattern is only four eighth-notes long, and begins with the bell. He is responded to by kidi with a pattern that fills in sogo's rests while doubling sogo's beats with muted beats. After many repetitions with ample improvised variation by sogo, the changing signal of unbroken eighth-notes is sounded by sogo telling all the musicians and dancers that a new pattern will begin. This second pattern is six eighth-notes long, and once again sogo begins with the bell, with kidi responding on the second quarter-note of the bell pattern.

My teacher told me that all drum patterns in Ewe music not only have a series of "nonsense syllables" associated with them to help remember their rhythm but also have a literal meaning. For instance, the gong-gong pattern in Agbadza means, "Do mayi makpo tefe mava" in Ewe or "Let me go and witness this myself and return," while the rattle means "Tso, miayi miakpo nusia tefe" or "Stand up and let us go and witness this ourselves." The kagan pattern means "Kaba" or "Quickly," kidi is saying "Midzo" or "Let us go," and sogo's first pattern is "Do va" or "Get out and come here." These patterns may refer to the Ewe's hasty departure from Benin in Nigeria sometime probably in the nineteenth century.

When it is remembered that there is no indigenous written language in Africa, and when the talking drums are considered, it may be seen that not only are the dances the choreographic reenactments of important historical events in the history of the tribe, but also that there is actually a literal recorded history of these people in the drum patterns themselves.

DRUMMING (1971) 8

Drumming was composed during the period of over a year between Reich's return from Africa and the premiere in December 1971. Reich composed by taping patterns and playing against them, then rehearsing with members of his ensemble, now expanded to twelve musicians. Three premiere performances were given. The first was in the Museum of Modern Art Film Theater, the second was at the Brooklyn Academy of Music, and the third in New York's Town Hall. The third performance was recorded and published together with full score in 1972, in a signed and numbered special edition of 500, by John Gibson and Multiples, Inc.

For one year, between the fall of 1970 and the fall of 1971, I worked on what turned out to be the longest continuous piece I have ever composed. *Drumming* lasts from 55 to 75 minutes (depending on the number of repeats played) and is divided into four parts that are performed without pause. The first part is for four pair of tuned bongo drums stand-mounted and played with sticks, the second for three marimbas played by nine players together with two women's voices, the third for three glockenspiels played by four players together with whistling and piccolo, and the fourth section is for all these instruments and voices combined.

While first playing the drums during the process of composition, I found myself sometimes singing with them, using my voice to imitate the sounds they made. This involved using syllables like "tuk," "tok," "duk," and so on. I found that if I used a microphone to make the volume of my voice almost as loud as the drums, but no louder, I could then make some of the resulting patterns very much as if my voice were another set of drums, gradually bringing out one pattern after another.[1] I began to understand that this might also be possible for the marimbas and glockenspiels as well. Thus, the basic assumption about the voices in *Drumming* was that they would not sing words but would precisely imitate the sound of the instruments.

The problem then was to find out what sort of sounds were needed to best imitate these instruments. For the marimbas, the female voice was needed using consonants like "b" and "d" with a more or less "u" as in "you" vowel sound. In the case of the glockenspiels, the extremely high range of the instrument precluded any use of the voice and necessitated whistling. Even this form of vocal production proved impossible when the instrument was played in its higher ranges, and this created the need for a more sophisticated form of whistle; in this case, the piccolo. In the last section of the piece, these techniques are combined simultaneously with each imitating its particular instrument.

The women's voices sing patterns resulting from the combination of two or more marimbas playing the identical repeating pattern one or more quarter-notes out of phase with each other. By exactly imitating the sound of the instruments, and by gradually fading the patterns in and out, the singers cause them to slowly rise to the surface of the music and then to fade back into it allowing the listener to hear these patterns, along with many others, actually sounding in the instruments.

In the context of my own music, *Drumming* is the final expansion and refinement of the phasing process,[2] as well as the first use of four new techniques: (1) the process of gradually substituting beats for rests (or rests for beats); (2) the gradual changing of timbre while rhythm and pitch remain constant; (3) the simultaneous combination of instruments of different timbre; and (4) the use of the human voice to become part of the musical ensemble by imitating the exact sound of the instruments.

The very beginning of *Drumming* starts with two drummers constructing the basic rhythmic pattern of the entire hour and a quarter long piece from a single drum beat, played in a cycle of 12 beats with rests on all the other beats (see ex. 8-1). Gradually, additional drum beats are substituted for rests, one at a time,

1. An early version of the score has male voices singing resulting patterns in the first section of *Drumming;* these were removed by the composer in 1975 and, instead, one of the drummers plays resulting patterns on the drums.
2. Reich never used the phasing technique after *Drumming.*

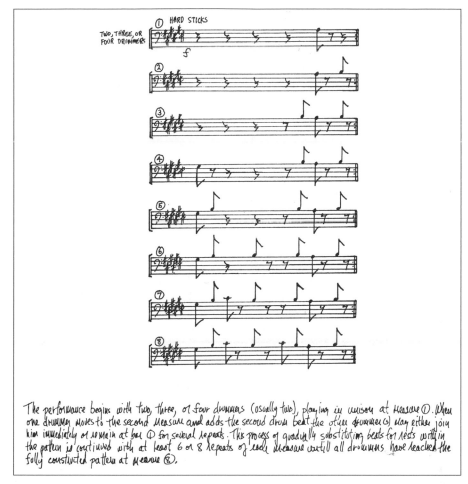

Example 8-1. *Drumming*, bars 1–8. COPYRIGHT © 1973 BY HENDON MUSIC, INC., A BOOSEY & HAWKES COMPANY. COPYRIGHT RENEWED. REPRINTED BY PERMISSION.

until the pattern is constructed. The reduction process is simply the reverse, where rests are subsituted for beats, one at a time, until only a single beat remains (see ex. 8-2).

The sections are joined together by the new instruments doubling the exact pattern of the instruments already playing. At the end of the drum section, three drummers play the same pattern two quarter-notes out of phase with each other. Three marimba players enter softly with the same pattern also played two quarter-notes out of phase. The drummers gradually fade out so that the same rhythm and pitches are maintained with a gradual change of timbre. At the end of the marimba section, three marimbas played in their highest range are doubled by three glockenspiels in their lowest range so that the process of maintaining rhythm and pitch while gradually changing timbre is repeated. The sections are

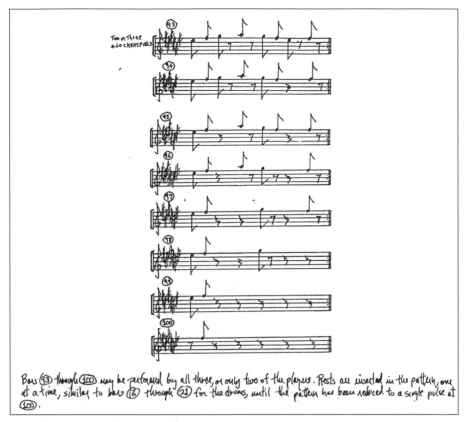

Example 8-2. *Drumming,* bars 93–100. Copyright © 1973 by Hendon Music, Inc., a Boosey & Hawkes company. Copyright Renewed. Reprinted by permission.

not set off from each other by changes in key, the traditional means of gaining extended length in Western music. *Drumming* shows that it is possible to keep going in the same key for quite a while if there are instead considerable rhythmic developments, together with occasional, but complete, changes of timbre to supply variety.

One of the most noticeable aspects of my music has been that it is written for ensembles of two or more *identical* instruments. Starting with *It's Gonna Rain* for identical tape loops moving out of phase with each other, through the other tape pieces *Come Out* and *Melodica,* and into the instrumental pieces, *Piano Phase* for two pianos, *Violin Phase* for four violins, *Phase Patterns* for four electric organs, and the first three sections of *Drumming,* this was necessary because *the phasing process is only clearly audible when the two or more voices moving against each other are identical in timbre,* and therefore combine to form one complete resulting pattern in the ear. To play *Piano Phase* on one piano and one harpsichord would just not work, but to play it on two harpsichords might be very interesting. Because of this necessary matching of timbres, a unique body of

Figure 8-1. *Drumming* performed by Steve Reich & Musicians at Loeb Student Center, New York University, 1973. Left to right: Russell Hartenberger, Joseph Rasmussen, Bob Becker, Leslie Scott, Timothy Ferchen, Joan LaBarbara, Janice Jarrett, Steve Reich, Steve Chambers, Glen Velez, Ben Harms, and James Preiss. PHOTO BY GIANFRANCO GORGONI.

work has been written for multiples of the same instrument. In the last section of *Drumming*, however, the drums, marimbas, and glockenspiels are combined simultaneously for the first time in my music. All the instruments play the same rhythmic pattern, but the drums play it with one set of notes, the marimbas with a second, and the glockenspiels with a third. When one marimba phases against another, they create an overall marimba pattern that is clearly distinguishable from the drums and glockenspiels. It is a similar situation when one drummer phases against the other drummers, or when one glockenspiel player moves ahead of another. The overall sound, of course, becomes considerably richer.

The question often arises as to what influence my visit to Africa in the summer of 1970 had on *Drumming?* The answer is *confirmation*. It confirmed my intuition that acoustic instruments could be used to produce music that was genuinely richer in sound than that produced with electronic instruments, as well as confirming my natural inclination toward percussion. I chose instruments that are all now commonly available in Western countries, (although the history of bongo drums leads back to Latin America, that of the marimba goes back to Africa, and the glockenspiel ultimately derives from Indonesia), tuned to our own tempered diatonic scale, and used them within the context created by my own previous compositions (fig. 8-1).

9 CLAPPING MUSIC (1972)

In 1972, I composed *Clapping Music* out of a desire to create a piece of music that would need no instruments at all beyond the human body. At first I thought it would be a phase piece, but this turned out to be rather inappropriate, since it introduces a difficulty in musical process (phasing) that is out of place with such a simple way of producing sound. The solution was to have one performer remain fixed, repeating the same basic pattern throughout, while the second moves abruptly, after a number of repeats, from unison to one beat ahead, and so on, until he is back in unison with the first performer. The basic difference between these sudden changes and the gradual changes of phase in other pieces is that, when phasing, one can hear the same pattern moving away from itself with the downbeats of both parts separating further and further apart, while the sudden changes here create the sensation of a series of variations of two different patterns with their downbeats coinciding. In *Clapping Music,* it can be difficult to hear that the second performer is in fact always playing the same original pattern as the first performer, although starting in different places (see ex. 9-1).

Clapping Music marks the end of my use of the gradual phase shifting process. First discovered in *It's Gonna Rain* in 1965, this process was then used in every piece from 1965 through *Drumming* in 1971, with the exception of *Four Organs.* Starting with *Clapping Music,* I felt a need to find new techniques. *Six Pianos, Music for Mallet Instruments, Voices and Organ,* and *Music for Pieces of Wood,* all composed in 1973, use the process of rhythmic construction, or substitution of beats for rests, first used in *Drumming,* as well as the process of augmentation similar to that in *Four Organs.*

The gradual phase shifting process was extremely useful from 1965 through 1971, but I do not have thoughts of ever using it again. By late 1972, it was time for something new.

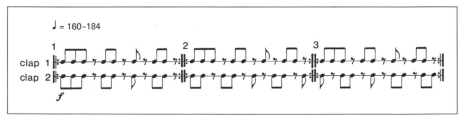

Example 9-1. *Clapping Music,* bars 1–3. Copyright © 1980 by Universal Edition (London) Ltd., London. Reproduced by kind permission.

Originally published in slightly different form under the title "A Composer Looks East" in the *New York Times*, Sunday, September 2, 1973.

During the summer of 1973, I studied Balinese Gamelan Semar Pegulingan with I Nyoman Sumandhi, a Balinese musician in residence at the American Society for Eastern Arts Summer Program at the University of Washington in Seattle. Earlier (in the summer of 1970) I had studied African drumming in Ghana.[1] I studied Balinese and African music because I love them, and also because I believe that non-Western music is presently the single most important source of new ideas for Western composers and musicians.

Although earlier generations of Western musicians *listened* to many non-Western musics, live or in recordings, it is now becoming increasingly possible to learn how to *play* African, Balinese, Javanese, Indian, Korean, and Japanese music, among others, directly from first-rate native teachers, here in America or abroad. A Western musician can thus begin to approach non-Western music as he would his own; he learns to play it through study with a qualified teacher, and in that process can also analyze the music he is playing in detail to understand how it is put together. During the process of performance and analysis, he will find basically different systems of rhythmic structure, scale construction, tuning, and instrumental technique. Knowledge of these different systems also sheds light on our own Western system, showing it to be one among many.

It was my personal desire to understand the basic differences between African drumming and Balinese mallet playing, on the one hand, and Indian drumming, on the other. After a bit of reading in Walter Kaufman's books on North Indian music, and in Robert E. Brown's Ph.D. thesis *The Mrdanga—A Study of Drumming in South India*, together with some discussions with Indian musicians and students at Wesleyan University, I came to the conclusion that there are three main differences, and that they are closely related. First, Indian drumming, both in the Hindustani (Northern) and Carnatic (Southern) traditions, is basically a solo music, while African drumming and Balinese mallet playing are basically ensemble musics. Second, Indian drumming is improvised within a given framework of a particular tala (rhythmic cycle), while Balinese mallet playing is composed and allows no improvisation. In African drumming, all the musicians have fixed parts, with the exception of the master drummer, who improvises on traditional patterns. Third, the basic rhythmic structure of any tala in Indian drumming, Northern or

---

1. See the essay *Gahu*, p. 55.

Southern, has one main down beat at the beginning of the cycle, whereas African drumming has multiple downbeats, often one for each member of the ensemble. In this respect, Balinese music is similar to Indian in that it has one main downbeat for the entire ensemble at the beginning of a cycle. It is no surprise then that Indian drumming is for the solo virtuoso, while in African drumming and Balinese mallet playing the individual parts, with the exception of the African master drum, are all relatively simple, and it is in the precise rhythmic blending of the ensemble that the virtuosity lies. Not being a virtuoso, not being interested in improvisation, and being thoroughly committed to my own ensemble that performs music I have composed with repetitive patterns combined so that their downbeats do not always coincide, it may be natural for my interests to run strongly toward Balinese and African music.

Not only African, Balinese, and Indian music, but also Javanese, Korean, Japanese, and many others are having a strong effect on Western musicians. This very real interest in non-Western music can be seen now in composers, performers, and even universities, where the interest in electronics, so marked in the '60s, is gradually giving away to an interest in world music. Along with the obvious benefits of this interest, which include a strong belief in live performance, and the aural or rote teaching of music instead of the exclusive use of scores, there are also some problems. The most difficult of these is the problem of Western composers, like myself, absorbing non-Western music. What can a composer do with this knowledge? One possibility is to become an ethnomusicologist, using the talents of analysis that composers often have to transcribe non-Western music into Western notation and analyse it. This is work of the utmost value, producing masterpieces of scholarship, like Colin McPhee's *Music in Bali,* but it is not musical composition. Alternately, a composer can give up composing and devote himself to trying to become a performer of some non-Western music. This will take many years of study and may, even then, only lead to mediocre performing abilities when judged by appropriate native standards. (If the performance of non-Western music were available for musically gifted Western children and teenagers to study, this would undoubtedly lead to American and European-born virtuosos of non-Western music.) Lastly, one may continue composing, but with the knowledge of non-Western music one has studied, and this is the case for myself and most other composers in this situation.

The question then arises as to how, if at all, this knowledge of non-Western music influences a composer. The least interesting form of influence, to my mind, is that of imitating the *sound* of some non-Western music. This can be done by using non-Western instruments in one's own music (sitars in the rock band), or in using one's own instruments to sound like non-Western ones (singing "Indian style" melodies over electronic drones). This method is the simplest and most superficial way of dealing with non-Western music, since the general sound of these musics can be absorbed in a few minutes of listening without further study. Imitating the sound of non-Western music leads to "exotic music"—what used to be called "Chinoiserie."

Alternately, one can create a music with own's sound that is constructed in the light of one's knowledge of non-Western *structures*. This is similar, in fact, to learning Western musical structures. The idea of canon or round, for instance, has influenced the composition of Renaissance motets, baroque fugues, and then, among others, the music of Anton Webern and my own phase pieces. The precise influence of this, or any structural idea, is quite subtle, and acts in unforseen ways. One can study the rhythmic structure of non-Western music and let that study lead one where it will, while continuing to use the instruments, scales, and any other sound one has grown up with. This brings about the interesting situation of the non-Western influence being there in the thinking, but not in the sound. This is a more genuine and interesting form of influence, because while listening one is not necessarily aware of some non-Western music being imitated. Instead of imitation, the influence of non-Western musical structures on the thinking of a Western composer is likely to produce something genuinely new.

NOTES ON MUSIC AND DANCE (1973) 11

Written for *Writings*, 1974, but prepublished in *Ballet Review*, vol. IV, no. 5, New York, Fall, 1973.

For a long time during the 1960s, one would go to the dance concert where nobody danced, followed by the party where everybody danced. This was not a healthy situation. Using rock and roll in a dance concert is not the answer, although it would probably be (and actually was) the first superficial answer one might come up with. The real answer is to create a genuinely new dance with roots that go back thousands of years to the basic impulse at the foundation of all dance: the human desire for regular rhythmic movement, usually done to music.

The avant garde dance of the 1960s focused on nondance movements to be performed in concert situations. Walking, running, working with objects, and performing specific tasks were among the genuinely new alternatives to the modern dance of expressive movements of an earlier generation. The basic of the idea of the Judson dance group (Steve Paxton, Yvonne Rainer, etc.) as well as the contribution of Simone Forti, could be summed up as: Any movement is dance. This is the precise equivalent to the basic idea of the composer John Cage: Any sound is music.

There is, however, another and primary sense of these words, where one can say that all sounds are obviously not music, all movements are not dance, and most children can usually tell the difference between one and the other.

While the Judson group was the dance equivalent to John Cage (even more so, curiously, than Merce Cunningham—think of Paxton's *Satisfyin' Lover*, the walking piece, and Cage's *4'33"*, the silent piece), presently what is needed is the dance equivalent of music composed with regular rhythmic repetition of a single musical pattern. Laura Dean is the first choreographer/dancer to work with such extreme regular rhythmic repetition as a fundamental technique and soon, hopefully, there will be others.

Somehow in recent years movements in music have preceded similar developments in dance. Hopefully in the future they will occur simultaneously.

In the last few years, there have been and still are a number of dance performances (largely by those formerly associated with the Judson group) based on improvisation and group dynamics. The momentary state of mind of the individual or group during performance creates or strongly influences the structure of the dance. Now we have an alternative to this where the predetermined structure of the dance creates or strongly influences the state of mind of the performers while performing. While this alternative is new for us at this particular time, it has existed in other cultures for thousands of years.

Unfortunately, there may soon be a number of choreographers who will present imitation Oriental, African, or American Indian dances. This exoticism will be as vulgar and inappropriate as its musical equivalent.[1] What is needed is neither exoticism nor a return to the modern dance of earlier decades but, rather, a return to the roots of dance as it is found all over the world: regular rhythmic movement, usually done to music, and performed by members of our own culture within the context of our own high art tradition.

When I was in Ghana in 1970, I found there was a clear distinction between social popular dances and high art religious dances. The obvious differences lay in the formal or informal movement and dress of the performers, as well as the location, time of day, and social-religious context of the performance. But all of the dances, popular and classical, had a strong rhythmic pulse.

For music and dance to go together, they must share the same rhythmic structure. This common rhythmic structure will determine the length of the music and dance, as well as when changes in both will occur. It will not determine what sounds are used in the music nor what movements are used in the dance.

In 1944, John Cage wrote, ". . . a dance, a poem, a piece of music (any of the time arts) occupies a length of time, and the manner in which this length of time is divided . . . is the work's very life structure."[2] In the same article, he said, "Personality is a flimsy thing on which to build an art." Cage understood that rhythmic structure was impersonal and therefore universal, that is, understood by all. He also understood that a rhythmic structure did not dictate particular sounds for a piece of music nor a set of movements for a dance. *Those* elements *were* the manifestations of personality. What Cage put less emphasis on in the 1940s, and

---

1. Discussed in "Postscript to a Brief Study," (no. 10), p. 70.
2. John Cage, "Grace and Clarity," originally published in *Dance Observer*, 1944, reprinted in *Silence*, Wesleyan University Press, 1961.

apparently still less as time went on, was the underlying impulse for dance: the natural human desire for regular rhythmic movement. He also turned away from the reality that people do in fact dance *to the music*—that music can and does supply rhythmic energy for dance.

What is needed is a genuinely new Western high art dance with movements natural to the personality of someone living here and now, organized in a clear (i.e., universal) rhythmic structure, and satisfying the basic desire for regular rhythmic movement that has been and will continue to be the underlying basic impetus for all dance.

SIX PIANOS (1973) 12

For several years, I had the idea of composing a piece for all the pianos in a piano store. The Baldwin Piano and Organ Company, through their artist's representative, Mr. Jack Romann, made it possible for me to try and realize this idea during many evening rehearsals at their New York store during the fall and winter of 1972–73. The piece that resulted was more modest in scope, since too many pianos, especially if they are large grands, can begin to sound thick and unmanageable. Using six small spinet pianos, or small grands, made it possible to play the fast, rhythmically intricate kind of music I am drawn to, while at the same time allowing the players to be physically close together so as to hear each other clearly.

Six Pianos was completed in March 1973. It begins with three pianists all playing the same eight-beat rhythmic pattern but with different notes for each player. Two of the other pianists then begin in unison to gradually build up the exact pattern of one of the pianists already playing by first playing the notes of his fifth beat on the seventh beat of their measure, then his first beat on their third beat, and so on, until they have constructed the same pattern with the same notes, but two beats out of phase (see ex. 12-1).

This is the same process of substituting beats for rests as appears for the first time in *Drumming* but here, instead of the process happening by itself, it happens against another performer (or performers) already playing that pattern in another rhythmic position. The end result is that of a pattern played against itself but one or more beats out of phase. Although this result is similar to many of the older pieces, the process of arriving at that result is new. Instead of slow shifts of phase, there is a percussive build-up of beats in place of rests. In contrast to the smooth movements of *Piano Phase,* the use of the piano here is truly more like a set of tuned drums.

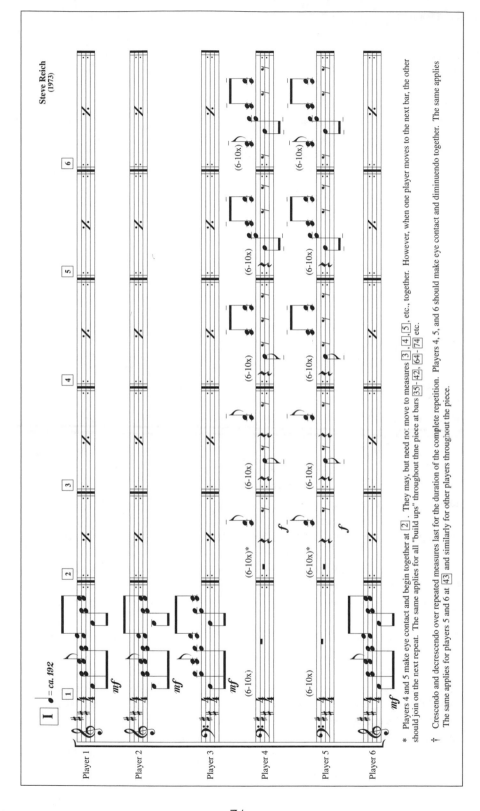

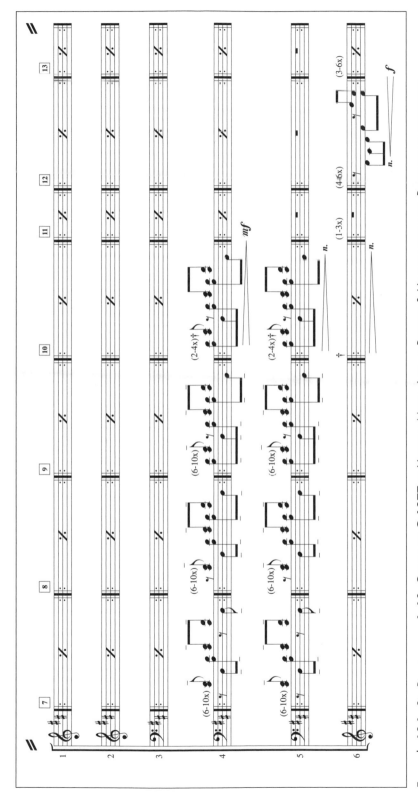

Example 12-1. *Six Pianos*, mm. 1–13. Copyright © 1977 by Hendon Music, Inc., a Boosey & Hawkes Company. Reprinted by permission.

In 1973, I began work on a piece that grew very spontaneously from one marimba pattern to many patterns played by other mallet instruments. While working out the marimba patterns, I found myself spontaneously singing long held tones. By May 1973, *Music for Mallet Instruments, Voices, and Organ* was completed.

The piece deals with two simultaneous and interrelated musical processes. The first is the building up, beat by beat, of a duplicate of a preexisting repeating marimba or glockenspiel pattern, with the duplicate being one or more beats out of phase with the original. This then triggers the second process of augmenting or lengthening the repeating chord cadences in the woman's voices and organ. The first process of rhythmic construction in the marimbas and glockenspiels has the effect of creating more fast-moving activity, which then triggers the voices and organ into doubling, quadrupling, and further elongating the duration of the notes they sing and play.

When the marimbas and glockenspiels have built up to maximum activity, causing the voices and organ to elongate to maximum length and slowness, then a third woman's voice doubles some of the short melodic patterns resulting from the interlocking of the four marimba players, using her voice to precisely imitate the sound of these instruments (exactly as happens in *Drumming*).

In its use of instruments of different timbre paired off against each other, this piece is an extension of the last section of *Drumming*. In the augmentation of the organ and voices, it is a simplification of the gradual augmentation found in *Four Organs*. In the combination of these processes, it is new.

The piece is in four sections marked off by changes in key and meter. The first is in F dorian $\frac{3}{4}$, the second A♭ dorian $\frac{2}{4}$, the third B♭ minor $\frac{3}{4}$, and the fourth is D♭ $\frac{3}{4}$. The duration is about 17 minutes (see ex. 13-1).

One of the most important aspects of this piece for me is the use of voices to double the electric organ and produce a new timbre that is both instrumental and vocal at the same time. The choice of two women's voices and electric organ took several months of experimentation to arrive at. My first impulse was *not* to use the electric organ because I wanted to avoid working with electronic instruments. Since I had written a series of four-note chords, I began with four wind instruments and four voices, two men and two women, with one instrument and one voice for each note. Each instrument and each voice had its own microphone so as to blend all the vocal and instrumental timbres. At one early rehearsal, there were even two bass clarinets and two clarinets doubled by two men's and two women's voices. At another time, there was bass trombone, trombone, fluegelhorn, and trumpet, doubled by bass, tenor, alto, and soprano voices. Unfortunately, when the chords grew long in duration, both winds and voices had diffi-

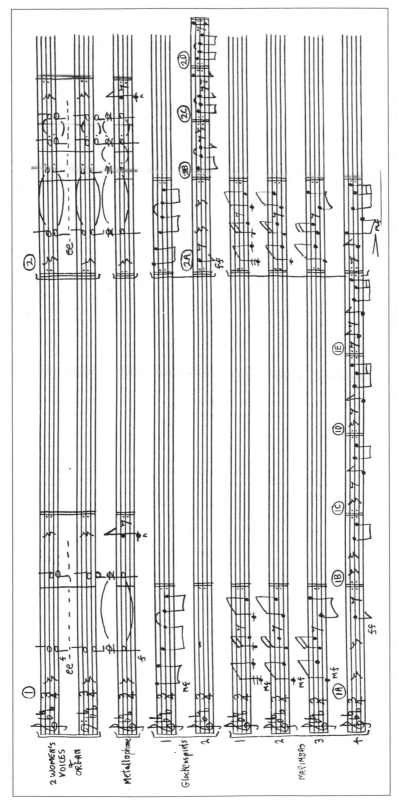

Example 13-1. *Music for Mallet Instruments, Voices, and Organ,* bars 1–2. Copyright © 1977 by Hendon Music, Inc. A Boosey & Hawkes Company. Reprinted by permission.

culty keeping in tune, and the effect became ponderous and heavy. I eliminated the wind instruments and substituted the electric organ, while keeping all four voices. There was an improvement in the stability of tuning, but the sound was still too heavy and slow moving. Finally, I tried only the soprano and alto doubling the top two notes of the organ chords, and eliminated the men's voices. The vowel sung was "ee." The two women adjusted their tuning far more precisely, the organist and singers moved more closely together rhythmically, and the electric organ was infused with the sound of the human voice. The idea of occasionally using the voice to exactly imitate the sound of an instrument playing short repeating melodic patterns, which first appeared in *Drumming*, was extended in *Music for Mallet Instruments, Voices, and Organ* to a constant vocal-instrumenal blend as one of the basic timbres of the entire piece.

14 MUSIC FOR PIECES OF WOOD (1973)

Music for Pieces of Wood grows out of the same roots as *Clapping Music:* a desire to make music with the simplest possible instruments. The claves, or cylindrical pieces of hard wood, used here were selected for their particular pitches (A, B, C♯, D♯, and D♯ an octave above), and for their resonant timbre. This piece is one of the loudest I have ever composed, but uses no amplification whatsoever.

The rhythmic structure is based entirely on the process of rhythmic "build-ups" or the substitution of beats for rests, and is in three sections of decreasing pattern length: $\frac{6}{4}, \frac{4}{4}, \frac{3}{4}$.

15 STEVE REICH AND MUSICANS (1973)

Originally written for *Writings*, 1974.

Since late in 1966, I have been rehearsing and performing my music with my own ensemble.

In 1963, I first decided that despite my limitations as a performer I had to play in all my compositions. It seemed clear that a healthy musical situation would only result when the functions of composer and performer were united.

In San Francisco in 1963, I formed my first ensemble, which was devoted to free, and sometimes controlled, improvisation. This quintet met at least once a week for about six months, but because we were improvising on nothing but spur of the moment reactions I felt there was not any musical growth except when I brought what I called *Pitch Charts,* which gave all the players the same notes to play at the same time, but with free rhythm. Even with these charts the musical growth was much too limited, and the group was disbanded.

In the fall of 1965, I returned to New York, and by late 1966 I had formed a group of three musicans: the pianist Art Murphy, the woodwind player Jon Gibson, and me playing piano. This ensemble was able to perform *Piano Phase* for two pianos; *Improvisations on a Watermelon* for two pianos (later discarded); *Reed Phase* for soprano saxophone and tape (later discarded); and several tape pieces. This trio remained intact with occasional additions, notably that of the composer/pianist James Tenney in 1967 to play a four piano version of *Piano Phase* and other pieces, until 1970 when the composition of *Phase Patterns* for four electric organs, and *Four Organs* for four electric organs and maracas created the need for a quintet adding the pianist Steve Chambers and occasionally the composer/performer Phil Glass. In 1971, with the composition of *Drumming,* the ensemble underwent a significant expansion to 12 musicians and singers. At this time I sought out and found a number of fine percussionists, the most outstanding of whom, Russ Hartenberger and James Preiss, continue to play in the present ensemble[1]. Also and for the first time, I had to find singers who had the sense of time, intonation, and timbre necessary to blend in with the sound of the marimbas in *Drumming.* Joan LaBarbara and Jay Clayton proved to be perfectly suited to this new vocal style. It was in 1971 that the name of the ensemble, Steve Reich and Musicians, was first adopted.[2]

I have thus become a composer with a repertory ensemble. Each new composition is added to the repertoire and our concerts present a selection of new and older works.

The question often arises as to what contribution the performers make to the music. The answer is that they select the resulting patterns in all compositions that have resulting patterns, and that certain details of the music are worked out by members of the ensemble during rehearsals. Resulting patterns are melodic patterns that result from the combination of two or more identical instruments playing the same repeating melodic pattern one or more beats out of phase with each other. During the selection of resulting patterns to be sung in the second section of *Drumming,* Joan LaBarbara, Jay Clayton, Judy Sherman, and I all contributed

---

1. Two other percussionists who have played in the ensemble for almost as long are Bob Becker and Garry Kvistad.
2. This name is still used when the composer participates on stage as a performer. The name Steve Reich Ensemble has been introduced for those occasions when he is not performing but overseeing the performance from the sound mixing board.

various patterns we heard resulting from the combination of the three marimbas. These patterns were selected, and an order for singing them worked out, with the help of tape loops of the various marimba combinations played over and over again at my studio during rehearsals held throughout the summer of 1971. Similarly, in the resulting patterns for *Six Pianos,* Steve Chambers, James Preiss, and I worked out the resulting patterns and the order in which to play them during rehearsals at the Baldwin Piano Store during the fall and winter of 1972–73.

During the summer of 1973, in Seattle, I worked with different singers in the marimba section of *Drumming* who heard and sang very different resulting patterns than the singers in New York. When I returned to New York, I showed the new resulting patterns to Jay Clayton and Joan LaBarbara, who decided to incorporate some of these patterns into their own version. The details of the music changed when the performers changed.[3]

Selecting resulting patterns is not improvising; it is actually filling in the details of the composition itself. It offers the performers the opportunity to listen to minute details and to sing or play the ones he or she finds most musical.

There's a certain idea that's been in the air, particularly since the 1960s, and it's been used by choreographers as well as composers and I think it is an extremely misleading idea. It is that the only pleasure a performer (be it musician or dancer) could get was to improvise, or in some way be free to express his or her momentary state of mind. If anybody gave them a fixed musical score or specific instructions to work with this was equated with political control and it meant that the performer was going to be unhappy about it.[4] John Cage has said that a composer is somebody who tells other people what to do, and that it is not a good social situation to do that. But if you know and work with musicians you will see that what gives them joy is playing music they love, or at least find musically interesting, and whether that music is improvised or completely worked out is really not the main issue. The main issue is what's happening *musically;* is this beautiful, is this sending chills up and down my spine or isn't it?

The musicians play in this ensemble, usually for periods of three to five years or more, because, presumably, they like playing the music, or at least because they find it of some musical interest. They do not make all their income from playing in this ensemble. Some have been doctoral candidates in the study of African, Indonesian, and Indian music, some teach percussion, and all perform in a variety of musical ensembles including orchestras, chamber groups, medieval music ensembles, South Indian, African, and Indonesian classical ensembles, free improvisation and jazz groups. It is precisely the sort of musician who starts with a strong Western classical background and then later gravitates toward these other types of music that I find ideally suited for this ensemble.

---

3. This remains a possibility even with the publication of a score of the early works—but most performers will probably want to follow the given resulting patterns unless they have an unusual amount of time for creative rehearsal.

4. The situation has, of course, changed but was still very much in evidence at the time of writing.

The presence of musicians who play certain instruments or sing encourages me to write more music for those instruments or voices. The percussionists and singers I began working with in *Drumming* encouraged me to write more percussion and vocal music. *Music for Mallet Instruments, Voices, and Organ* is one of the results.

These musicians are also my first and most important critics. During early rehearsals when a first version of a new piece is being tried out, the reactions of the players will often tell me whether the new piece really works, or not. Not only direct verbal comments during or after a rehearsal but also an appreciative laugh or an embarrassed averted glance may be enough to let me know when I am on the right or wrong track. This was particularly the case in the early fall of 1972, when the reactions of James Preiss, Russell Hartenberger, and Steve Chambers were enough to make me throw away several attempts at multiple piano pieces that preceded the finished version of *Six Pianos*.

There is also the question of frequency of rehearsals. Most new pieces of about 20 minutes in length will be rehearsed once or twice a week for two or three months. *Drumming*, which lasts about an hour and 20 minutes, took almost a year of weekly rehearsals. This amount of rehearsing allows for many small compositional changes while the work is in progress and at the same time builds a kind of ensemble solidity that makes playing together a joy.

MUSIC AND PERFORMANCE (1969–74; 1993) 16

I–III were printed in *Writings*, 1974, under the title "From Program Notes"; IV—Statement about Time—was written for *Dance Ink* magazine October 1993.

(I)

I am not interested in improvisation or in sounding exotic.

One hardly needs to seek out personality as it can never be avoided.

Obviously music should put all within listening range into a state of ecstasy.

I am interested in music which works exclusively with gradual changes in time.

(II)

A performance for us is a situation where all the musicians, including myself, attempt to set aside our individual thoughts and feelings of the moment, and try to focus our minds and bodies clearly on the realization of one continuous musical process.

This music is not the expression of the momentary state of mind of the performers while playing. Rather the momentary state of mind of the performers while playing is largely determined by the ongoing composed slowly changing music.

By voluntarily giving up the freedom to do whatever momentarily comes to mind, we are, as a result, free of all that momentarily comes to mind.

(III)

As a performer what I want is to be told exactly what to do within a musical ensemble, and to find that by doing it well I help make beautiful music. This is what I ask of my own compositions, and those of any other composer, and this is what I looked for and found when I studied Balinese and African music. The pleasure I get from playing is not the pleasure of expressing myself, but of subjugating myself to the music and experiencing the ecstasy that comes from being a part of it.

(IV)

Music Dance Theatre Video and Film are arts in time. Artists in those fields who keep this in mind seem to go further than those mainly concerned with psychology or personality.

17a VIDEOTAPE AND A COMPOSER (1975)

Written in September 1975, this essay was in included in *Video Art—An Anthology*, compiled and edited by Ira Schneider and Beryl Korot, and published in New York in 1976. Thus, it dates from the beginning of Reich's association with his future wife and clearly maps out the area in which they would eventually collaborate as artists. Beryl Korot's own essay in the same book offers a fascinating account of her approach to video art, and this takes on added resonance when considered in the context of their later collaboration. Her essay is reprinted here in full as number 17b. In both essays, ideas are glimpsed that will be further developed in *The Cave* and *Three Tales*.

There are two ways I've worked or thought of working with videotape. The first is videotaping performances of musical compositions and the second is composing pieces for videotape.

1. For me, with few exceptions, the effect of watching and listening to a musical performance on a television screen and loudspeaker is one of trivializing the music. This trivialization happens because the sound quality is poor and the image small and also not of high quality. Can you ever remember a musically moving experience you had while watching and listening to a television receiver?

What are the "few exceptions" just mentioned? These tend to be those cases where the instrumentation is relatively simple, the number of performers relatively few, and the bodies of the performers readily observable so that their posture, gestures, and general psychophysical presence can be seen and felt while they play. It seems to me that the medium of television, whether as commercial broadcast, art gallery installation, or whatever, is the most psychological medium I have ever encountered. By that I mean that it is, for me, more important to see and feel the presence of the performer on a television broadcast or recording than it is in live performance, or on an audio broadcast or recording, where it may be preferable to simply close one's eyes and listen.

As examples of the above I have made videotapes of performances of my compositions *Clapping Music* (1972) and *Music for Pieces of Wood* (1973). The instrumentation of the former is simply two musicians clapping, that of the latter, five musicians playing tuned claves, or small tuned cylinders of hard wood. In both cases, the sound sources are relatively simple compared to the acoustic spectrum of a piano, marimba, violin, or other musical instrument, and in both cases the number of performers is small enough so that the viewer can enjoy their posture, gestures, and presence. I should add that, in accord with these ideas, *Clapping Music*, which is the simpler of the two both in instrumentation and in number of performers, seems the more effective on videotape (see fig. 17-1).

2. In the 1950s and 1960s, composers began composing pieces on magnetic audiotape. More recently, a few composers have begun to work with videotape as the medium of a particular musical work. As in relation to taped performances, I believe that for videotape compositions the most interesting image is that of the human body and face, close up; and the most interesting sound is that of human speech. As a composer, the image in a videotape composition, for me, is simply the "sync image" of the soundtrack.

As examples of videotape compositions, I have two closely related multichannel pieces in mind to be realized, I hope, in the future.

The first, *My Name Is* (video), is simply the video version of my piece of the same name of 1967 for three or more audiotape recorders. In the video version, the faces of three or more men, women, or children are videotaped close up saying, "My name is . . ." and their first name. Each "My name is . . ." is then made into a loop by dubbing it over and over again onto another reel or cassette for one or two minutes. Then the completed reel or cassette of three or more people each saying "My name is . . ." is itself reproduced three or more times. These duplicate reels or cassettes are then played on three or more separate decks into three or more monitors simultaneously, all beginning at exactly the same instant. The identical sound and image loop plays on three or more monitors simultaneously

Figure 17-1. *Clapping Music* performed in 1974 by, left to right: Russell Hartenberger, Steve Reich. STILL FROM VIDEO BY STEVE REICH.

and, due to minute differences in motor speed, tape imperfections, and so on, the tapes begin to gradually move in and out of phase with each other, producing audiovisual canons, or rounds.

The second piece, *Portraits,* is identical in form and only slightly different in content. In this piece, three or more people are videotaped close up saying words or making sounds that give some direct intuitive insight into who they are. A casual remark accompanied by a typical gesture or a habitual speech melody might contain the brief (one to three seconds or so) sound and image necessary for the portrait. Each brief videotape is then duplicated as a loop, as mentioned above, and played on three or more decks and monitors, as described for *My Name Is.* Again, slight differences in motor speed of the decks, minute differences in the tapes, and so on, will produce gradually shifting phase relations perceived as audio-visual canons or rounds.

In making the four-channel video work *Dachau 1974*, my experience as a weaver directly influenced the basic structuring of the work. The content itself was taped in 1974 at the former concentration camp, Dachau. The symmetry of the architecture and the *present* ambience of this space were the focus of the recordings. The past was recorded only insofar as the sounds of the voices of the present commingled with the feeling absorbed in the wood and revealed in the structure of forms which no amount of time can erase. In retrospect, from a historical perspective, what seems most unique about Dachau symbolically is the expression of that darker side of the human spirit, manifested here through the use of specific tools and techniques of a highly sophisticated and efficient nature.

Once the material for the work was gathered, I turned to the ancient technology of the loom to help solve problems I'd long been having in working with video.

The technology of the loom and the art of weaving both literally and metaphorically represent the combining of many separate elements (literally in the form of threads) to develop patterns that evolve in time to create fabric. That is, the rhythmic body time (as expressed through hand movements)/eye/mind relationship of the individual weaver works in harmony with the laws of the machine itself. For a particular work, the weaver passes weft threads over and under the warp threads of the loom, which has been threaded (programmed) by the weaver so that preselected pattern possibilities remain for the weaver to develop, or ignore, when creating a work.

The tactile relationship of the hand and mind working cooperatively within the ancient and sophisticated parameters of this earliest of *threaded* technologies has created indispensable objects of mundane use as well as works of great beauty, endurance, and complex visual structuring.

Just as the spinning and gathering of wool serve as the raw material for a weave, so the artist working with video selects images to serve as the basic substance of the work. All technology, in its capacity to instantly reproduce, store, and retrieve information, has moved continually in a direction that seeks to free us from laboring with our hands by giving us greater conceptual freedom to organize, select, and judge. For me, it's become clear that the greater my understanding of the role of craftsmanship in working with the video medium, and the more manually active I remain in the selection processes, the greater the possibility for making a technological work true to my intentions.

In the actual making of the work I sought primarily to: (1) introduce a patient, molding attitude toward selection and structuring of the recorded images, and (2) to work with time on multiple channels in such a way that carefully composed image/time relationships would seem live and present to the viewer.

Ultimately, I structured the work for four channels. (Working with multiple channels, in general, permits a richness of input and variables, as well as a simultaneity of action that I feel can give this type of work vitality, greater spatial scale, and potential structural substance.) Selecting specific image/time relationships for each channel in the editing process, working with small sections of time repeated with slight variations played against one another on different channels, and editing from a drawn sketch of the overall structure of the work permitted the physical/ conceptual relationship I was seeking.

In the actual construction of the work, my concern was to re-present the space of Dachau through the development of time patterns. This was accomplished by assigning specific time values to specific images (per channel) and by repeating images to create image blocks.

Each channel was conceived as representing a thread. Channels (1 and 3) and (2 and 4) form the interlocking thread combinations that bind the work as it proceeds in time. The same apparent image block always plays on channels 1 and 3, and another on 2 and 4, for predesignated amounts of time. After 3 minutes, say, and at slightly different moments, the image block on channels 1 and 3 changes to the same apparent one as on 2 and 4; in a while, 2 and 4 change to another block while 1 and 3 hold; and, again, 1 and 3 change while 2 and 4 hold, and so on.

As these two sets of corresponding images proceed in time, they always share a direct contextual relationship (e.g., you might be inside the barracks on 2 and 4 while on 1 and 3 you are outside looking in). In addition to this vertical block progression of time, and although channels (1 and 3) and (2 and 4) always show the same apparent image (facilitated since most images were shot on tripod), each channel has been given a slightly different rhythm that remains constant for the work's 24 minutes. (In other words, channel 1 always has 15 seconds of image and a 1-second pause; channel 2, 11 seconds and a 1-second pause; channel 3, 7 seconds and a 1-second pause; and channel 4, 15 seconds and a 1-second pause. The pause is represented by gray leader tape edited in for 1 second after each duration of 15, 11, or 7 seconds.) This concept of playing back preselected time/ image segments on itself was my way of infusing the work with liveness and presence.

As for the audio, it was all recorded and edited in sync with the images. Thus, image and sound together, through constant repetitions of small sections of time within the larger image blocks, reinforce each other and, for me, the feeling of this particular place.

In the exhibition space where the work was presented, four 22″ monitors were cut into a white false wall (approx. 10′ × 10′), easily constructed from foam board. A small wooden bench was placed in front of this wall at a comfortable viewing distance.

Written as a program note for the first performance at New York Town Hall on April 24, 1976.

Music for 18 Musicians is approximately 55 minutes long. The first sketches were made for it in May 1974 and it was completed in March 1976. Although its steady pulse and rhythmic energy relate to many of my earlier works, its instrumentation, harmony, and structure are new.

As to instrumentation, *Music for 18 Musicians* is new in the number and distribution of instruments: violin, cello, two clarinets doubling bass clarinet, four women's voices, four pianos, three marimbas, two xylophones, and metallophone (vibraphone with no motor). All instruments are acoustical. The use of electronics is limited to microphones for the voices and some of the instruments, in order to obtain a balance in the overall sound.

There is more harmonic movement in the first five minutes of *Music for 18 Musicians* than in any other complete work of mine to this date. Although the movement from chord to chord is often just a revoicing, inversion, or relative minor or major of a previous chord, usually staying within the key signature of three sharps at all times, nevertheless, within these limits, harmonic movement plays a more important role here than in any of my earlier pieces.

Rhythmically, there are two basically different kinds of time occurring simultaneously in *Music for 18 Musicians*. The first is that of a regular rhythmic pulse in the pianos and mallet instruments that continues throughout the piece. The second is the rhythm of the human breath in the voices and wind instruments. The entire opening and closing sections plus part of all sections in between contain pulses by the voices and winds. They take a full breath and sing or play pulses of particular notes for as long as their breath will comfortably sustain them. The breath is the measure of the duration of their pulsing. This combination of one breath after another gradually washing up like waves against the constant rhythm of the pianos and mallet instruments is something I have not heard before and would like to investigate further (see ex. 18-1).[1]

The structure of *Music for 18 Musicians* is based on a cycle of 11 chords played at the very beginning of the piece and repeated at the end (see ex. 18-2). All the instruments and voices play or sing pulsing notes within each chord. Instruments like the strings that do not have to breathe nevertheless follow the rise

1. See Reich's comments on Michael Snow in "Excerpts from an interview in Art Forum," #2A, p. 33.

Example 18-1. *Music for 18 Musicians*, mm. 624–25. COPYRIGHT © BY HENDON MUSIC, INC., A BOOSEY & HAWKES COMPANY. REPRINTED BY PERMISSION.

Example 18-2. *Music for 18 Musicians,* cycle of chords.

and fall of the breath by following the breath patterns of the bass clarinet. Each chord is held for the duration of two breaths, and the next chord is gradually introduced, and so on, until all 11 are played and the ensemble returns to the first chord. This first pulsing chord is then maintained by two pianos and two marimbas. While this pulsing chord is held for about five minutes a small piece is constructed on it. When this piece is completed there is a sudden change to the second chord, and a second small piece or section is constructed. This means that each chord that might have taken 15 or 20 seconds to play in the opening section is then stretched out as the basic pulsing harmony for a five-minute piece, very much as a single note in a cantus firmus or chant melody of a twelfth-century organum by Perotin might be stretched out for several minutes as the harmonic center for a section of the organum. The opening 11-chord cycle of *Music for 18 Musicians* is a kind of pulsing cantus for the entire piece.

On each pulsing chord one or, on the third chord, two small pieces are built. These pieces or sections are basically either in the form of an arch (ABCDCBA), or in the form of a musical process, like that of substituting beats for rests, working itself out from beginning to end. Elements appearing in one section will appear in another but surrounded by different harmony and instrumentation. For instance, the pulse in pianos and marimbas in sections 1 and 2 changes to marimbas and xylophones and two pianos in section 3A, and to xylophones and maracas in sections 6 and 7. The low piano pulsing harmonies of section 3A reappear in section 6 supporting a different melody played by different instruments. The process of building up a canon, or phase relation, between two xylophones and two pianos, which first occurs in section 2, occurs again in section 9, but building up to another overall pattern in a different harmonic context. The relationship between the different sections is thus best understood in terms of resemblances between members of a family. Certain characteristics will be shared, but others will be unique.[2]

One of the basic means of change or development in many sections of this piece is to be found in the rhythmic relationship of harmony to melody. Specifi-

---

2. A concept Reich first encountered in Wittgenstein's *Philosophical Investigations*, 1953.

cally, a melodic pattern may be repeated over and over again, but by introducing a two- or four-chord cadence underneath it, first beginning on one beat of the pattern, and then beginning on a different beat, a sense of changing accent in the melody will be heard. This play of changing harmonic rhythm against constant melodic pattern is one of the basic techniques of this piece, and one that I had never used before. Its effect, by change of accent, is to vary that which is in fact unchanging.

Changes from one section to the next, as well as changes within each section, are cued by the metallophone, whose patterns are played once only to call for movements to the next bar—much as in a Balinese Gamelan a drummer will audibly call for changes of pattern, or as the master drummer will call for changes of pattern in West African music. This is in contrast to the visual nods of the head used in earlier pieces of mine to call for changes and in contrast also to the general Western practice of having a nonperforming conductor for large ensembles (fig. 18-1). Audible cues become a part of the music and allow the musicians to keep listening.

PH: How was *Music for 18 Musicians* composed—I think you told me there was a lot of collaboration in putting it together?

SR: It was composed during 1974–75 and at that point there were more regular rehearsals with the ensemble than at any other time. In those days I wasn't commissioned, but there was a clear understanding that there were concerts available. It was first done as a work-in-progress in 1975.

PH: Did the musicians work for free during the rehearsals?

SR: Yes, basically—they were mostly then students—Russ Hartenberger and Bob Becker were studying non-Western music at Wesleyan University [about a two-hour drive north of New York City in Middletown, Connecticut], and I paid the bus fare. I lived across the street from here in a loft and I rented four spinets for the rehearsals, which took place every two to four weeks. I would write a lot in my notebook in shorthand and then transfer it to individual parts for the musicians, just adding occasional notes in the parts. Then there was a lot of discussion in rehearsal: "No, no, you come in here," and the musician would just write it on his part. So this oral tradition grew and the notation shrunk; the parts had everything on them that the musicians needed to play the piece, but no bar numbers common to all players. There are 11 sections with Roman numerals that mark off the sections, but once you're into a section there's no number to call out. We just continued working that way and the piece was going well, and when the piece was done, that's what there was. I started to make a score. I got to section 2 and I began realizing I wasn't even sure how to notate everything, and there were hundreds of pages to go, so I stopped. Basically there were 22 years without a score: between 1976 and 1998, when Marc Mellits finally made the score (in conjunction with me) for Boosey & Hawkes.

—From a discussion with the editor.

Figure 18-1. *Music for 18 Musicians* performed by Steve Reich & Musicians at Town Hall, New York City, 1976. Left to right: Nurit Tilles, Shem Guiborry, Elizabeth Arnold, Jay Clayton, Ken Ishii, Larry Karush, Gary Schall, Russell Hartenberger, Glen Velez, Bob Becker, Steve Chambers, David van Tiegham, Pamela Wood, James Preiss, Steve Reich, Richard Cohen, and Leslie Scott. PHOTO BY PAMELA MAGNUS.

SECOND INTERVIEW WITH MICHAEL NYMAN (1976) 19

This interview, which is primarily concerned with *Music for 18 Musicians,* took place at La Rochelle, France, on June 26/27, 1976. It was published in the art magazine *Studio International* (November/December 1976, vol. 192, no. 984). The composer has very slightly emended some of his comments.

NYMAN: When you wrote *Music as a Gradual Process,* were you aware of Sol LeWitt's *Paragraphs on Conceptual Art?* Because it seems to me that there are some very striking parallels.

REICH: I wrote *Music as a Gradual Process* in New Mexico in the summer of 1968 in complete isolation from everybody except the composer/pianist James Tenney, who paid me a visit and looked over the manuscript and offered some good comments. I discovered Sol LeWitt's *Paragraphs* a couple of years later when he gave me the catalogue for his exhibition at the Gemeente Museum in The Hague.

NYMAN: He says in the opening paragraph, for instance, that "When an artist uses a conceptual form of art, it means that all of the planning and decisions are made beforehand and the execution is a perfunctory affair."

REICH: I don't agree. Execution is hardly a perfunctory affair and never has been in my music. Also, I'm not a conceptual artist, because the concept does not necessarily precede the work but, rather, as I said in *Music as a Gradual Process,* not only may the form precede the content but the content may precede the form. In my music, the musical material has usually become clear before the form. In *It's Gonna Rain,* the material, the original loop, preceded the phasing idea. I knew I was going to work with Brother Walter's voice. I knew it was that material that was generating my excitement. So it was a sound that was in my ear, and later I discovered the process of phasing. For me, sound has been uppermost in my mind, and even in *It's Gonna Rain* the question of how long the execution of the phasing would be (in other words, does it go round from unison to unison in two minutes or does it take nine minutes or does it take seven minutes)—that decision was crucial. So the execution is never perfunctory. As you know my ensemble will rehearse a large new piece like *Music for 18 Musicians* for two years. So I would completely disagree with what Sol says here—at least as far as my own music is concerned.

NYMAN: What struck me was the similarity between LeWitt's "all the planning and decisions are made beforehand" and your "once the process is set up and loaded it runs by itself."

REICH: Well, my decisions weren't all made beforehand. The only times that I composed a phase piece that goes from unison to unison was in the first section of *It's Gonna Rain* and the individual sections of *Piano Phase.* Every other piece of mine has some aesthetic decision in it as to exactly how many beats out of phase a pattern will shift against itself and when the two voices will become four voices, and when the four voices will become eight voices, and when the melodic resulting patterns will be doubled. Even in *It's Gonna Rain* where you have the "pure" process, yes, there's a pure process, but how long does it take? That's an aesthetic decision.

NYMAN: But surely you'd admit that the tone and purpose of *Music as a Gradual Process* were very close to that of the *Paragraphs?*

REICH: Yes, but we're talking now in 1976, and at the time I was writing, in 1968, much of the stress in new music was on chance and free improvisation and I was trying to separate myself from that and to show that one could work in a more traditional way. What I wanted was a blend of controlled individual choice and impersonality. You're doing something that is working itself out and yet because you've chosen the material and the process it is also expressive of yourself and you needn't meddle with it any further for it to express your personality. But surely what you say is true that the thrust of my essay, and the tersely worded style, was to drive home an idea of *im*personality, which I thought was important at the time. And now it's eight years later and I don't feel like making that point any more because it's so well understood. In fact, I've changed musically quite a bit and I'd like to bring my words up to date, too.

NYMAN: To return to the LeWitt *Paragraphs,* he says, "If the artist wishes to explore his idea thoroughly, then arbitrary or chance decisions would be kept to a minimum, while caprice, taste, and other whimsies would be eliminated from the making of the art."

REICH: Certainly there's no place for chance in my music beyond the traditional place for it; namely, after the rehearsals, one can never know exactly how a live performance will go. The idea of composing through tossing coins, or oracles, or other chance forms I would reject now, as I did in 1967, and as I did in 1958 when I first heard John Cage's retrospective concert.[1] But there is a great difference between chance and choice, and what I was trying to do in my earlier pieces was, to some extent, eliminate personal choices as a composer. Now, especially in *Music for 18 Musicians,* I have made a great deal more choices. There still isn't one iota of chance in my music and I don't foresee that there will be.

NYMAN: LeWitt also says, "once out of his hand the artist has no control over the way a viewer will perceive the work." That certainly applies to your earlier work, but it's surely true of traditional music too?[2]

REICH: Yes, but it's particularly true of music that works with short repeating patterns. In the phase pieces you can't possibly know all that people may hear. First, there are two, three, or four identical repeating patterns playing canonically against each other in different phase positions and, at times, on different groups of identical instruments simultaneously—as at the end of *Drumming.* Second, there are acoustic by-products of this repetition and phasing. For instance, in the first section of *Drumming* for tuned bongos, one may be listening to the little "tkk" of the stick hitting the skin that bounces off the ceiling at the rear of the concert hall and focusing in on that rhythmic pattern. That may be more present for one listener than the fundamental pitch of the drums. Similarly with the attack of the wooden mallets hitting the metal keys of the glockenspiels later in the piece. These acoustic by-products are particularly audible when there is rhythmic repetition and a constant key center, as is often found in Balinese and African music. As to the fundamental phase relationships, these are basically a variation of canonic technique and resemble Western musical techniques of the medieval and baroque periods. In listening to

---

1. This famous event, a 25-year retrospective concert, took place in New York Town Hall on May 15, 1958. The recording of that event is now available on CD, and the original LP box set with photographs by Robert Rauschenberg has become something of a collector's item.

2. Lewitt also writes ("Sentences on Conceptual Art" in Lewitt, 1978): "The words of one artist to another may induce an idea chain, if they share the same concept. . . . Perception is subjective. . . . The concept of a work of art may involve the matter of the piece or the process in which it is made. . . . The process is mechanical and should not be tampered with. It should run its course."

any canonic music, one will naturally focus on one of the two or more simultaneous voices—and this focus will shift depending on the listener.

NYMAN: You would obviously disagree with LeWitt's statement that "It doesn't really matter if the viewer understands the concepts of the artist by seeing the art."

REICH: Well, in 1968 through about 1972, I would have. What I said in 1968 was that I wanted the process to be perceptible. It was very important to me that the listener be able to perceive precisely what was going on in the music and I hope that I succeeded.

NYMAN: But do you still hold that position? Even with the program notes in front of me I find it very difficult to follow the process of *Music for 18 Musicians*.

REICH: Let's put it this way: in *Music for 18 Musicians* you can hear what's going on in the sense in which you can hear that the melodic pattern is getting longer. You may not realize that the melodic pattern is being repeated over and over again and is being reaccented, and that's *how* it's getting longer. So in a sense you're right, I'm not as concerned that one hears *how* the music is made. If some people hear exactly what's going on, I'm glad of it, and if other people don't, but they still like the piece, that's fine with me. I think *Music for 18 Musicians* was consciously composed with a feeling of liberating myself from strict structures. I had to have some strong formal organization because I hear that way, but once I'd established those 11 chords at the beginning, each section was in a sense an invention. Within some sections you'll still find strict build-ups working in strict canonic relationships, and then they'll be harmonized, absolutely as a question of taste with no other justification. Nevertheless, the 11 different sections do relate to each other as members of a family: Certain characteristics will be shared, others will be unique.[3]

NYMAN: But one finds that as the texture of your music becomes richer amd more seductive, not only is there less possibility of following the process but also there seems to be less necessity.

REICH: You're right. There was a didactic quality to the early pieces, I think. When you discover a new idea, it may be very important to present that idea in a very forceful and pared-down way. My early pieces are very clear examples of a strict working-out of certain musical ideas that were new, although they did have strong relationships to canonic structure and augmentation. But once you've done that for a while—you can't write the same piece over and over again. The artists I admire are the ones that move on. There's no point in simply rehashing those same principles in another orchestration. Would you really have wanted me to sit there cranking out just one perfect phase piece after another?

NYMAN: So in fact variety of materials is important to you?

REICH: Yes, it's been very important to me to work with different kinds of instruments (or the lack of them in the case of *Clapping Music*). It's very important

3. Cf. Wittgenstein, 1953.

for me to work in successive different media because the formal necessities of dealing with the voice, as opposed to dealing with the clapping of the hands, as opposed to working with marimbas, or pianos, or strings, or with bass clarinets, all produce very different basic musical assumptions. Mallet percussion and bare hands produce short tones, whereas voices, bass clarinets, and strings can produce longer ones, and that leads to basic decisions about duration of notes, the human breath, and so on. Plus, the sheer beauty of sound these instruments can produce, especially in combination.

NYMAN: You're not interested in genuinely minimal music?

REICH: No, I'm not. I'm interested in music in a more traditional sense of that word, and I really always have been. By "traditional," I mean several of the world's musical traditions including that of Europe from about 1200 to 1750, that of Balinese gamelan music as it has survived, West African music as it is found now, American jazz from about 1950 to 1965, the music of Stravinsky, Bartók, and Webern, and the traditional cantillation of the Hebrew Scriptures.

NYMAN: You've often referred to the lead pieces of Richard Serra.

REICH: I would say that the relationship between Serra and me is lodged in *Pendulum Music.* I gave him the original score of *Pendulum Music* as a gift; in exchange, he gave me a piece called *Candle Rack,* which is simply a piece of wood with 10 holes drilled in it that holds candles and sits on the floor. Actually, my ensemble rarely performs *Pendulum Music* any more.

NYMAN: Some of my students did it at Nottingham last year, unprompted by me.

REICH: Really, well, it's very easy to do, one can say that for it. I prefer the low-fi version. You can do it beautifully on small, inexpensive loudspeakers because then you get a sort of series of bird calls and I much prefer that to hi-fi shriek.

NYMAN: *Pendulum Music* is the only piece of yours that one can talk of in terms of a *natural* process, because the other pieces, as you've admitted, all have some degree of personal intervention on your part.

REICH: And not only that, they're *musical* in the sense that *Pendulum Music* is strictly *physical.* A pendulum is not a musician. So of all my pieces, that was *the* most impersonal, and was the most emblematic and the most didactic in terms of the process idea, and also most sculptural. In many ways, you could describe *Pendulum Music* as audible sculpture, with the objects being the swinging microphones and the loudspeakers. I always set them up quite clearly as sculpture. It was very important that the speakers be laid flat on the floor, which is obviously not usual in concerts.

NYMAN: So if someone composed it now, it would be called performance art.

REICH: Exactly—but I'm more interested in music.

NYMAN: Do you find that your attitude toward the art world is changing?

REICH: It may be that after a period of much activity as there was in the 1960s, things are naturally slowing down, starting about 1970.

NYMAN: Do you see the same thing happening in music?

REICH: Well, music has always moved slower—there aren't the same expectations. In the 1960s, everyone thought it was great that there was one art movement following another in quick succession. For instance, there was a two- or three-year period between the emergence of Pop Art as a dominant form and the emergence of Minimal Art as a dominant form; and then after that you have the process art that I was tied in with. Things moved very rapidly.

NYMAN: But the pace of music is slower?

REICH: It has accelerated from what it was in the Middle Ages, but it's still considerably slower than the three- or four-year generation period in the visual arts. I composed *It's Gonna Rain* in 1965, so this kind of music has been going on for well over 10 years and it's only now gaining serious attention and consideration.

Now, frankly, I think this slower movement is more healthy. It's harder to get accepted in serious music. There are a lot of people around playing Bach, so you've got to deal with them. They're not going to accept your music without careful and repeated listenings. If you want to be taken seriously by musicians in general, and not just a small coterie on the outside, it's going to take a while.

NYMAN: But when your music becomes available for anyone to play, it ceases to have the exclusivity that it has at the moment.

REICH: Well, that exclusivity is something I really don't believe in. I *want* other musicians to play my music.

NYMAN: You say that you're primarily interested in younger musicians getting to know your music.

REICH: Yes, I'm interested in other musicians *playing* my music. If a piece of music is going to survive, who's going to make that decision? It's not going to be painters or sculptors or music critics, it's going to be other musicians. If musicians like a piece of music they will continue to play it, and it will continue to live. Otherwise it's like pop music, it comes and it goes.

NYMAN: What about the question of scale and duration in your music? Taking a particular phase relationship in *Drumming,* for instance, once you've made the phasing shift, there's no *inner* reason—nothing within the music—that dictates how long you stay where you are and when to move on.

REICH: Yes, there is. What I mean by that is that if you take *Piano Phase* and you make it last for three hours, you're creating a scandal and you're not playing the piece seriously. *Piano Phase* could take, if you were really tearing along, about 16 minutes, and if you're going incredibly slowly, 22 to 24 minutes. It's a pretty wide latitude. But, on the other hand, you can't play it in seven minutes or play it in an hour without hurting the music.

NYMAN: Why not?

REICH: Because we're human beings and in many respects we're very similar, and at a certain point boredom sets in even if you're an aficionado. At a certain point, you've heard the relationship long enough to appraise it carefully, to appraise what the upper resulting patterns are, what the lower resulting patterns are, what the middle resulting patterns are, and it's time for a change.

NYMAN: *Piano Phase* is not the best example, because the texture's pretty bare. What about *Drumming?*

REICH: *Drumming* will vary in concert performance from about 70 to 80 minutes. That's the most latitude that I'm aware of—10 minutes in what is generally an 80-minute piece. On the other hand, if you played *Drumming* for two hours, that's a mistake, it's just wrong—you've grossly elongated something that shouldn't take that long.

NYMAN: Have you tried it?

REICH: We've not tried it that long, but we've played the piece many, many times without fixing it; so that, in other words, without consciously trying to do it, we've simply allowed ourselves the human situation of having no rules. I've never told anyone in my ensemble how long or how short to go on for. The singers have *x* amount of patterns to sing and they pace themselves slightly differently each night. The duration does vary, but never has it taken two hours and never has it taken 30 minutes. If you did it in 30 minutes, you'd be moving along at such a clip that no one really could get a grasp on what they heard—they wouldn't be able to hear those relationships clearly. And if you played it for two hours, it would just be a bore.

Some musicians in my ensemble have perfect pitch, as you know, and other musicians have what you could say is an absolute sense of tempo—given a piece of music they know really what the right tempo is. And this relates to the number of repetitions in my music. There is latitude, but there are limits to that latitude.

MUSIC FOR A LARGE ENSEMBLE (1978) 20

Music for a Large Ensemble was commissioned by the Holland Festival and completed in December 1978. It was premiered in June 1979 by the Netherlands Wind Ensemble under the direction of Reinbert de Leeuw at the Holland Festival. The piece is a development of two of my earlier works, *Music for Mallet Instruments, Voices, and Organ* and *Music for 18 Musicians*. The instrumental forces are the largest I have ever used and include all the orchestral families plus women's voices. All instruments are acoustical, and electronics are limited to microphones for the strings, winds, voices, and pianos.

The piece is structured in four sections, each of which is an arch form (ABCBA) beginning with shorter phrases that grow longer by augmentation and then, by diminution, return to their original length, at which point there is a change of key or meter and the next section begins. In the middle of each section, there are somewhat longer and ornate melodic lines in the violins and clarinets. This interest in more extended melodies is continued further in *Octet*.

The use of four trumpets continues my interest in the human breath as the measure of musical duration, since the chords played by the trumpets are written to take one comfortable breath to perform.

This piece may be conducted, or, if there is sufficient rehearsal time, the cues from the vibraphone will enable the musicians to know when to move on to the next bar by listening, and the piece can thus be played without conductor as a large chamber work.

21 OCTET (1979)

Octet was commissioned by Radio Frankfurt (Hessischer Rundfunk) and completed in April 1979. It was premiered on June 21, 1979, by members of the Netherlands Wind Ensemble under the direction of Reinbert de Leeuw at Radio Frankfurt. *Octet* grows out of musical material for two pianos, four hands that was suggested by the two-piano writing in *Music for a Large Ensemble*. This two-piano writing is the most difficult I have written for individual performers, and basically transfers the interlocking rhythmic complexities I had previously discovered with multiples of marimbas and xylophones to two pianos. *Octet* also reflects my ongoing interest in traditional Western acoustical instruments. Electronics are optional and are limited to microphones for amplification. The ensemble consists of string quartet, two pianos and two clarinets doubling both bass clarinet and flute as well as piccolo. I have had the good fortune to perform with several fine woodwind players over the years who play both clarinets and flutes, and saxophones as well. If musicians like these are not available, however, the piece is simply played by nine or ten musicians, adding one or two flutists to the two clarinetists. (The piece was performed by 10 musicians at its premiere in Frankfurt, and shortly afterward in Paris.) Since at no time are there more than eight musical voices playing, whether there are eight, nine, or ten performers, the piece is always musically an octet.

The piece is structured in five sections, of which the first and third resemble each other in the fast-moving piano, cello, and bass clarinet figures on the bass, while the second and fourth sections resemble each other in the longer held tones in the cello. The fifth and final section combines these materials. Perhaps more interesting, however, is that the division between sections is as smooth as possible with some overlapping in the parts, so that it is sometimes hard to tell exactly when one section ends and the next begins.

In the first, third, and fifth sections, there are somewhat longer melodic lines in the flute or piccolo. This interest in longer melodic lines, composed of shorter patterns strung together, has its roots in my own earlier music—particularly *Music for a Large Ensemble*—as well as my studies in 1976–77 of the cantillation (chanting) of the Hebrew Scriptures (see "Hebrew Cantillation," no. 24, p. 105).

VARIATIONS FOR WINDS, STRINGS, AND KEYBOARDS (1979) 22

Variations is dedicated to Betty Freeman. It was completed in December 1979 and is approximately 25 minutes long. The work was performed in a chamber orchestral format at its world premiere on February 19, 1980. The full orchestral version, commissioned by the San Francisco Symphony (Edo de Waart, Music Director), was premiered in San Francisco under Mr. de Waart's direction May 14–17, 1980.

This piece introduces markedly new harmonic, formal, and timbrel material into my music. The constant yet slow harmonic change (there are no repeat markings in this score), the slow recurrence of materials from variation to variation, and the scoring for oboes, flutes, full brass, strings, and acoustic and electric keyboards all give this piece a sound quite different from my earlier music.

These variations are on an harmonic progression somewhat in the manner of a chaconne, but with a considerably longer harmonic progression than the four- or eight-bar progressions customarily found in the chaconne. The progression begins in C minor (or C dorian) and makes its way into C♭, and then, by gradually dropping sharps or adding flats, moves slowly through several keys and back to C minor (or C dorian). There are three variations on the complete cycle lasting approximately six, ten, and nine minutes each. The harmonic progression is followed in the middle register so that, from time to time, the bass may vary from variation to variation.

The rhythm of the melodic patterns in the winds remains more or less constant throughout each variation, while the notes slowly yet constantly change to match the changing harmony. In the first variation, the rhythmic pattern for the winds is two bars long, changing meters back and forth between $\frac{6}{4}$ and $\frac{5}{4}$. The second variation begins as two bars of alternating $\frac{5}{4}$ and $\frac{6}{4}$ and, after about a minute, changes into two bars of $\frac{8}{4}$, each divided into five plus three. The final third variation pattern is four bars long, changing meters $\frac{4}{4}$, $\frac{6}{4}$, $\frac{4}{4}$, and $\frac{3}{4}$. Since the first variation uses only quarter- and eighth-notes, while the second and third introduce an increasing amount of sixteenths, the effect is one of becoming more and more florid and melismatic. At all times throughout the piece there are at least two wind instruments playing the melodic pattern in harmony with each other, while a third plays in canon with the upper voice.

The winds, three oboes doubled by electric organs, or three flutes doubled by two pianos and electric organs, play the melodic material throughout while the slowly changing harmonies are played by the strings also doubled by electric organs. During the first and last variations, a full brass section of three trumpets, three trombones, and tuba gradually fades in and out to complete the harmony of the middle register strings and organs.

23 TEHILLIM (1981)

Tehillim (pronounced teh-hill-*leem*) is the original Hebrew word for Psalms. Literally translated, it means *praises* and derives from the three-letter Hebrew root *hey, lamed, lamed (hll)*, which is also the root of halleluyah. *Tehillim* is a setting of Psalms 19:2–5 (19:1–4 in Christian translations), 34:13–15 (34:12–14), 18:26–27 (18:25–26) and 150:4–6.

The ensemble version is scored for four women's voices (one high soprano, two lyric sopranos, and one alto), piccolo, flute, oboe, english horn, two clarinets, six percussion (playing small tuned tambourines with no jingles, clapping, maracas, marimba, vibraphone, and crotales), two electric organs, two violins, viola, cello, and bass. The voices, winds, and strings are amplified in performance. In the orchestral version, there are full strings and winds with amplification for the voices only.

The first text begins as a solo with drum and clapping accompaniment only. It is repeated with clarinet doubling the voice and with a second drum and clap in canon with the first. It then appears in two-voice canon and at last the strings enter with long held harmonies. At this point, all four voices, supported by a single maraca, doubled by two electric organs and harmonized by the strings, sing four four-part canons on each of the four verses of the first text. When these are completed, the solo voice restates the original complete melody with all drums and full string harmonization. The second text begins immediately after a short drum transition. Here, the three verses of text are presented in two- or three-voice harmony in a homophonic texture. Sometimes the voices are replaced by the english horn and clarinet or by the drums and clapping. Soon the melodic lines begin augmenting (or lengthening) and then adding melismas. The effect is of a melodic line growing longer and more ornate. After a pause, the third text begins in a slower tempo and with the percussion changed to marimba and vibraphone. The text is presented as a duet first between two and then all four voices. This third text is not only the first slow movement I have composed since my student days but also the most chromatic music I have ever composed (with the possible exception of *Variations*). The fourth and final text resumes the original tempo and key signature and combines techniques used in the proceeding three movements. It is, in effect, a recapitulation of the entire piece that then, in a coda based solely on the word halleluyah, extends the music to its largest instrumental forces and its harmonic conclusion. This last movement affirms the key of D major as the basic tonal center of the work after considerable harmonic ambiguity earlier.

The tambourines without jingles are perhaps similar to the small drum called *tof* in Hebrew in Psalm 150 and several other places in the biblical text. Hand clapping as well as rattles were also commonly used throughout the Middle East in the biblical period, as were small pitched cymbals. Beyond this, there is no musicological content to *Tehillim*. No Jewish themes were used for any of the melodic material. One of the reasons I chose to set Psalms as opposed to parts of the Torah or Prophets is that the oral tradition among Jews in the West for singing Psalms has been lost. (It has been maintained by Yemenite Jews.) That means that, as opposed to the cantillation of the Torah and Prophets, which is a living 2,500-year-old oral tradition throughout the synagogues of the world, the oral tradition for Psalm singing in the Western synagogues has been lost. This meant that I was free to compose the melodies for *Tehillim* without a living oral tradition to either imitate or ignore.

In contrast to most of my earlier work, *Tehillim* is not composed of short repeating patterns; although an entire melody may be repeated either as the subject of a canon or variation, this is actually closer to what one finds throughout the history of Western music. While the four-part canons in the first and last movements may well remind some listeners of my early tape pieces *It's Gonna Rain* and *Come Out,* which are composed of short spoken phrases repeated over and over again in close canon, *Tehillim* will probably strike most listeners as quite different from my earlier works. There is no fixed meter or metric pattern in *Tehillim* as there is in my earlier music. The rhythm of the music here comes directly from the rhythm of the Hebrew text and is consequently in flexible changing meters. This is the first time I have set a text to music since my student days and the result is a piece based on melody in the basic sense of that word. The use of extended melodies, imitative counterpoint, functional harmony, and full orchestration may well suggest renewed interest in classical—or, more accurately, baroque and earlier Western musical practice. The nonvibrato, nonoperatic vocal production will also remind listeners of Western music prior to 1750. The overall sound of *Tehillim*, however, and, in particular, the intricately interlocking percussion writing that, together with the text, forms the basis of the entire work, marks this music as unique by introducing a basic musical element that one does not find in earlier Western practice including the music of this century. *Tehillim* may thus be heard as traditional and new at the same time.

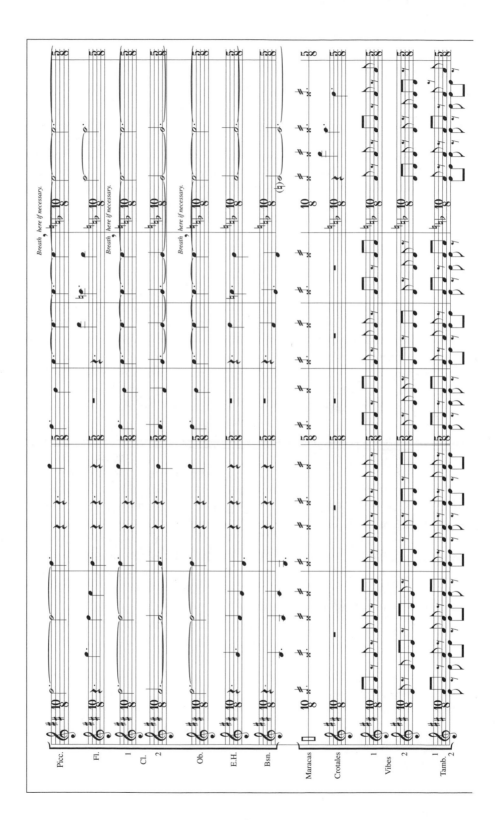

Example 23-1. *Tehillim*, from fourth movement. COPYRIGHT © 1981 BY HENDON MUSIC, INC., A BOOSEY & HAWKES COMPANY. REVISED VERSION COPYRIGHT © 1994 BY HENDON MUSIC, INC. REPRINTED BY PERMISSION.

A further question may arise for some listeners familiar with any earlier music: Why is there no repetition of short patterns in Tehillim? The basic reason for avoiding repetition in *Tehillim* was the need to set the text in accordance with its rhythm and meaning. The Psalm texts set here not only determine the rhythm of the music (which is basically combinations of two or three beats throughout the piece combined so as to form constantly changing meters) but also demand appropriate setting of the meaning of the words. In this respect, I have tried to be as faithful to the Hebrew text as possible, and some examples of "word-painting" should be pointed out. In the second text, "Sur may-rah va-ah-say-tov" ("Turn from evil and do good") is set with a descending melodic line on "Sur may-rah" ("Turn from evil"), and a strongly rising line for "va-ah-say-tov" ("and do good"), ending in a crystal clear A♭ major triad on the word "tov" ("good"), with the third of the chord voiced as a high C in the high soprano voice. In the third text, the verse "Va-im-ee-kaysh, tit-pah-tal" ("and with the perverse You are subtle") is set in C♯ minor with a strong G natural (lowered fifth, tritone, or diabolus in musica) on the word "ee-kaysh" ("perverse"). Another example is found in the first movement on the words "Ain-oh-mer va-ain deh-va-rim, Beh-li nish-mah ko-lahm" ("Without speech and without words, Nevertheless their voice is heard"), which is set with only four notes, G, A, D, and E. Although the original key signature is one flat and seems to be D minor, these four tones alone can be interpreted (especially when they are repeated over and over again in the four-part canons) as either in D minor, C major, G major, or D major (among others), depending on their rhythm and the chords harmonizing them. They are interpreted, at least in the first movement, as being in D minor and then in G major, but their basic ambiguity suggests that when we hear a voice without speech and words we are not only hearing music but also music of the most open sort that is consonant with many harmonic interpretations. This four-note scale—recurring later on "Halleluya" at the end of the piece—supplies one of the basic means of harmonic change and was suggested by the text. Returning then to the question about repetition as a musical technique, my reason for limiting it to repetition of complete verses of the Psalm text is basically that, based on my musical intuition, *the text demanded this kind of setting.* I use repetition as a technique when that is where my musical intuition leads me, but I follow that musical intuition wherever it leads (see ex. 23-1).

Tehillim was commissioned by the South German Radio, Stuttgart (SDR); the West German Radio, Cologne (WDR): and The Rothko Chapel, Houston. Additional support was received from Betty Freeman, The Rockefeller Foundation, and The Memorial Foundation for Jewish Culture.

The first two movements of *Tehillim* were premiered by the South German Radio Orchestra and soloists in Stuttgart conducted by Peter Eötvös in June 1981. The world premiere of the completed work was given at the West German Radio in Cologne by Steve Reich and Musicians conducted by George Manahan and was subsequently performed in London, Paris, Frankfurt, Munich, Utrecht, and Vienna by the same ensemble.

The American premiere of *Tehillim* was presented at The Rothko Chapel in Houston in November 1981 as part of the tenth Anniversary of that institution, performed by Steve Reich and Musicians conducted by George Manahan.

The New York premiere performances of *Tehillim* were presented by the same ensemble at the Metropolitan Museum of Art on March 15, 1982, in the Museum's Twentieth Century Galleries, and on April 19, 1982, in the Museum's Grace Rainey Rogers Auditorium.

The orchestral premiere of *Tehillim* was presented by the New York Philharmonic conducted by Zubin Mehta on September 16, 17, 18, and 21, 1982, on the opening concerts of the orchestra's 1982–83 subscription season.

HEBREW CANTILLATION AS AN INFLUENCE ON COMPOSITION (1982) 24

Reich wrote "Hebrew Cantillation" a few years after coming back from a visit to Israel in 1977 when he recorded Sephardic Jews from Bagdad, Yemen, Kurdistan, and Cochin, India, all chanting the same opening verses of Bereshith (Genesis). "I was very interested in the structure of the cantillation that was constant, though the melodies varied from culture to culture, and wanted to present it to musicians who were not aware of it, or at least not aware of its structure. I had no specific plans for publication. I assumed something would just come up." In fact, it was first published in French (Reynaud, 1981) and Italian (Restagno, 1994). This is its first publication in English.

Cantillation is the word given to the chanting of the Hebrew Scriptures. In the late 1970s, it was an influence on one of my compositions. Before discussing it, however, I would like discuss briefly two earlier influences: West African drumming and Balinese gamelan music.

In the case of West African drumming, my acquaintance with it began, as with most musicians in the West, via recordings, which I heard during the late 1950s and early 1960s. In 1963, while attending a conference on contemporary music at Ojai, California, I heard the American composer Gunther Schuller speak of his attempts to find out more about African music as preparation for his *History of Early Jazz*. He said that the most important book he had found was the two-volume *Studies in African Music* by the Englishman A. M. Jones.[1] In this book, which I bought immediately after the Ojai conference, I found complete scores of music by the Ewe tribe in Ghana. These scores made clear what records did not reveal; they showed how the music was made. Briefly, it is made of short repeat-

---

1. Jones, 1959.

ing patterns, generally of two, three, four, six, or twelve beats, played simultane-ously but *so that their downbeats do not coincide*. This struck me as a radically different way of organizing music and together with other influences including tape loops and the musics of Terry Riley and John Coltrane, led to my compos-ing *It's Gonna Rain* for tape, in January of 1965. Between 1966 and 1970, I com-posed *Come Out, Melodica, Piano Phase, Violin Phase, Four Organs,* and *Phase Patterns,* among other pieces, and many of these works developed my discovery of gradually shifting phase relations between two identical repeating patterns—a process that is *not* found in African music or any other Western or non-Western music. Finally, in the summer of 1970, I traveled to Ghana to study drumming first hand.[2] While there I took daily lessons from Ghanaian master drummers, particularly from the Ewe tribe, and transcribed the patterns and their relation-ships into Western notation. The effect of my visit was basically *confirmation:* that writing for acoustic instruments playing repeating patterns of a percussive nature was a viable means of making music, and had an ancient history. Thus, my visit to Africa did not directly influence my composition *Drumming*. That piece was mostly the result of my having studied drumming when I was 14 with Roland Kohloff. My studies of Western drumming as a teenager together with my undying attraction for percussion and my discoveries of phase shifting with short repeating patterns led to the composition of *Drumming* in 1971. The influence of African music on my composition really had happened much earlier in 1963 and '64, and from that point, as an influence, it diminished.

Around 1966, I began to take an interest in Balinese music as well. I had heard recordings of it much earlier while a student of Professor William Austin's at Cor-nell University in the mid-1950s. While listening to the recordings I had no idea how the music was produced. Once again, it was a book (Colin McPhee's *Music in Bali*[3]) that opened the door to Balinese musical techniques. The use of inter-locking rhythmic patterns of short duration that I discovered in McPhee's book were already in my music, and again it was a case of *confirmation* that other mu-sicians elsewhere in the world were using musical techniques related to those that I was using. I briefly studied Balinese Gamelan Semar Pegulingan and Gamelan Gambang during the summers of 1973 and '74 with Balinese teachers in Seattle and Berkeley. Again, while the study of the music through playing it was enjoy-able, the techniques were already present in my music well before 1973.

While studying both African and Balinese music, it became clear to me that I was not interested in imitating the *sound* of those musics. I thought briefly about using some African gong-gong bells in my own music, but soon rejected the idea because to me these instruments have their own history and purpose, and to retune them and use them in my own music would have seemed a kind of musi-cal rape. Similarly, with the very beautiful Balinese instruments, I felt no interest

2. See "Gahu" (no. 7), pp. 55–63.
3. McPhee, 1966.

in using them in my own music. Rather, I felt at home with marimbas, glocken-spiels, and vibraphones—*Western* percussion instruments whose tuning and sound were something that I had grown up with—something that was natural to my ear. The only aspect of African and Balinese music that I found exportable, and therefore of possible significance to Western composers, was their *structure*. The polyrhythmic interlocking patterns found in Balinese and African music seemed of great interest because they could be created by pianos, clarinets, and violins playing our own tempered scale. In that way, a Western composer might continue to use the pitches and timbres that are in his ear since birth but with the added re-source of a new compositional technique. This is, in fact, very similar to the learning of Western compositional techniques, particularly contrapuntal ones like canon, by a Western music student. One learns basic structural techniques that a good student will use with their own very personal choices of pitch, tim bre, and precise working out of the structure.

In 1974, the seeds of my interest in Hebrew cantillation began with my desire to learn more about my own ethnic and religious background. What I had ad-mired greatly in African and Balinese music was the preservation of an ancient oral musical tradition and, indeed, the preservation of many other ancient tradi-tions within tribes or communities. In 1974, I began to miss the fact that my own extremely ancient tradition was one that I had lost touch with. I was brought up with only a superficial exposure to Judaism. I did not learn any Hebrew, any Torah, or any traditional chanting. After a "lip-sync" Bar Mitzvah, in which I pointed at Hebrew words I could not read but said from memory of a transcrip-tion into the English alphabet, I lost interest in Judaism, with the exception of reading Martin Buber during my teens. Much later, at the age of 37, I decided that my desire for ancient tradition and religious practice might very well be sat-isfied by Judaism, provided I got some long overdue education. In 1975, I began to study Hebrew and Torah at Lincoln Square Synagogue in Manhattan, an out-standing center of adult education within traditional Judaism. While studying biblical Hebrew, I asked my teacher about the biblical accents or ta'amim and was informed that these were, among other things, the musical notation for the chanting of the Torah and Prophets and several other books of the Hebrew scrip-tures. This explanation led to further study of these biblical accents, in both New York and Jerusalem during 1976 and 1977. I worked briefly with Cantor Edward Berman from the Jewish Theological Seminary and also spoke several times with Dr. Johanna Spector of that same institution. In Jerusalem, my wife, the video artist Beryl Korot, and I had the good fortune to work with Dr. Avigdor Herzog of the Phonoteka of the National Library at the Hebrew University, as well as with Dr. Israel Adler and other musicologists at the Hebrew University. Once again a book played an important role; *Jewish Music* by Abraham Idelsohn.[4]

The ta'amim, or accents, serve three functions in the biblical Hebrew text.

4. Idelsohn, 1929.

First, they show the accented syllable. For example, the first word in the Torah is Bereshíth and not Béreshith.[5] Second, the ta'amim are the punctuation marks for the Hebrew text. All in all, there are 28 different ta'amim. Nineteen of these serve as disjunctive punctuation to show separations of varying degrees between parts of a sentence and eight are connectives.[6] (To appreciate the degree of nuance such a large number of punctuation marks can create, bear in mind that there are only 12 punctuation marks on an English-language typewriter.) As with all punctuation, the biblical accents are used to clarify the meaning of the text. Third, the ta'amim serve as the musical notation for the chanting of the Hebrew biblical text. How exactly do the ta'amim serve as musical notation and what is their history?

The word ta'amim derives from the three letter Hebrew root—tet, ayin, mem—meaning to taste or discern. Consequently, ta'amay hamikrah would translate literally as the "taste of the writing" or "taste of scripture." The Talmud says, "He who reads the Torah without tune shows disregard for it" (Bab. Megilla, 32a). Abraham Idelsohn, the founder of modern Jewish musicology, explains as follows:

> The Biblical intonations preserved in the memory of the people, were transmitted orally from generation to generation. Yet an attempt was made in the early centuries to find a way by which these intonations could be preserved. Similar attempts, as we know, were also made by all the other ancient nations, such as the Indians and the Greeks; and were the beginnings of musical notation, which, after a long development, resulted in the modern system of writing music. The earliest system was the notation of the rise and fall of the voice . . . with . . . hand-signs, in Greek cheironomia, made by the teacher or musical leader. . . . We notice this custom in ancient Egypt, shown on the wall-pictures of the pyramids. The Talmud gives evidence of the custom of using finger-motions in the air in Palestine and in Babylonia in the beginning of the Christian Era. (P. Berachoth, 62a reported in the name of Rabbi Akiba 40–135 C.E.). . . . In some countries, like Yemen, the custom is still in vogue. For these movements of the hand descriptive names were invented. . . . During the Talmudic period only three names were known, marking the beginning, half-stops, and end of the verse. In like manner we find among other nations: udata, svarita and anudata among the Hindus; acutus, circumflex and gravis among the Greeks; and shesht, kurr, and butu among the Armenians. The names employed by the Jews were kadma—ascending, atnah—resting half-stop, and sof—conclusion. Gradually, there developed the system of naming each detail of the nuances marked by voice and hand. But not satisfied with the cheironomia, every nation mentioned above in-

5. By the way, this does not translate into "In the beginning" but rather "In the beginning of." This suggests a process that may well have been going on for some time before the six "days" of creation. If one understands this correct translation as well as the inferences in Psalm 90:4, "For a thousand years in Your eyes are but a bygone day, like a watch in the night," the "days" of creation can more accurately be understood as geological ages. The supposed conflict between Darwin and the Bible only exists on the most naive and literal reading of the text. Evolution can be properly understood as a theory of one tiny aspect of how G-d works. All science makes us more and more precisely aware of G-d's work. The Torah itself is most certainly not a science text about how the world was formed; it is about why and for what purpose it, and especially we, were created. (SR)
6. According to Rosofsky, 1957.

vented *written signs* independently which were *imitations* of the *hand-marks*. . . . The development (among Jews) continued for several centuries until the system received its finishing touches in Tiberias and was introduced in the Bible in the ninth century as a means by which the Scripture should be chanted. However, the use of an accented Bible for public reading in the service was not permitted. For this purpose only the original Scroll without vocalization or accents had to be used.[7]

One may wonder how a movement of the hand or a written sign imitating such a hand movement can possibly serve as musical notation. Again Idelsohn explains:

. . . the accents indicate small patterns . . . but they show neither notes nor exact intervals. Only for those who know the mode and its motives and characteristics do the accents serve their purpose. They are rather reminders of the motives. . . . They indicate neither scale nor rhythm, neither tonality nor tempo, neither intervals nor steps. Even at the time they were introduced, people who did not know the modes beforehand could learn nothing from this system.[8]

In technical terms, the ta'amim are classified as "ecphonetic notation" or "early neumes." They are defined as follows:

Ecphonetic notation: Term for certain primitive systems of musical notation, consisting only of a limited number of conventional signs designed for the solemn reading of a liturgical text. Originally they were simply signs added to the text in order to clarify its sentence structure, comparable to present-day punctuation marks. Signs also were added to individual syllables . . . to be emphasized. Later these signs adopted a musical significance. . . . Ecphonetic signs occur in Syrian, Jewish, Byzantine and Coptic manuscripts from c. 600 to 1000 and later. In Jewish chant they developed into fuller musical notation, the ta'amim which is used to the present day.[9]

The term neume is clearly defined by Eric Werner as follows: "The basic distinction between a neume and a note is that: the former usually stands not for a single note, but for a whole phrase, whereas the modern notation has one sign for each individual note."[10]

To learn how to use the ta'amim, one must therefore rely on oral tradition. In my own case I learned the ta'amim for the reading of the Torah on the Sabbath from Cantor Edward Berman, who learned them from his teacher, Solomon Rosofsky, who taught what he referred to as the Lithuanian tradition. Of this tradition Rosofsky writes: "The Lithuanian is the principal type in the large Ashkenazic family of cantillations. . . . It is by no means confined to the territorial limits of Lithuania. It is adhered to by Jews of Poland, Russia . . . various European countries, North and South America, South Africa, and by a number of Ashkenazic communities in Israel."[11]

7. Idelsohn, 1929, pp. 67–68.
8. Ibid., p. 69.
9. *Harvard Dictionary of Music*, p. 252.
10. Werner, 1959, p. 105.
11. Rosofsky, 1957, pp. 1–2.

Not only did my teacher Cantor Edward Berman teach me the ta'amim for Torah reading on Sabbath by singing them, but he also gave me a written table of accents using modern musical notation. Example 24-1 gives the table of Sabbath Torah Tropes or Ta'amim.

Of course, this is only the beginning. Within the Lithuanian tradition, different melodic patterns are chanted to the same ta'amim, according to whether the reading is from the Prophets or the Torah. There also are particular ta'amim for the Five Megilot or scrolls, Song of Songs, Ruth, Lamentations, Kohelet (or Ecclesiastes), and Esther. While the melodic structure of Torah accentuation is basically in major, the Prophets are basically in minor. In the case of the Song of Songs, some of the accents are in major, others in minor, and some in the Phrygian mode. To show this difference in modality between chanting for Torah, Prophets, and Song of Songs all within the Lithuanian tradition, example 24-2 compares the five most common groupings of accents.

However, this is not all. We have so far considered only the Lithuanian tradition. Let us now consider the same text but in different physical locations. Geographical differences will be reflected in the use of different melodic patterns for the various ta'amim. As Dr. Johanna Spector has observed:

> In looking for the oldest musical heritage in any Jewish community the researcher goes to the synagogue. It is here that he hopes to find old melodies handed down from generation to generation, which may contain ancient elements reaching back to the Temple times before the destruction of ancient Israel by the Romans (about 70 C.E.). . . . Music of the synagogue is divided into 1) cantillation of the Bible, and 2) prayer-song. Of the two, cantillation is by far the more important traditionally and the less changeable. . . . While the . . . ta'may hamikra (or Biblical accents) are fixed and identical in all the Jewish communities regardless of geography, their melodic interpretation, which has always been transmitted orally, varies from place to place, and it is possible to detect by melodic structure alone where in the world this particular cantillation is practiced.[12]

Unfortunately, it is not possible to represent accurately in Western notation the ta'amim of Jews living in Iraq (the modern Babylonia) or Yemen or other Middle Eastern countries, because the notes in their scale (tuned microtonally) are not the same as the tempered tuning we find on our piano keyboard.

A second—and, to me, more important—observation is that although melodies vary from place to place, the overall melodic *structure* is constant. By this, I mean that an opening series of motives like mercha-tipcha will vary as to the melody from location to location, but that its basic character as an opening motive, within the given mode of a particular community, is maintained. Similarly, an etnach is always a semi-cadence and a sof pasuk is always a full cadence, regardless of what notes are used to create that semi-cadence or full cadence. A further and less musicologically explored suggestion is that there may be similarities

12. Spector, 1973, pp. 245–46.

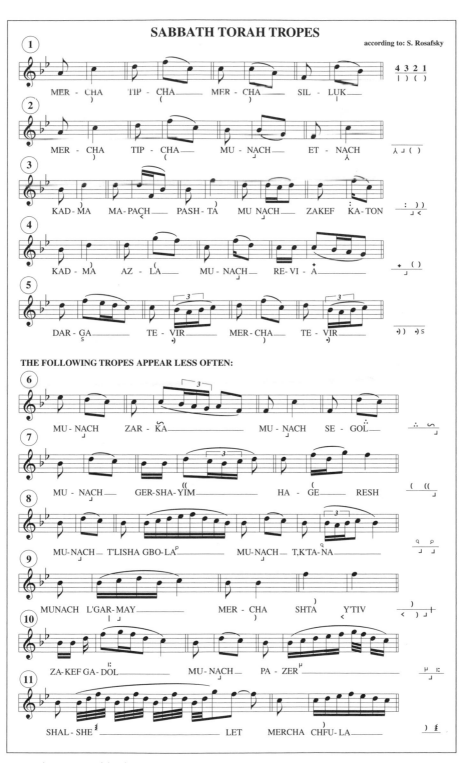

Example 24-1. Sabbath Torah Tropes.

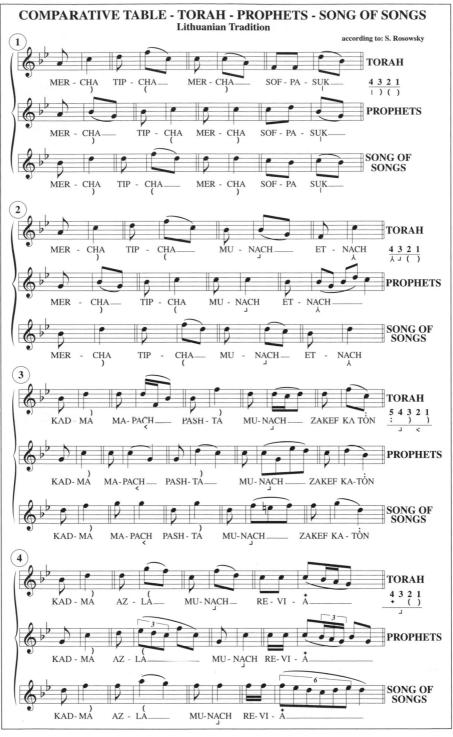

Example 24-2. Comparative table of Torah, Prophets, and Song of Songs.

of structure between other traditions and the Jewish tradition. Dr. Avigdor Herzog, in his article on the biblical accents in the *Encyclopedia Judaica*, (1972) observes as follows:

> A comparison with practices of scriptural reading in other religious traditions such as Vedic recitation in India or Buddhist recitation in Japan and other countries reveals that none is spoken or sung but they are cantillated; that this cantillation is based upon strict conventions handed down by oral tradition (which were described explicitly only in the respective Middle Ages of each culture): and, most important, that a basic *similarity of constructive principles, not of melodic content,*[13] can still be recognized in all such practices throughout the Asian continent, including all Jewish traditions throughout the Diaspora. . . . This "pan-Asiatic" style must already have been present in cantillated Bible reading in the synagogue preceding the period in which the system of written accents began to be developed.[14]

A final consideration, certainly of major importance, is that the ta'amim form the historical basis for Gregorian Chant and thus stand at the earliest period in Western musical history. "Although no manuscripts of early Jewish music exist, the state of music in the late pre-Christian era has been clarified considerably by Idelsohn, who examined the musical traditions of Jewish tribes in Yemen, Babylonia [now Iraq], Persia, Syria, etc. A startling similarity was found among the chants sung by these tribes, who, living in strict isolation, had no contact with one another after leaving Palestine. Therefore these melodies probably antedate the destruction of the Temple and have been preserved for 2,000 years with only slight alterations. They thus are thought to approximate very closely the Jewish chant of the pre-Christian era. No less interesting is the close resemblance between some of these melodies and certain melodies of Gregorian chant. For instance, a chant used by the Jews of Yemen for the recitation of the Pentateuch (as well as certain Psalms) shows a striking similarity to the Gregorian Psalm tones."[15]

In a similar vein, the musicologist Curt Sachs says: "Almost half a century ago, the late Abraham Z. Idelsohn began to record an impressive amount of tunes sung in the archaic communities of the Middle East. Hidden among the thousands of sacred songs, he found in the liturgies of the Babylonian and Yemenite Hebrews melodic patterns so close to the Catholic chant that a connection could not be disclaimed. . . . Idelsohn's pioneering discoveries proved to be an epochal link between Antiquity and the Middle Ages."[16]

It now remains to see how cantillation of the Hebrew Scriptures can act as an influence on a composer. In my own case, cantillation influenced my composition *Octet* (later called *Eight Lines*) and perhaps other works through its *struc-*

---

13. SR's emphasis.
14. Avigdor Herzog, 1972, pp. 1099–100.
15. *The Harvard Dictionary of Music*, 1969.
16. Curt Sachs, "Forward," in Werner, 1959.

ture and not its sound. Just as I had found it inappropriate to imitate the sound of African or Balinese music, I found it similarly inappropriate to imitate the sound of Hebrew cantillation. It is true that I am Jewish, but I did not grow up with the sound of cantillation, and really only discovered it in my late 30s. Even more important, though, is that the *sound* of Hebrew cantillation is not perhaps the most fruitful form of influence, and that by imitating it one could easily end up with merely a "Jewish sounding piece" much as one could end up with an African or Balinese sounding piece. These are merely updated versions of chinoiserie—the wearing of colorful cloths on the surface of a piece of music to make it sound like something exotic. In contrast to this, it seems to me far more fruitful and certainly more substantial to try and understand the structure of Hebrew cantillation, to apply that to the pitches and timbres one has grown up with, and so hopefully to create something new.

Octet was composed in 1979 and the influence of cantillation is in the flute and piccolo melodies. This can be seen at several places in the score: example 24-3 shows the last 10 bars of the flute and piccolo parts in relation to the two pianos.

The first two bars of the flute part double piano 1's right hand more or less exactly, with an octave displacement here and there. The second two bars of the flute part begin with the first four notes again from piano 1, but the flute then diverges for the rest of bar three and all of bar four into notes taken from pianos 1 and 2, together with several that do not exist in either piano part. The fifth bar is a repeat of bar one, while the sixth bar is a repeat of bar four. The seventh bar is another repeat of the first bar, and the eighth bar is a slight variation of bar two. The ninth and tenth bars are repeats of bars three and four. Treating each bar as a self-contained motif, the ten-bar pattern is: 1, 2, 3, 4, 1, 4, 1, 2′, 3, 4. The piccolo part basically doubles piano 2 with small variations. Again looking at each bar as a motive to be joined to others the overall pattern is: 1, 2, 1′, 3, 1″, 2, 1″, 2, 1′, 3. Since the two piano part is only two bars long while the string parts are all 10 bars long, the flute and piccolo take the two-bar piano part and, by putting shorter motives together, create two 10-bar melodies in counterpoint. Although the *sound* of this music is not at all like Hebrew cantillation, its *construction* in the flute and piccolo parts resembles the *construction* of motives in Hebrew chant. It is a small influence but a real one, and interesting in that it lends itself to further and unforeseen developments in the future.

As a postscript, I would like to briefly discuss my composition *Tehillim*, written in 1981. *Tehillim* is a setting of verses from Psalms 19, 34, 18, and 150 (see "Tehillim," no. 23, p. 100). Before choosing these Psalm texts, I had thought of setting the Book of Jonah, but the more I thought about it the more difficult the idea became, because Jonah is one of the Prophets and the book is chanted in the synagogue on the afternoon of Yom Kippur. Having heard this chanted, and knowing the ta'amim for the Prophets, made me feel that all that was necessary was simply to *transcribe* Jonah exactly as it is chanted in synagogues. To compose a setting for this text seemed problematical—perhaps similar to the difficulty I felt

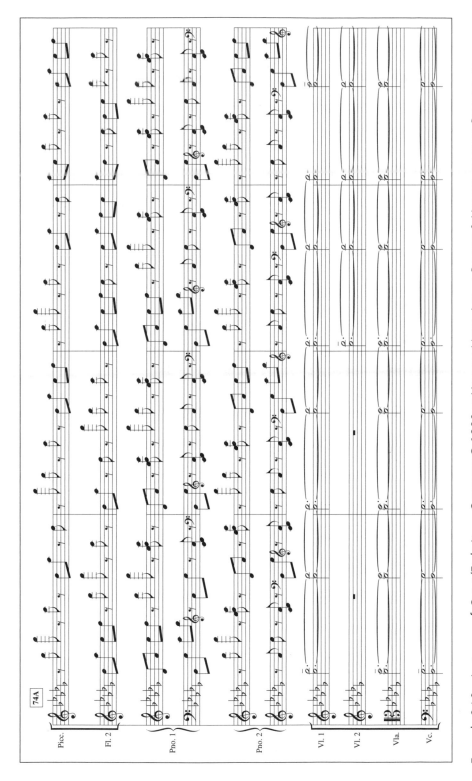

Example 24-3a. Last page of *Octet/Eight Lines*. Copyright © 1980 by Hendon Music, Inc., a Boosey & Hawkes company. Reprinted by permission.

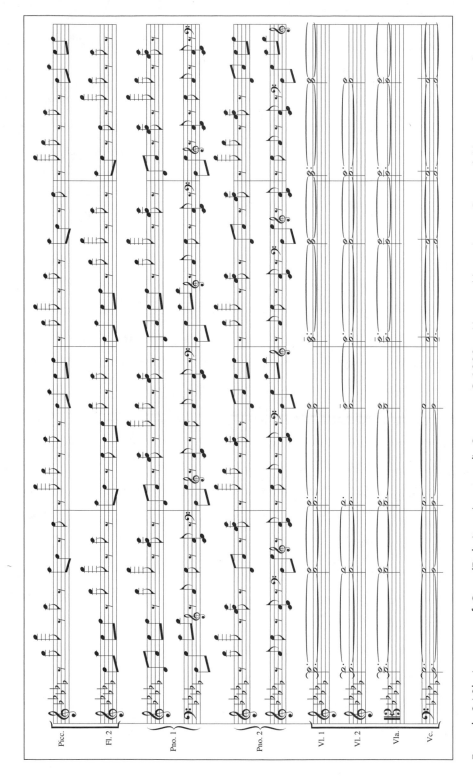

Example 24-3b. Last page of *Octet/Eight Lines* (continued). COPYRIGHT © 1980 BY HENDON MUSIC, INC., A BOOSEY & HAWKES COMPANY. REPRINTED BY PERMISSION.

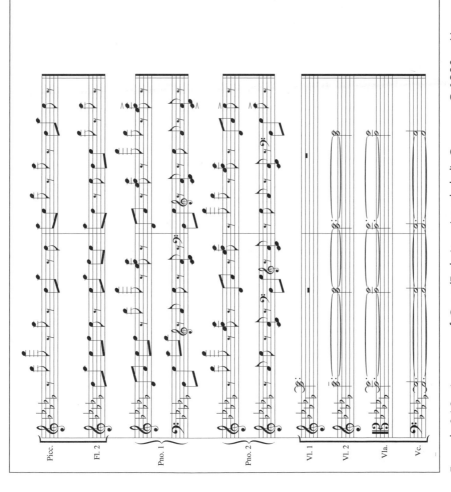

Example 24-3c. Last page of *Octet/Eight Lines* (concluded). Copyright © 1980 by Hendon Music, Inc., a Boosey & Hawkes Company. Reprinted by permission.

in using an African bell in my own music. Another factor for me was the fact that the custom of the traditional synagogue has been to *preserve* the original cantillation, which is quite different from the Christian Church, where new settings of the Mass and other texts are part of a tradition of always creating new compositions for liturgical use. In short, there is *no need* of new musical compositions in the traditional synagogue, and even to write a concert piece using Jonah as text made me feel that I would be taking something that goes a certain way and changing it in a manner that made me feel uncomfortable.

While pursuing this line of thought, I then remembered that the cantillation for the Psalms has been lost in the Western synagogues. As Dr. Avigdor Herzog notes in the *Encyclopedia Judaica:* "Among the Ashkenazi communities hardly any true psalmodies have survived, and the home rituals for the singing of the psalms have absorbed many folk tunes from the surrounding cultures. . . . In the 'ordered hazzanut' of the 19th century in Western Europe, the Psalms were set to music in a manner not different from the style of the prayers and often as showpieces for the choir, somewhat in the manner of the Anglican anthem. In Reform Judaism where the text was paraphrased as a rhymed poem in Western meters, the result followed the precedents of the Protestant chorale and even utilized its tunes."[17]

The great nineteenth-century Christian scholar William Wickes notes that "the Jews themselves allow that a musical value of the accents for the three Poetical Books (Job, Proverbs, and Psalms) is altogether lost. Such is the testimony of the European Jews. But . . . the Jews of Yemen have still a particular melody for the three books."[18]

With this in mind, and coupled with the fact that the Psalms were obviously as musical a text as the Hebrew Scriptures had to offer, I decided to choose Psalm texts that attracted me and then feel free to *compose* a setting for them without the constrictions of a living oral tradition over 2,000 years old to either imitate or ignore.

The result has been a melodic piece in the basic sense of that word. If you have heard examples of cantillation, I think you will quickly note that there is no audible connection in *Tehillim.* Even the principles of motivic combination basic to the structure of cantillation, which begin to appear in the flute and piccolo parts of my *Octet*, are not present in *Tehillim.*

A familiarity with the basic construction of Hebrew cantillation should be of considerable interest to music students, both for its value as the root of Gregorian chant and for its connection to musical constructions used in the Middle East. It also may be of interest to other Western composers as a potential compositional tool.

17. Avigdor Herzog, 1972, p. 1333.
18. Wickes, 1881.

Vermont Counterpoint was commissioned by Ransom Wilson and is dedicated to Betty Freeman. It is scored for three alto flutes, three flutes, three piccolos, and one solo part all prerecorded on tape, plus a live solo part. The live soloist plays alto flute, flute, and piccolo, and participates in the ongoing counterpoint as well as contributing more extended melodies. The piece can be performed by 11 flutists but is intended primarily as a solo with tape. The duration is approximately nine minutes. In that comparatively short time, four sections in four different keys are presented, with the third in a slower tempo. The compositional techniques used are primarily building up canons between short repeating melodic fragments by substituting notes for rests and then playing melodies that result from their combination. These resulting melodies or melodic patterns then become the basis for the following section as the other surrounding parts in the contrapuntal web fade out. Although the techniques used include several that I discovered as early as 1967, the relatively fast rate of change (there are rarely more than three repeats of any bar), metric modulation into and out of a slower tempo, and relatively rapid changes of key may well create a more concentrated and concise impression.

Eight Lines is exactly the same piece as my *Octet* (1979) with the addition of a second string quartet. These additional four strings were added because of problems in performing the piece with only one player to a part. For the two violins, this problem was the difficulty of playing rather awkward double stops in tune. This was solved by having two first violins and two seconds so that each player could play one note at a time. For the viola and cello, a second player was added to each to allow the rapid eighth-note patterns to be broken up between the two players thus preventing fatigue. This small change in instrumentation has proved to make a large difference in performance and for that reason *Eight Lines* is the only version of the piece suitable for performance.

The Desert Music was written partly at the suggestion of Wolfgang Becker in Cologne, who had commissioned Coro from Berio and wanted another work of similar proportions. Reich's first thought was, "Why don't I set Wittgenstein." He also thought of using tapes from World War II: Hitler's voice, Truman's voice after dropping the A-bomb, or going back to the tape pieces. Then he came across the William Carlos Williams poem "The Orchestra," where he found material that best suited his purpose. Some of these preoccupations (and the comment about Wagner in the Cott interview, no. 46, p. 171) will resurface later in Three Tales.

"The very center of the piece is a cluster of canons on the word difficult (see ex. 27-1). It's the most difficult part of the piece—when the Grove Dictionary asked me for a score page, I unhesitatingly gave them a page from that canon and jokingly told Beryl that if I die in the middle of this piece put that on my gravestone. So for me that's the very center of the work. There's something self-referential about the repeating—it refers to the music itself but also to the persistence of the problems. That's the fulcrum, after which you have the same texts coming back, but coming back differently than when they were first presented."[1]

The Desert Music—Note by the Composer

The Desert Music was begun in September 1982, and completed in December 1983. Work on the orchestration continued through February 1984. It was commissioned by the West German Radio, Cologne, which gave the world premiere conducted by Peter Eötvös, and by the Brooklyn Academy in New York, where the Brooklyn Philharmonic, Michael Tilson Thomas conducting, presented the first American performance. It is a setting of parts of poems by the American poet William Carlos Williams. The duration is about 48 minutes.

The title is taken from Dr. Williams's book of collected poems, The Desert Music. From this collection I chose parts of The Orchestra and Theocritus: Idyl I—A version from the Greek. From another collection, I chose a small part of Asphodel, That Greeny Flower. There are no complete poems used and the arrangement of parts is my own. This arrangement was my first compositional activity and the form of the piece into a large arch follows the text.

As indicated in the text, there are five movements forming a large arch A–B–C–B–A. The first and fifth movements are fast and use the same harmonic cycle. The second and fourth are at a moderate tempo, share the identical text, and also

1. From an interview with Edward Strickland published in Fanfare, March/April 1987, vol. 10, no. 4.

share a common harmonic cycle, which is different from the one used in the outer movements. The third—middle—movement is the longest (18 minutes) and is itself an arch form A B A, on which the A sections are slow and the B section moves up to the moderate tempo of the second and fourth movements. It also has its own harmonic cycle. There are no pauses between movements and the piece is played *attacca* from beginning to end. The changes of tempo between movements are made suddenly by metric modulation, always using the 3:2 relationship either to get slower (dotted quarter equals quarter), or faster (eighth note triplet equals eighth note).

Following the arrangement of the text, three cycles of harmonies were composed to serve as the basis for the individual movements. I chose to present these cycles as a series of pulsing chords, similar in rhythm to the pulses in my earlier *Music for 18 Musicians,* but more chromatic and "darker" in harmony than the earlier piece, to suit the text of *The Desert Music.* The harmonic cycle of the outer movements cadences, although with some ambiguity, on a D dorian minor center.

This ambiguity resides in the fact that a prominent A altered dominant chord follows the D but an F altered dominant precedes it. The cycle of the second and fourth movements does not clearly cadence on any center, although it, too, contains a prominent altered A dominant chord. The cycle for the large third movement is the most ambiguous of all, since all the chords are altered dominants, with their roots moving in major and minor thirds, making a clear V–I or IV–I cadence impossible. Thus, the overall harmonic movement of *The Desert Music* is from the possibility of a D dorian minor center to more and more ambiguity, until in the third movement, where the text would seem to suggest it, there is no clear harmonic center at all. This ambiguity more or less remains until well into the fifth movement when, just before the chorus enters, there is a large orchestral cadence—albeit coming from the F altered dominant—to D dorian minor. The only chord present in all movements is the A altered dominant. This chord is then used to move from one movement to the other at each change of tempo. The piece ends with the women's voices, violins, and mallet instruments pulsing the notes (reading up) G, C, F, A, which are the common tones to the A altered dominant, the D dorian minor, and the possible F major. The piece therefore ends with a certain harmonic ambiguity, partially, but not fully, resolved.

In the orchestration of *The Desert Music,* I wanted to use all the orchestral instruments to play the repeating interlocking melodic patterns found in much of my earlier music. The strings begin this kind of polyrhythmic interlocking shortly after the opening pulses of the first movement, just before the chorus enters singing "Begin, my friend." To give the strings the extra "snap" needed in this kind of rhythmic interplay, they are doubled by the synthesizers. The chorus, throughout the piece, is doubled for support either by the woodwinds or muted brass. This is, of course, an old technique, but one that here helps create that mixture of vocal and instrumental sound I have been working with since *Drumming.*

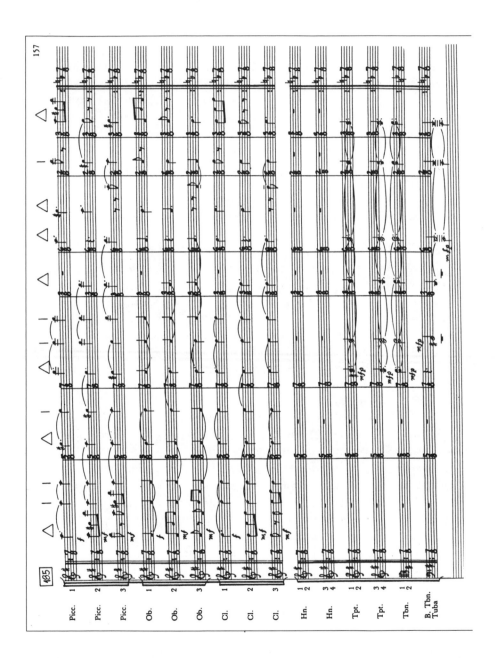

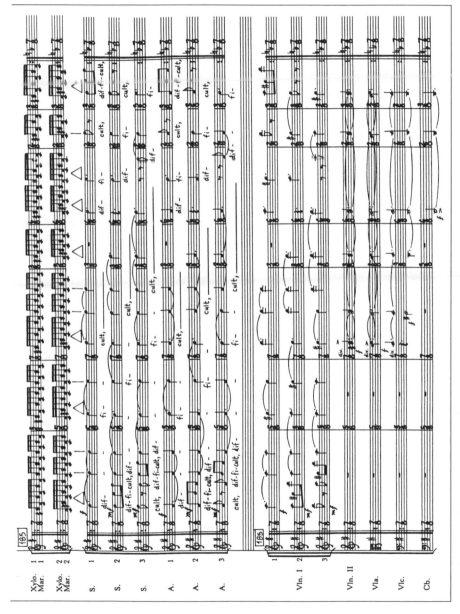

Example 27-1. *The Desert Music*, rehearsal no. 185. Copyright © 1984 by Hendon Music, Inc., a Boosey & Hawkes company. Reprinted by permission.

To further enhance this mix of vocal-instrumental sound, both the chorus and the woodwinds are amplified and mixed together. The percussion is omnipresent, usually playing mallet instruments to supply the ongoing pulse. Here and there one will also hear maracas, clicking sticks, bass drums, timpani, and tam-tam.

The pulse that begins, ends, and recurs throughout *The Desert Music* is significant both musically and as a kind of wordless response to and commentary on the text itself. Musically, it presents the harmonic cycles of the movements like a pulsing chorale. The pulse also is developed in the second and fourth movements, from a simple eighth-note pulsing in all voices and instruments, to interlocking groups of two and three beats, each forming overall polyrhythmic pulses; this grows out of the two- and three-beat groupings found in *Tehillim*. In terms of the text, the vocalise syllables are a kind of wordless response to "Well, shall we/ think or listen?" in the second and fourth movements. That constant flickering of attention between what words mean and how they sound when set to music is one main focus of *The Desert Music*.

While composing the last part of the slow movement during the summer of 1983 in a small town in Vermont, the local fire siren went off. I thought to myself, "That's it," and resolved to put a siren in the last part of the third movement. After some reflection, I decided that instead of a mechanical or electric siren, the violas, who were not playing at the time, could play glissandos that, with contact microphones attached, would rise and fall over the entire orchestra and chorus.

As to the meaning of the text and music, I hope that it speaks for itself. I have loved Dr. Williams's poetry since I was 16 years old, and I picked up a copy of his long poem, *Paterson,* just because I was fascinated by the symmetry of his name. I have continued reading his work to the present. I find Dr. Williams's best work to be his late poetry, written between 1954 and his death in 1963 at age 80. It is from this period in the poet's work that I have selected the texts for *The Desert Music*—a period after the bombs were dropped on Hiroshima and Nagasaki. Dr. Williams was acutely aware of the bomb, and his words about it, in a poem entitled *The Orchestra,* struck me as to the point: "Say to them: / Man has survived hitherto because he was too ignorant / to know how to realize his wishes. Now that he can realize / them, he must either change them or perish." When I began work on *The Desert Music,* I thought those words were too grave to be set and thought I would use a tape of Dr. Williams reading them instead. When the time came to compose the third movement in the summer of 1983, the character of the movement's harmony seemed to generate just the right setting. I am very glad now that I did not resort to using a tape.

In the center of the piece is the text, also from *The Orchestra,* which says "it is a principle of music / to repeat the theme. Repeat / and repeat again, / as the pace mounts. The / theme is difficult / but no more difficult / than the facts to be resolved." Those at all familiar with my music will know how apt those words are for me, and particularly for this piece, which among other things addresses that basic ambiguity between what the texts says and its pure sensuous sound.

The Desert Music — Text

I—*Fast*

"Begin, my friend
for you cannot,

        you may be sure,

take your song,

      which drives all things out of mind,

         with you to the other world."

                    from: Theocritus: *Idyl I*
                    A version from the Greek

II—*Moderate*

        "Well, shall we
think or listen? Is there a sound addressed

      not wholly to the ear?

        We half close

our eyes. We do not

      hear it through our eyes.

        It is not

a flute note either, it is the relation

      of a flute note

         to a drum. I am wide

awake. The mind

      is listening."

                    from: *The Orchestra*

IIIA—*Slow*

"Say to them:
Man has survived hitherto because he was too ignorant
to know how to realize his wishes. Now that he can realize
them, he must either change them or perish."

                    from: *The Orchestra*

IIIB—*Moderate*

        "It is a principle of music
to repeat the theme. Repeat

      And repeat again,

as the pace mounts. The
theme is difficult
     but no more difficult
        than the facts to be
resolved."

from: *The Orchestra*

IIIC—*Slow*

"Say to them:
Man has survived hitherto because he was too ignorant
to know how to realize his wishes. Now that he can realize
them, he must either change them or perish."

from: *The Orchestra*

IV—*Moderate*

    "Well, shall we
think or listen? Is there a sound addressed
    not wholly to the ear?
       We half close
our eyes. We do not
    hear it through our eyes.
       It is not
a flute note either, it is the relation
    of a flute note to a drum. I am wide
awake. The mind
    is listening."

from: *The Orchestra*

V—*Fast*

"Inseparable from the fire
    its light
        takes precedence over it.
who most shall advance the light -
    call it what you may!"

from: *Asphodel, That Greeny Flower*

JC: All great events, William Blake once stated, start with the pulsation of an artery. It's almost as if one could say, "In the beginning was the Pulse." And in the beginning of *The Desert Music,* one immediately enters the realm of pulsation.

SR: Purely. And without anything else added. The opening of the piece is a kind of chorale, only instead of individual chords sounding for a given length of held notes, they're pulsed; instead of a steady tone, you get rapid eighth-notes repeating over and over again, which sets up a kind of rhythmic energy that you'd never get if the notes were sustained. And that energy is maintained in different ways by the mallet instruments throughout the work. *The Desert Music* begins with this pulsation in order to set up the feeling, structure, and harmony of the entire piece.

JC: In fact, the Williams poems you've chosen for your text aren't about the desert at all. But I was wondering whether the *idea* of the desert—that irredeemable terrain that confronts a traveler only with himself and whose silence makes him listen only to the inwardness of his being—has anything to do with the title and atmosphere of your piece.

SR: There were a number of things that went through my mind as I worked on the composition and as the title kept working on *me.* And they were related to very particular deserts. One of them was the Sinai. When the Jews entered the Sinai 3,500 years ago in their exodus from Egypt, they were going into a land where life was insupportable, where they should have died, and the only thing that kept them alive was divine intervention. It is also important to remember that the divine revelation wasn't given in the land of Israel but in the *desert,* in a land belonging to no one. Later, in the New Testament, Jesus goes to the desert to confront his visions, to overcome his temptations, to struggle with the devil, to fight madness—and you find this idea in the stories of Paul Bowles in our time. The desert is associated with hallucinations and insanity. It threatens one's normal thinking.

In this regard, I remember taking many trips years ago, to and from California, and traveling through the Mojave. Sometimes I'd begin to feel very strange there because I'd get so dehydrated, I'd have to drink enormous amounts of fluids just to keep going and keep my mind functioning normally.

Finally, there is another desert that is central to *The Desert Music:* White

Sands and Alamagordo in New Mexico, where weapons of the most intense and sophisticated sort are constantly being developed and tested. Hidden away from the eyes of the rest of the world are these infernal machines that could lead to the destruction of the planet—and it is to this possibility that the words of William Carlos Williams, which I set in the third movement, refer. So it was these images that particularly struck me, although they seem to be ingrained in people's thinking generally when the idea of the desert comes to mind.

JC: How did these associations connect to the music?

SR: Well, there's no portrayal of the desert in my piece as there is in, say, the *Grand Canyon Suite*—no picturesque evocation of sand dunes! I don't think there's any direct correlation between the title and the music, except as regards the setting of the text. Now that I think of it, though, the last movement has a very long opening orchestral section. And when I first played a taped version of that section to David Drew—from my publisher, Boosey & Hawkes—I remember turning to him and saying, "Out on the plain, running like hell." And that's the image—it's as if you're in the desert and you're running as fast as you can. There are these very large clouds of harmony that seem to tilt the entire rhythmic structure in different directions until rehearsal number 318 of the score, when, finally, after about 40 minutes, we return to the tonal center of the piece. For me, this is an extremely emotional moment. And the chorus enters and sings, "Inseparable from the fire / its light / takes precedence over it. / Who most shall advance the light— / call it what you may!" That last line is just thrown out, and then you return to the pulse—the pulsation we talked about in the beginning. So, yes, in a sense, at least for me, there is a desert in this piece; and it's in the opening of the last movement, where there are no words at all.

JC: When we're first introduced to the chorus in the first section of *The Desert Music*, we hear singing but no words.

SR: Right. The chorus begins wordlessly. You know, a voice can sing words—but does one hear the voice or the words? At certain points in *The Desert Music*, there's no more to be said—there are things that can only be said musically. So the voices continue, without words, as part of the orchestra. The text emerges out of a completely nonverbal, totally abstract sound into something that says "Begin, my friend." Maybe it's fitting that the piece begins *and* ends with a totally abstract use of the voice, going into a text and then out of it again.

JC: In your previous work for voices and instruments, *Tehillim,* you set a psalm from the Bible that reads, "The heavens declare the glory of God, / the sky tells of His handiwork. / Day to day pours forth speech, / night to night reveals knowledge. / Without speech and without words, / nevertheless their voice is heard."

SR: Yes, that's from the nineteenth Psalm. The "voice" here refers to the voice of the sun and moon and stars. And what is happening is that the patriarch Abraham is looking up at the sky and thinks, "There's an intelligence behind all of this"—he hears the voice of the perceivable universe. But instead of saying, "Let's worship the sun or moon or stars," Abraham realizes that he's the recipient of a wordless communication, he has an insight into things that is basically nonverbal, but which make him aware that there is a divine intelligence behind all of nature.[1] All pieces with texts—operas, cantatas, whatever—have, in my opinion, to work first simply as pieces of music that one listens to with eyes closed, without understanding a word. Otherwise, they're not musically successful, they're dead "settings." To the composer, the text may be a kind of a goad, as the Williams poems were to me. *The Desert Music* grew out of the text; I picked out passages by Williams, organized them into a shape, and then the music started coming. So the words were the motor or the driving force, but the listener doesn't have to know that. He or she merely has to listen and hopefully, if moved, will follow the text as well.

JC: "I am wide / awake. The mind / is listening" is one of the passages by Williams that you've set in *The Desert Music.*

SR: You know, some critics of my earlier pieces thought I was intending to create some kind of "hypnotic" or "trance" music. And I always thought, " No, no, no, no, I want you to be wide awake and hear details you've never heard before!" People listen to things any way they wish, of course, and I don't have anything to say about it, even if I *have* written the pieces. But I actually prefer the music to be heard by somebody who's totally wide awake, hearing more than he or she usually does, rather than by someone who's just spaced-out and receiving a lot of ephemeral impressions.

JC: This suggests that Buddhist idea of the mind that *attends.*

SR: One has to be in relative stillness to hear things in detail. All meditative practices are based on some sort of silence—inner and outer. Williams says "We half close / our eyes"—you're closing your eyes to hear more intently. And Williams continues "We do not / hear it through our eyes. / It is, not / a flute note either, it is the relation / of a flute note to a drum." And then, suddenly, the eyes are open, "I am wide / awake." He sort of reaches out and grabs you "The mind / is listening." At which point the chorus sings "dee-dee-dee-dee-dee-dee." It goes into something completely nonverbal, it leaves language behind.

JC: It becomes pulsation again.

SR: Pulsation and vocalise, pure sound. "I am wide / awake. The mind / is listening." And off you go into pulsation. Words come to an end, and musical communication takes over.

JC: Two of the things that contribute to musical communication in *The Desert Music* are the amazing ways you use and develop a kind of rhythmic ambiguity that occurs in a good deal of African music, as well as a kind of simultaneous elaboration of simple musical materials at different speeds— something that is at the heart of Balinese music.

1. See also no. 46, p. 171.

SR: Listening to *umm*-pah-pah, *umm*-pah-pah over and over again is intolerable and, indeed, a mistake. So if you want to write music that is repetitive in any literal sense, you have to work to keep a lightness and constant ambiguity with regard to where the stresses and where the beginnings and endings are. Very often, I'll find myself working in 12-beat phrases, which can divide up in very different ways; and that ambiguity as to whether you're in duple or triple time is, in fact, the rhythmic life-blood of much of my music. In this way, one's listening mind can shift back and forth within the musical fabric, because the fabric *encourages* that. But if you don't build in that flexibility of perspective, then you wind up with something extremely flat-footed and boring.

As for your second point about combining different musical speeds: Years ago, someone said rather testily to me, "Don't you ever write any *slow* music?" Actually, it was a good question. What I asked that person in response was, "In my *Octet,* are you going to concentrate on listening to the pianos—that's the rhythm section of fast eighth notes that never let up—or to the strings, which are playing much more spaciously?" Sustaining instruments like strings or the electric organ often move at a very slow rate of change in my pieces while chattering in their midst is a thriving anthill—the metropolis is buzzing, but the clouds overhead are passing calmly over a field. And that gives the listener the possibility of not necessarily listening just to one thing or the other; it allows them to realize that different things are happening *at the same time.* What I'm trying to do is to present a slow movement and a fast movement simultaneously in such a way that they make music together.

JC: It's often been pointed out that a good deal of contemporary painting can be seen as a process of enlarging upon certain particularized textured and ornamental aspects of the works of the old masters. This also seems to be true of your music as well.

SR: Certain musical passages that suggest the kind of music I write have existed in the Western musical tradition for some time. The C major Prelude that begins Book I of *The Well-Tempered Clavier* for example, is all sequences—it's all the same rhythm over and over, but the notes keep changing. Another example is the Prelude to *Das Rheingold,* where a long E-♭ major chord is sustained from the very beginning for several minutes with very small slow changes. But these passages are done en passant, as special cases within a basically different musical language. In Bach's case, he is beginning a series of keyboard preludes and fugues in all the 24 major and minor keys. He begins in C, the basic key, with a basic prelude written in imitation of lute playing. He then goes on to more complex pieces in other keys. In Wagner's case, he sets up the held E-♭ tonality as a kind of musical metaphor for the rolling river with rising mists. Some annotaters speak of this held E-♭ as Wagner's "Nature *Leitmotiv.*" In any case, as we all know Wagner is basically about extreme chromoticism that eventually led to Schönberg. It's only now that we've come to focus on this kind of repeating melodic pattern or long-held tonality as the center of compositional interest—as the main dish so to speak. And this has given birth to a lot of new music.

JC: Ultimately, it seems to me that both the music and the text of *The Desert Music* are really about hearing and seeing, sound and light.

SR: I once had a vision where light became a metaphor for harmony, for tonality. You know, of course, that the notes on the piano aren't all there are—there's a continuity of vibration from the lowest to the highest sounds we can hear. Slowly, over more than a thousand years, out of this complete continuity of vibration from low to high, musicians in the West have evolved the selection and ordering of notes we find on the keyboard and in all our other instruments. These notes, and the harmonic system we have used to order them, struck me as a light radiating out of the dark infinitude of available vibrations. And when listening in particular to two pieces—Handel's *The Water Music* and Stravinsky's *The Rake's Progress*—I used to get a vision of a kind of barge of light, floating down a river in very dark surroundings, in complete darkness.

You see, I understood that human conventions are, in a sense, the *light*—a kind of conveyance in which we ride, in which we live, and without which we die. And the human construct that we call our *music* is merely a convention—something we've all evolved together, and that rests on no final or ultimate laws. And it sails, in my mind, like a ship of light down an endlessly dark corridor, preserving itself as long as it can. And no more and no less.

SEXTET (1985) 29

Sextet was commissioned by Laura Dean Dancers and Musicians, and by the French government for the Nexus percussion ensemble[1]. The first performance under the title *Music for Percussion and Keyboards* was given by Nexus at the Centre Pompidou in Paris on December 10, 1984, with guest artists playing keyboards. The last movement was then revised in January 1985 and the title shortened to *Sextet*. The American premiere was presented by Laura Dean Dancers and Musicians at Brooklyn Academy of Music's Next Wave Festival on October 31, 1985, as the music for Ms. Dean's *Impact*. The American concert premiere by Steve Reich and Musicians was performed on the Great Performers Series at Avery Fisher Hall January 20, 1986. *Sextet*—for four percussionists and two keyboard players—is scored for three marimbas, two vibraphones, two bass drums, crotales, sticks, tam-tam, two pianos, and two synthesizers. The duration is about 28 minutes.

1. Two members of the Toronto-based Nexus, Bob Becker and Russell Hartenberger, are also regular members of Steve Reich and Musicians.

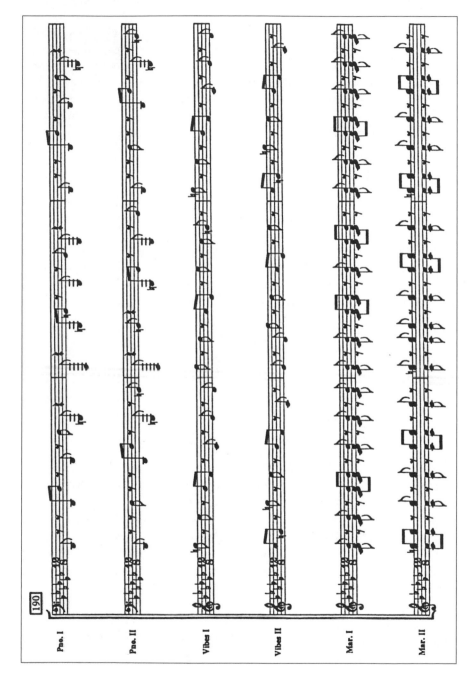

Example 29-1a. *Sextet*, rehearsal no. 190. Copyright © 1986 by Hendon Music, Inc., a Boosey & Hawkes Company. Reprinted by permission.

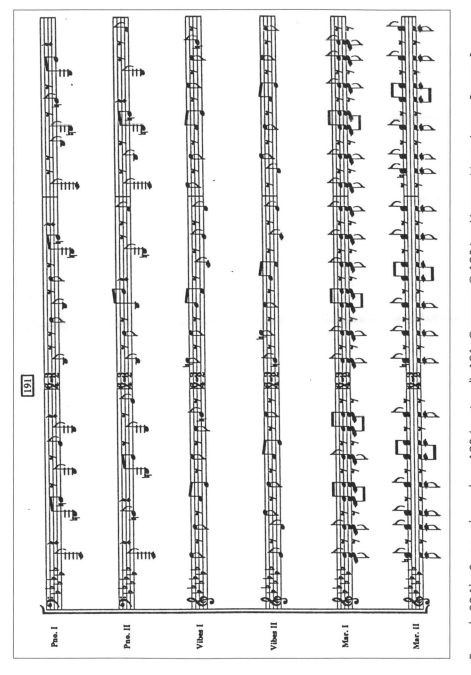

Example 29-1b. *Sextet*, rehearsal no. 190 (continued), 191. Copyright © 1986 by Hendon Music, Inc., a Boosey & Hawkes company. Reprinted by permission.

The work is in five movements played without pause. The relationship of the five movements is that of an arch form, A–B–C–B–A, in which the outer movements (A) are fast, the second and fourth movements (B) moderate, and the third (C) slow. Changes of tempo are made abruptly at the beginning of new movements by means of metric modulation, to get either slower or faster. Movements also are organized harmonically, with one chord sequence for the first and fifth movements, another for the second and fourth, and yet another for the third. The harmonies used are largely dominant chords with added tones creating a somewhat darker, chromatic, and more varied harmonic language than in my earlier works. Both the cyclical movement and structure, and the general harmonic language were suggested by *The Desert Music*.

Percussion instruments mostly produce sounds of relatively short duration. In this piece, I was interested in overcoming that limitation. The use of the bowed vibraphone—not merely as a passing effect, but as a basic instrumental voice in the second movement—was one means of obtaining long sustained sounds not possible with a piano. The mallet instruments (marimba, vibraphone, etc.) have basically a high and middle register without a low range. To overcome this, I used the bass drum to double the lower registers of the piano or synthesizer—particularly in the three central movements.

Some of the compositional techniques used were introduced in my music as early as *Drumming* (1971). In particular, the technique of substituting beats for rests to build up a canon between two or more identical instuments playing the same repeating pattern is used extensively in the first and last movements. Another is the sudden change of rhythmic position (or phase) of one voice in an overall repeating contrapuntal web, which first occurs in my *Six Pianos* (1973) and is used throughout this work. Double canons, where one canon moves slowly (the bowed vibraphones) and the second moves quickly (the pianos), first appear in my music in *Octet* (1979). Techniques influenced by African music—where the basic ambiguity in meters of 12 beats is between three groups of four and four groups of three—appear in the third and fifth movements. In the third movement, a rhythmically ambiguous pattern is played by vibraphones and accented, sometimes in four, sometimes in three, by the pianos. This pattern returns in the fifth movement, but at a much faster tempo (see ex. 29-1). Related to this is another more recent technique, appearing near the end of the fourth movement, in which the melodic material played by one pair of instruments (the synthesizers) is gradually removed, leaving the accompaniment played by another pair (the vibraphones) to become the new melodic focus. Similarly, the piano accompaniment in the second movement becomes the synthesizer melody in the fourth movement. This creates an ambiguity between what is melody and what is accompaniment. In music that uses a great deal of repetition, I believe it is precisely these kinds of ambiguities that give vitality and life.

New York Counterpoint is a continuation of ideas found in *Vermont Counterpoint* (1982), in which a soloist plays against a prerecorded tape of him- or herself. In *New York Counterpoint*, the soloist prerecords ten clarinet and bass clarinet parts and then plays a final eleventh part live against the tape. The compositional procedures used include several that occur in my earlier music. The opening pulses ultimately come from the opening of *Music for 18 Musicians*. The use of interlocking melodic patterns played by multiples of the same instrument can be found in my earliest works such as *Piano Phase* and *Violin Phase*, both of which date from 1967. But in the nature of its patterns and their harmonic combination, and also in the faster rate of change, the piece reflects my more recent works, particularly *Sextet*.

New York Counterpoint is in three movements—fast, slow, fast—played straight through without a pause. The change of tempo is abrupt and in the simple relation 1:2. The piece is in $\frac{12}{8}$ meter and exploits the ambiguity between whether one hears measures of three groups of four eighth-notes, or four groups of three eighth-notes (ex. 30-1):

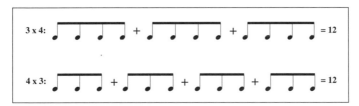

Example 30-1. *New York Counterpoint,* analysis.

In the last movement, the function of the bass clarinets is to accent first one and then the other of these possibilities, while the upper clarinets essentially do not change. The effect is to vary the perception of what is in fact not changing.

Three Movements for orchestra was commissioned by the St. Louis Symphony. It was begun late in the summer of 1985 and completed the following March. It is scored for a normal orchestra, with triple winds, and is approximately 16 minutes long.

The arrangement of the orchestra on stage is somewhat unusual and follows the layout of the orchestra for my previous work with orchestra, *The Desert Music*.[1] The purpose of this is to clarify the counterpoint between the two equal groups of strings, which are divided right and left, somewhat as one finds in Bartók's *Music for Strings, Percussion, and Celeste*. Each group can bow together and be heard more distinctly by the audience. In the work's opening pulse section, each gradual change in harmony is alternated in a gently overlapping way between the two string groups. This slow change from chord to chord may suggest the changing light as clouds move slowly across the sky or, in musical terms, it may recall the middle piece of Schoenberg's *Five Pieces for Orchestra*—Farben or *Summer Morning by a Lake*.

The opening harmonies are mostly altered dominant chords with their roots moving in minor thirds E, D♭, B♭, G, and back to E. This harmonic movement is used throughout the piece until, at the very end, it finally resolves to A minor. The three movements, fast-slow-fast, are played without pause. The tempo of the slow middle movement is exactly half that of the first movement, and the final third movement resumes the tempo of the opening movement.

After the opening pulse section, the remainder of the first movement gradually moves from pulse to melodic pattern in such a way that it may be difficult to say when the pulses end and the melodic patterns begin.

The second movement comes directly from my earlier *Sextet*. In the fourth movement of that piece, I wrote a two-part canon using slow melodic patterns played by synthesizers, which seemed to suggest oboes and clarinets. Here one can hear those wind instruments along with quiet violins playing this material, and supported by two vibraphones, bass drum, and low strings and winds. Eventually the woodwinds and violins fade away and the accompaniment of vibraphones, bass drum, and low strings and winds becomes the new melodic focus.

The fast final movement draws on both my *Sextet* and *New York Counterpoint*. After the upper voices of the orchestra have built up a two-part canonic texture, the lower voices begin accenting this material so that it is perceived alternately as three groups of four beats each and then as four groups of three beats each. The piece is concluded with a kind of mensuration canon—in which the

---

1. See *On the Size and Seating of an Orchestra*, no. 41, pp. 162–64.

subject appears simultaneously in two or more speeds—the subject being a rhythmic pattern found in the high bell part of some West African music. This canon involves the entire orchestra and moves gradually upward, leaving the bass behind to cadence on a high A minor.

SIX MARIMBAS (1986) 32

Six Marimbas, 1986, is a rescoring for marimbas of my earlier *Six Pianos* (1973).[1] The idea came from my friend the percussionist James Preiss, who also contributed the hand and mallet alternations that are used in this score.

TENNEY (1986) 33

First appeared as part of a tribute to James Tenney in *Perspectives of New Music,* vol. 25, nos. 1 and 2, Winter–Summer 1987.

In 1965, I returned to New York City from four years in San Francisco. I didn't know too many people there any more. I don't remember exactly how, but I was told to contact James Tenney. He was living near the lower east side at the time. He was immediately interested in what I had to say and in the tape piece I played for him, *It's Gonna Rain.* In the years that followed, I began to find out more about Tenney.

First, he was a fine composer, pianist, and conductor who was championing the works of (among others) Ives, Varèse, Cage, Feldman, Brown, and Wolff. Second, he was involved in very high-powered computer music research at Bell Laboratories. Later, I understood that he was involved with the basic analog to digi-

1. See p. 73.

tal and digital to analog sound conversion experiments, which were to form the foundation of both the telephone system and eventually the digital recording of music and sound sampling instruments. It soon turned out that I was working with Jim in both these capacities.

When I was offered a chance to perform three evenings of my music at the Park Place Gallery in downtown Manhattan in 1967, I immediately asked Jim if he would join my ensemble (which then consisted only of Art Murphy, Jon Gibson, and myself) to play a four electric piano version of a two-piano piece I was working on (which later became *Piano Phase*). He immediately agreed and suggested Phil Corner as the fourth keyboard player. We rehearsed intensively and in March 1967 presented three performances of the piece at the end of each concert. It was quite an experience and Jim put himself totally into the music, so much so that he became a regular member of my ensemble for the next few years.

Shortly after this time, Jim offered to teach a group of artists Fortran. This group included John Cage, Nam June Paik, Dick Higgins, Allison Knowles, and myself, among others. We met at Dick and Allison's home and if you think this sounds like a strange context in which to study Fortran, you're right.

Jim seemed to be a natural teacher. He always got to the point of things whether he was at rehearsal or explaining about computers. I particularly remember a visit from him when I was spending the summer of 1968 in Northern New Mexico. He was passing through, on the way to visit his parents if I remember correctly, and I was writing an essay, *Music as a Gradual Process*. I showed him what I had so far and his comments were immediate and clarifying. I was writing about how I wanted the compositional process to be heard in the sounding music and he said, "Then the composer isn't privy to anything." Exactly so, I don't know any secrets of structure that you can't hear. Eighteen years later, that certainly doesn't describe my music the way it did in 1968, but the memory of Jim getting to the point remains with me.

A few years later Jim composed his piece of constantly rising oscillator glissandos in canon (first referred to by him as "The Barber Pole Piece" and by me as "Busy Day at JFK") called *For Ann Rising*, which struck me as an extremely intelligent and amusing piece and was also a kind of comment on my own work and on canon in general. (The form is fixed, but open to any sound in the world.) Still later, Tenney became interested in piano rags and composed several of his own, which he performed with great charm.

Through it all, he always seemed to remain a natural teacher and champion of all sorts of new music. All sorts, that is, except his own. While he could courageously defend and perform Ives or Cage or Rhudyar he wouldn't try and get his own work performed beyond what he could play himself or with friends. That he left to others.

In 1979, members of my ensemble presented two evenings of his music at The Paula Cooper Gallery (Paula was the one who ran the old Park Place Gallery back in '67) and at Carnegie Recital Hall. They were two great evenings with many of his percussion pieces (dedicated to Varèse, Ives, and Nancarrow among others) and rags and tape pieces. Will some other ensembles please take note? And record companies as well? James Tenney has a fine body of work, which needs performing and recording.

Now it's 1986. High time to say, thank you, Jim—for the good performances, for the basic acoustic research, for the first-rate teaching and good advice, and most of all for your music, which must now get out there in the world for the benefit of all concerned.

TEXTURE—SPACE—SURVIVAL (1987) 34

Originally written for a composers' conference in New Hampshire; published in *Perspectives of New Music*, vol. 26, no. 2, Summer 1988.

Texture

When I was asked to give this talk, I was told that the three topics under consideration would be Texture, Space, and Survival.

Under the word "texture" in *The New Harvard Dictionary of Music,* one finds the following: "the texture of a work that is perceived as consisting of the combination of several melodic lines is said to be contrapuntal or polyphonic. A work consisting primarily of a succession of chords sounded as such is said to have a chordal or homophonic texture." Given this traditional distinction, there is no question that by far the greater part of my own music is contrapuntal in texture. The period in Western musical history where I find the most useful information is that from 1200 to 1750—the contrapuntal period. Musics outside the West that I have learned a great deal from are West African and Balinese, both of which are contrapuntal in nature. And, yes, their counterpoint was developed quite independently from ours and the myth that counterpoint was invented exclusively by Europeans is just that, a myth.

The technique I first discovered in 1965 while working with tape loops I called "phasing." It was later, in 1967, applied to live performance. In fact, "phasing" is a process for composing canons at the unison where the subject is short and the rhythmic interval between the subject and its answers is variable.

Canon, as you know, is a technique beginning in the thirteenth century, and instances of it can be found from the Middle Ages to the present. Although the principle of canonic technique is fixed this says nothing about the sound. Canons can be found from *Sumer Is Icumen In,* to Bach's *Musical Offering,* to Bartók's *Mikrokosmos,* and Webern's *Symphony Op.21.* While the procedure is basically the same, the sounds are extremely different.

My work is based on canon. I used infinite canon as an example of what I was talking about in my 1968 essay *Music as a Gradual Process.* My first tape pieces back in 1965 and '66 use one tape loop gradually going out of phase with itself in two or more voices. Canons are thus produced with gradually changing rhythmic distances. In the first piece of live music to use this technique, *Piano Phase* (1967), each phase position is just a short unison canon with a slightly different rhythmic interval. Although I stopped using the phasing technique after *Drumming,* I found other ways to gradually build up canons at the unison between two or more identical repeating patterns. The most productive of these is to gradually substitute notes for rests—sound for silence—until a canon is constructed. People became aware of my use of canonic structure much later with *Tehillim* because the subjects were longer and more traditionally melodic. Basically I was working as I always had, and what is new in *Tehillim* is its specifically homophonic sections. The same can be said of *Desert Music.* The homophonic aspects of these pieces result completely from the fact that they each set a text. In the works following these, I returned to basically contrapuntal textures.

Starting in 1982, I began my "Counterpoint" series with *Vermont Counterpoint,* written for Ransom Wilson in response to his original request for a flute concerto—which I was not interested in writing since its conception of soloist with accompaniment was not something I have any attraction for. *Vermont Counterpoint* refers back to the early works like *Violin Phase,* where a violinist plays against prerecorded tracks of him- or herself. The overall texture is made up entirely of multiples of the same timbre, which texture highlights the overall contrapuntal web with its many resulting patterns that the listener can hear. That is to say that my early works like *Violin Phase* and *Piano Phase* were written for multiples of identical instruments because if, for instance, in *Piano Phase* I play piano and you play harpsichord or synthesizer, we will hear the separate timbres moving out of phase without the complete blending between the two to produce a contrapuntal web in the way we would if we use two pianos or two harpsichords or two synthesizers. Thus, multiples of identical instruments with the same timbres were acoustically necessary in my early pieces to create the overall contrapuntal web and particularly the ambiguity as to where the downbeat is, since two or more equal downbeats are always sounding with the same timbre throughout. Now, in the '80s, the same principles apply with the addition of more developed melodic patterns and changes of harmony, as in a piece like *New York Counterpoint* for multiple clarinets and bass clarinets, composed for the clarinetist Richard Stolzman.

Texture can also refer to "heavy" or "light" texture. *The New Harvard Dictionary of Music* describes Sibelius's symphonies as "heavy" and Stravinsky's *Histoire* as "light." Following this line of thought, you might describe John Adams's *Harmonielehre* as "heavy" and my *Sextet* as "light." This line of thought obviously suggests how different composers deal with the orchestra both according to size and placement. My own ideal is to have a "light" texture and to achieve this I prefer to write for a chamber orchestra and to redistribute the positioning of the players.[1]

Space

When I was asked to give this talk and was told the three topics under discussion, I found that I remembered "texture" and "survival" and could not remember the third. On calling back to refresh my memory I was reminded that the other topic was "space." I looked in *The New Harvard Dictionary of Music* once again, both in the 1969 and 1986 editions, and found that the word "space" was not to be found in either. I called back again and was told there were three kinds of musical space under discussion: (1) physical space as found in Gabrieli or Henry Brant; (2) ritual space as pertaining to certain non-Western musics, for example; and (3) electronic space as in moving sound around a hall via multiple speakers.

I remember in 1957 enjoying Gabrieli performed in St. Mark's Cathedral, Venice, at the opening of the concert that featured the premiere of Stravinsky's *Canticum Sacrum*. The antiphonal brass choirs were something the composer obviously had in mind for that particular church. But is Gabrieli a flop in mono recordings? I think not. As for Henry Brant, I cannot say, as I don't know any of his music. Certainly one could say that my ideas about orchestral seating are concerned with space. It is important that musicians playing my music sit close together so they can hear each other well, and this is quite the opposite from, say, John Cage's music, where spatial separation is often desired and rhythmic coordination is not. In this sense, "space" is a practical factor in performance, but seems peripheral to composition.

Ritual space calls to mind my trip to Ghana in 1970, where I studied with members of the Ghana Dance Ensemble. This ensemble is made up of musicians from at least five different tribes who originally lived far away from the capital city of Accra, where the ensemble is located. Prior to 1967, these musicians had lived in their own villages and had been employed as musicians by the local chief. In 1967, Nkruma came to power and established a government in Accra for the entire country; a modern state was born. But with this modern Western-style statehood, the local village chiefs remained only as figureheads. They had no money or power. This meant that local musicians could remain musicians but not professional ones. Instead of being employed by the chief, they had to find a day job in the chocolate factories or elsewhere to support themselves and their families. For those fortunate enough to be outstanding players, and to have the right political connections in Accra, they could become professionals once again—but this time in an ensemble that toured Europe and the Orient with versions of

---

1. See "*On the Size and Seating of an Orchestra*," no. 41, pp. 162–64.

music and dance where the duration of a piece might be condensed from three days to 20 minutes, and the musical space changed from a village to a proscenium stage. So, can one conclude that changing the space changed the music? No, one is dealing with a complete shift in social organization and economics as the real cause here. *That* caused the shift to the stage, which in turn brought about shortened versions of music. Space here seems incidental to more profound cultural changes.

The third sense of "space," electronic space, is something we are all familiar with, especially if you are old enough to have experienced the shift from mono to stereo. Since we do have two ears and the G-d-given ability to locate sounds with them, using two loudspeakers instead of one brought electronic musical reproduction closer to our normal everyday acoustical hearing. Then, in electronic music in the fifties with Varèse and on through the '60s to the present, the movement of sound around a hall via multiple loudspeakers has become a possibility for composers. It is a possibility I have not pursued because for me the main questions in composition are rhythm, pitch, and timbre—in that order. My use of electronics has been primarily amplification to create balances that would not be possible without amplification. Thus a woman's voice without vibrato and with a great deal of rhythmic clarity and detail can be heard over an ensemble as large as an orchestra with the help of amplification. The placement of loudspeakers is indeed crucial for the audience to hear well, but for me that placement is only an expedient to realize a composition, it is not in itself the compositional material or technique.

Physical space, while undoubtedly enhancing or detracting from a performance because of acoustics, seems peripheral to composition. A piece of music limited to a particular space is just that—limited. It would seem more worthwhile to try and write pieces that will work well in almost any space.

Ritual space seems to be the result of religious, social, and economic organization. Change the religion, social organization, or the economics, and the ritual space will change along with many other things. It is incidental to these basic forms of life.

Electronic space created by multiple loudspeakers is an important aspect of performance with electronics, but it does not seem to me worthwhile material to compose music with.

Survival

In 1963, I received my M.A. from Mills College and thus ended my formal Western education. At precisely this point, the question arose as to how to survive. I felt very clearly that I did not want to continue in an academic environment. In my few teaching experiences as a graduate assistant at Mills and as a theory and composition teacher at a communty school in San Francisco, I found that the very energy I needed as a composer was being expended on my students instead. I felt that to be a good teacher one had to expend that energy, that there was only so much of it, and that for me I simply could not teach and still give the necessary energy to my own composition. It also seemed clear to me that teaching was a talent quite different from composing and that my best teachers, Hall Overton and Vincent Persichetti, were not necessarily the best composers. What I learned from more outstanding composers like Berio, for example, was not about who I was as a composer but about who he was. At the time that was of interest, but it is not, I believe, what is basic for good musical education. What is a basic is a teacher who can give you the musical information you need given your own particular situation at a given time. This kind of teacher in a sense disappears into the various alter egos of the various students he or she teaches. This kind of teacher may be a great teacher just because he or she lacks the single-minded focus on a particular way of writing music a stronger composer may have. In any event, I felt I could not pursue an academic career.

What then? I took a job with the Yellow Cab Company in San Francisco in 1963. I found that this kind of job left my mind completely free to concentrate on composition and actually paid more money than a college instructor in theory or composition would make. While in San Francisco I composed at home and presented my music, including a tape piece composed of fragments recorded in the taxi I drove, at both the San Francisco Tape Music Center and the San Francisco Mime Troupe. My job as a cab driver ended in late 1964 and I moved to the U.S. Post Office, which proved to be somewhat less interesting though about the same in terms of income and certainly did not interfere with my composing. In 1965, I left the Bay Area and returned to New York City.

In 1966, in New York, I began rehearsing my musical ideas with two friends, Art Murphy, a composer and pianist from Juilliard, and Jon Gibson, a woodwind player from San Francisco who had come to New York at the same time. At the time, I didn't envision that this would eventually lead to a performing ensemble that would make it possible for me to survive by performing my own music. In 1966, I simply had musical ideas that I wanted to try and these were my friends who were interested in what I was working on. Meanwhile, I continued to support myself by taking a series of menial jobs. In 1967, my ensemble grew to four people including myself, and we started presenting concerts, usually in art venues such as the Park Place Gallery that were closely associated with what was to be called Minimal Art. Few well-known composers attended these events, although lots of artists did, and their success led to further invitations to perform my own music with my own ensemble.

In 1970–71, I worked on *Drumming,* which is the piece where I came to terms with my own background as a drummer, and for which my ensemble grew from five or six musicians to 12 and introduced percussionists Russ Hartenberger, Bob Becker, and James Preiss into my ensemble, where they still perform. In December 1971, the world premiere of *Drumming* was presented at the Museum of Modern Art in New York, and at about this time I also began writing letters to European concert sponsors in England, Germany, and France, and in 1971 we made our first European tour. That same year, with help from Jean Rigg, the administrator of the Cunningham Dance Foundation, the Reich Music Foundation was incorporated so that we could receive funds from the National Endowment for the Arts and the New York State Council on the Arts to pay for travel and rehearsal fees for musicians in the ensemble. Finally, in 1972, somewhat to my surprise, I found that at the age of 36 I was finally able to make a living as a composer who performed his music with his own ensemble.

Now, in 1987, what could a young composer about to finish his or her own schooling get from this personal history that might be of use? I'm not sure. The 1960s were perhaps more idealistic and also perhaps more foolish and unrealistic. Students in the 1980s are often extremely concerned with how they will survive economically starting from the time they leave school. This cannot be dismissed as a foolish concern. I would, however, venture a few thoughts I hope are of some practical use:

1. If you're not wholly committed to your own compositions, you will undoubtedly find that performers and audiences aren't either.

2. If you feel that teaching will eat up valuable time and energy that would be better spent composing, you might just be right.

3. If you're young and unknown and you want to get your compositions performed the way you know they should be performed, perhaps you should perform them with your friends. One good performance leads to another and gradually people get to hear what you really have in mind.

Thank you very much.

---

35 THE FOUR SECTIONS (1987)

The title refers to the four sections of the orchestra; strings, woodwinds, brass, and percussion. It also refers to the four movements of the piece; slow for strings (with woodwinds and brass), slow for percussion, moderate for woodwinds and brass (with strings), and fast for the full orchestra. And it also refers to the four harmonic sections into which each of the movements is divided.

Since each of the movements focuses on one or two of the orchestral sections one might be tempted to think of it as a concerto for orchestra. The focus here, however, is on the *interlocking* of voices *within* the sections rather than displaying their virtuosity against the rest of the orchestra. Those familiar with other pieces of mine will recognize this interlocking of similar instruments to produce a contrapuntal web filled with resulting melodic patterns.

In contrast to all other pieces of mine, *The Four Sections* begins slowly and gradually increases tempo as it goes along. The first movement begins in the first violins in three part canon joined shortly by the second violins and then violas, also divided in three canonic parts. The cellos joined by woodwinds then bring out some of the melodies resulting from this nine voice canon. Below and around all of this the brass, synthesizers, and double basses add long held chords.

After approximately 10 minutes, the second movement begins abruptly with two vibraphones, two pianos, and two bass drums. Although the tempo remains slow the bass drum and piano accents against the two interlocking vibraphones creates an extremely angular and irregular percussive music in sharp contrast to the first movement.

The third movement begins somewhat faster using the triplet rhythm at the end of the preceding movement as its eighth-note. As mentioned earlier, each movement is divided into four harmonic sections and in this movement each of those sections is devoted to a different instrumental grouping. The first is for a trio of interlocking oboes with resulting patterns played by flutes and two solo violins, and with pulsing chords from the other woodwinds and horns. The second is centered around a trio of smoothly interlocking clarinets, while the third is for a double trio of trumpets and clarinets. The tempo increases in the fourth section with the old quarter-note equaling the new dotted quarter. Here a double trio of flutes and clarinets is harmonized by the full string section while trumpets and oboes play resulting patterns.

The fourth movement begins abruptly with the vibraphones, marimbas, and pianos at a fast tempo arrived at by shifting the basic meter from a dotted quarter-note to a quarter-note. The first violins, violas, and vibraphones gradually construct a rapid repeating pattern while at the same time a high melody is built up, a note at a time, in the second violins and flutes. Suddenly, the pianos, bass drums, basses, and cellos begin adding low accents to reinterpret the metric stress. When this orchestral build-up is completed it then modulates through the four harmonies mentioned earlier, changing metrical accent and melodic shape as it goes. Finally the full ensemble cadences on F♯. The total duration of the piece is about 25 minutes.

The Four Sections was commissioned by the San Francisco Symphony in honor of its seventy-fifthth Anniversary. The world premiere was presented in San Francisco on October 7, 1987, conducted by Michael Tilson Thomas, to whom the piece is dedicated.

ELECTRIC COUNTERPOINT (1987) 36

Electric Counterpoint was commissioned by the Brooklyn Academy of Music's Next Wave Festival for the guitarist Pat Metheny. It was composed during the summer of 1987. The duration is about 15 minutes. It is the third in a series of pieces (preceded by *Vermont Counterpoint* and *New York Counterpoint*) all deal-

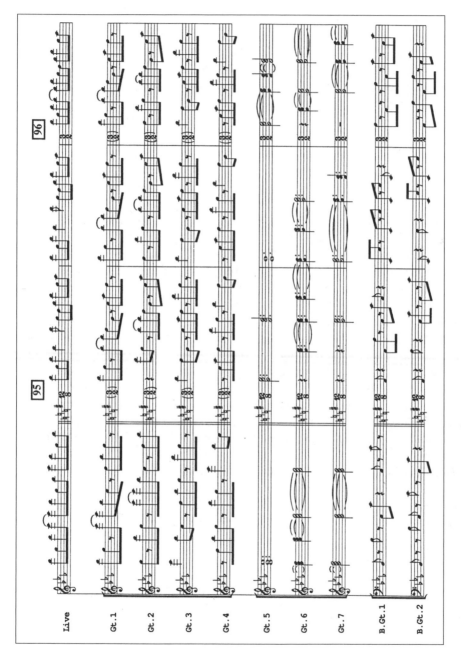

Example 36-1. *Electric Counterpoint*, rehearsal nos. 94–96. Copyright © 1987 by Hendon Music, Inc., a Boosey & Hawkes Company. Reprinted by permission.

ing with a soloist playing against a prerecorded tape of themselves. In *Electric Counterpoint,* the soloist prerecords as many as 10 guitars and two electric bass parts and then plays the final eleventh guitar part live against the tape. I would like to thank Pat Metheny for showing me how to improve the piece in terms of making it more idiomatic for the guitar.

The work is in three movements—fast, slow, fast—played one after the other without pause. The first movement, after an introductory pulsing section where the harmonies of the movement are stated, uses a theme derived from Central African horn music that I became aware of through the ethnomusicologist Simha Arom. That theme is built up in eight voice canon and, while the remaining two guitars and bass play pulsing harmonies, the soloist plays melodic patterns that result from the contrapuntal interlocking of those eight prerecorded guitars.

The second movement cuts the tempo in half, changes key and introduces a new theme, which is then slowly built up in nine guitars in canon. Once again, two other guitars and bass supply harmony, while the soloist brings out melodic patterns that result from the overall contrapuntal web.

The third movement returns to the original tempo and key and introduces a new pattern in triple meter. After building up a four-guitar canon, two bass guitars enter suddenly to further stress the triple meter. The soloist then introduces a new series of strummed chords that are built up in three-guitar canon. When these are complete, the soloist returns to melodic patterns that result from the overall counterpoint, suddenly, the basses begin to change both key and meter back and forth between E minor and C minor and between $\frac{3}{2}$ and $\frac{12}{8}$, so that one hears first three groups of four eighth-notes and then four groups of three eighth-notes (see ex. 36-1). These rhythmic and tonal changes speed up more and more rapidly until at the end the basses slowly fade out and the ambiguities are finally resolved in $\frac{12}{8}$ and E minor.

NON-WESTERN MUSIC AND THE WESTERN COMPOSER (1988) 37

First printed in *Analyse Musicale,* vol. 11, April 1988; Reich's contribution was made at the invitation of Simha Arom.

I first heard African music on recordings while I was at Cornell University in the mid-1950s. It impressed me enormously, but I had absolutely no idea how the music was made. Later, in 1962, I came across A. M. Jones's transcriptions of Ghanaian music in his *Studies in African Music,* and was amazed to see what could briefly be described as repeating patterns (often in what we would call a kind of $\frac{12}{8}$ meter) superimposed on each other so that their individual downbeats did not coincide. This was clearly a radically different way of making music. It also suggested the multiple simultaneous tape loops I was beginning to experiment with at the time. After having composed *It's Gonna Rain, Come Out, Piano Phase, Violin Phase, Four Organs, Phase Patterns,* and other works, I went to visit Ghana in the summer of 1970, where I studied with several musicians, mostly from the Ewe tribe. I took daily lessons and recorded each lesson. Afterward I would return to my room and, by playing and replaying the tape, sometimes at half or quarter speed, I was able to transcribe the bell, rattle, and drum patterns I had learned.[1]

When I returned to New York from Accra I brought with me several iron bells called "gong-gong" and "atoke." I thought I would use these bells in a composition of my own. One of my first considerations in this respect was tuning, since these bells obviously did not correspond to the notes in our scale. Because the bells were made of iron, a metal file would be necessary to retune them. The more I thought about this, the more it began to seem like a kind of musical rape. These bells came from a certain musical context and history and it seemed to me totally inappropriate to take a file and retune them. So, in order to get the desire to play them out of my system, I simply taught members of my ensemble how to play some of the *Hatsyiatsya* patterns for these bells I had learned in Ghana. The more I thought about the whole thing the clearer it became to me that I didn't want to use *any* African instrument in my own music. Shortly after that I began to work with glockenspiels for a section of my piece *Drumming*. The glockenspiel was *my* set of bells. It came from a shop in New York and was tuned to the same scale as all our other instruments. I was free to use it as I liked.

Later, in the summers of 1974 and 1975, I studied Balinese Gamelan Semar Pegulingan and Gamelan Gambang at the American Society for Eastern Arts summer sessions in Seattle and Berkeley. I was interested in doing this because earlier, in the late 1960s, I had read Colin McPhee's *Music in Bali*.[2] Once again the rhythmic structure of the music as shown in McPhee's transcriptions struck me. In this case interlocking metallophone patterns, some moving very quickly in what we would call eighth-notes and others, the large gongs, only playing once every 16 or 32 bars. Other musicians I knew at the time were fascinated with Balinese scales and particularly the timbres of their instruments. I realized that for me I had no desire whatsoever to imitate these scales or timbres. My interest was in the rhythmic structure of the music. I didn't want to *sound* Balinese or African, I wanted to *think* Balinese or African. Which meant that I would

1. These transcriptions form part of the essay *Gahu;* see no. 7, p. 55.
2. McPhee, 1966.

sound like myself while expanding my ideas about how to rhythmically structure my pieces.

This kind of learning is quite similar to what Western music students do when they are taught about canons for instance. They are shown examples from, let us say, Josquin, Bach, Bartók, and Webern. What do these examples have in common? Certainly not their sound! What these examples have in common is an imitative contrapuntal process in two or more voices where all voices are melodically the same. Variations on this technique may then be presented with the use of augmentation and diminution, retrograde or inverted forms of the subject, and so on. Thus, when a Western music student learns about canon and then later begins to compose them himself or herself the result in terms of sound will be *unforeseen*. The structure remains but the sound is (hopefully) new and expressive of the times and place the composer lives in.

In my own case, the influence of my trip to Africa on my composition was more in the nature of encouragement than change of direction. Since I had composed the formative works in my style (*It's Gonna Rain, Come Out, Piano Phase, Violin Phase*, etc.) in the 1960s prior to going to Ghana in 1970, my trip there basically *confirmed* the direction I was already going in. Specifically, it confirmed my interest in acoustic instruments as opposed to electronically generated sound and my basic concern with percussion, which began when I started studying drums at the age of 14. My basic insight into change of phase between two repeating patterns was made by observing two tape loops on two tape recorders. However, seeing the book of African transcriptions by A. M. Jones undoubtedly helped prepare me to take a strong interest in the phasing process when I discovered it.

Somewhat later, in 1975, I became aware of the work of the ethnomusicologist Simha Arom. While in Paris in 1976, presenting concerts with my own ensemble, I had an opportunity to meet with him briefly and become at least superficially aware of his work with multitrack recording and transcription in Central Africa. Later, in 1987, I received a copy of his magnum opus, *Polyphonies et Polyrythmies Instrumentales d'Afrique Centrale* (1985)[3]. Although my reading of French is quite limited I could see from the musical examples that this was obviously a contribution to ethnomusicology of the highest order.

I received a copy of this book while beginning work on *Electric Counterpoint* for electric guitar and tape, where the tape has up to 10 tracks of prerecorded guitar and bass guitar. The guitarist is thus playing in counterpoint with recordings of him or herself. While looking through Arom's book, one of the patterns for three horns on the top of page 569 caught my eye (see ex. 37-1).

3. Published in English, Arom, 1991.

Example 37-1. From Simha Arom's
Polyphonies et Polyrhythmies.

By more or less combining all three voices and extending the pattern with a slight variation to two bars, I had the theme for the first movement of *Electric Counterpoint* (ex. 37-2):

Example 37-2. Theme for *Electric Counterpoint,* first movement.

This theme was then worked out in close canon between a total of eight guitars plus the live player and three bass guitars. In this case, I used an African *theme* for the first time in a piece of mine. The fact that I found it in a book already in Western notation made questions of tuning irrelevant. On the other hand, I don't think *Electric Counterpoint* is any more "African" because it uses a theme derived from a book of African transcriptions. If it has any African quality, it lies perhaps in the fact that the close canon between voices makes it ambiguous as to where the downbeat is and that happens most ambiguously in the last movement of the piece where this African theme is not even used. If anything this theme seems a bit "un-African" in that it is in a very unambiguous $\frac{4}{4}$ meter instead of a more typically ambiguous $\frac{3}{2} = \frac{12}{8}$ Ghanaian meter.

If I compose music that is to use repeating patterns and is also to remain interesting I *must* build in rhythmic ambiguity to make it possible for the ear to hear a given pattern beginning and ending in different places depending on slight differences of accent and on how one listens. *This* is a lesson one can learn from African music. And it suggests what kinds of lessons Western composers can learn from non-Western musics. We all hear our Western scale before we learn to walk or talk. It is deeply programmed in our conscious and unconscious mind. To try, later in life, to imitate a scale from Bali or India is, it seems to me, rather problematic. To really do it best one needs to use the original non-Western instruments, which are best played by the original non-Western players, and so what exactly is one doing here? On the other hand, Western musical structures like canon, fugue, and others are learned considerably later in life and are really only learned well by professionals or well-trained amateurs. These ways of putting music together can thus be transported to another culture more easily because they are not as deeply ingrained in our minds. One can thus create music with one's own sound that is constructed in the light of one's knowledge of non-Western structures.[4]

DIFFERENT TRAINS (1988) 38

The material presented here is taken from record liner and program notes; the reader is also referred to "Answers to Questions about Different Trains," p. 180, which is placed there to preserve its position in the chronological sequence. All rights reserved. Used by permission.

Different Trains for string quartet and tape begins a new way of composing that has its roots in my early taped speech pieces *It's Gonna Rain* and *Come Out*. The basic idea is that speech recordings generate the musical material for musical instruments.

The idea for the piece comes from my childhood. When I was one year old, my parents separated. My mother moved to Los Angeles and my father stayed in New York. Since they arranged divided custody, I traveled back and forth by train frequently between New York and Los Angeles from 1939 to 1942, accompanied by my governess. While these trips were exciting and romantic at the time, I now look back and think that, if I had been in Europe during this period, as a Jew I would have had to ride on very different trains. With this in mind, I wanted to make a piece that would accurately reflect the whole situation. In order to prepare the tape, I had to do the following:

1. Record my governess Virginia, now in her seventies, reminiscing about our train trips together.

2. Record a retired Pullman porter, Lawrence Davis, now in his eighties, who used to ride lines between New York and Los Angeles, reminiscing about his life.

---

4. See no. 10, p. 69, *Postscript to a Brief Study.*

3. Collect recordings of Holocaust survivors Rachella, Paul, and Rachel—all about my age and now living in America—speaking of their experiences.

4. Collect recorded American and European train sounds of the 1930s and '40s.

In order to combine the taped speech with the string instruments, I selected small speech samples that are more or less clearly pitched, then transcribed them as accurately as possible into musical notation. For instance, see example 38-1.

Example 38-1. From *Different Trains,* first movement.

The strings then literally imitate that speech melody (ex. 38-2a). The speech samples as well as the train sounds were transferred to tape with the use of sampling keyboards and a computer. The Kronos Quartet then made four separate string quartet recordings, which were then combined with the speech and train sounds to create the finished work.

Different Trains is in three movements, although that term is stretched here, since tempos change frequently in each movement. They are:

1. America—before the war

2. Europe—during the war

3. After the war

The piece thus presents both a documentary and a musical reality, and begins a new musical direction. It is a direction that I expect will lead to a new kind of documentary music video theater in the not-too-distant future.[1]

Different Trains was commissioned by Betty Freeman for the Kronos Quartet. It was composed from January through August of 1988 and is about 27 minutes long. The transcript of the speech recordings used follows:

1. America—before the war

"From Chicago to New York" (Virginia)

"one of the fastest trains"

"the crack[2] train from New York" (Mr. Davis)

---

1. See *The Cave,* no. 45, and *Three Tales,* no. 59.
2. In the older sense of "best."

"from New York to Los Angeles"
"different trains every time" (Virginia)
"from Chicago to New York"
"in 1939"
"1939" (Mr. Davis)
"1940"
"1941"
"1941 I guess it must've been" (Virginia)

2. Europe – during the war

"1940" (Rachella)
"on my birthday"
"The Germans walked in"
"walked into Holland"
"Germans invaded Hungary" (Paul)
"I was in second grade"
"I had a teacher"
"a very tall man, his hair was concretely plastered smooth"
"He said 'Black Crows invaded our country many years ago' "
"and he pointed right at me"
"No more school" (Rachel)
"You must go away"
"and she said 'Quick, go!' " (Rachella)
"and he said, 'Don't breathe!' "
"into those cattle wagons" (Rachella)
"for four days and four nights"
"and then we went through these strange sounding names"
"Polish names"
"Lots of cattle wagons there"
"They were loaded with people"
"They shaved us"
"They tattooed a number on our arm"
"Flames going up to the sky—it was smoking"

3. After the war

"And the war was over" (Paul)
"Are you sure?" (Rachella)

"The war is over"

"going to America"

"to Los Angeles"

"to New York"

"from New York to Los Angeles" (Mr. Davis)

"one of the fastest trains" (Virginia)

"but today, they're all gone" (Mr. Davis)

"There was one girl, who had a beautiful voice" (Rachella)

"and they loved to listen to the singing, the Germans"

"and when she stopped singing they said, 'More, more' and they applauded"

Example 38-2a. *Different Trains,* from first movement. COPYRIGHT © 1988 BY HENDON MUSIC, INC., A BOOSEY & HAWKES COMPANY. REPRINTED BY PERMISSION.

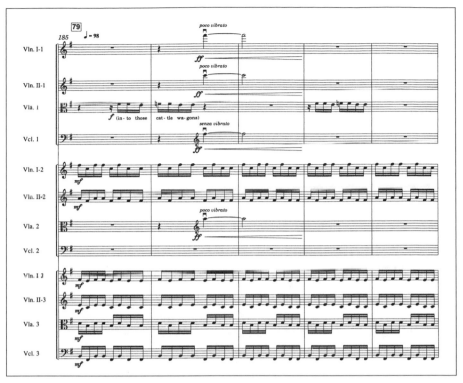

Example 38-2b. *Different Trains,* from second movement. Copyright © 1988 by Hendon Music, Inc., a Boosey & Hawkes company. Reprinted by permission.

Example 38-2c. *Different Trains,* from third movement. Copyright © 1988 by Hendon Music, Inc., a Boosey & Hawkes company. Reprinted by permission.

First publication in English. Originally read as the keynote address at the 1989 annual meeting of Chamber Music America.

I am a composer who has, among other things, written music for his own ensemble. This ensemble normally comprises between four to as many as nine percussionists (plus keyboards). When we perform it is common for audiences to see the stage decked out with multiple marimbas, vibraphones, glockenspiels, bass drums, and so forth—with or without the addition of strings, winds, or voices—and usually microphones, too. All in all, this is a different world from the string quartet or woodwind quintet; and yet we play one to a part and without a conductor.

In African and Balinese music, the rhythmic skills demanded from percussionists are formidable since they have the dominant role, comparable to that of the strings in Western classical ensembles. In my ensemble, percussion is often the dominant voice, although it is certainly not used to achieve an exotic effect. In works such as *Music for 18 Musicians,* one of the instruments gives audible cues to the other players to make a change to the next bar, which is similar to the practice used in African and Balinese music. The initial tempo is maintained throughout, and cues for entrances are given by the bass clarinettist simply by eye contact. These cueing systems replace the need for a conductor and the musicians work together in a chamber music manner—and yet with 18 musicians on stage, one doesn't think of "Chamber Music" as the descriptive term.

What sort of musicians are in this ensemble? First, they were all trained at Eastman, Curtis, Juilliard, Oberlin, Manhattan, and other conservatories. Later, many of them became involved in non-Western music, early music, or jazz. For example: the percussionist Russell Hartenberger did a Ph.D. in Mrdangham (the South Indian side drum) at Wesleyan University, while also playing African and Indonesian music; Bob Becker, another percussionist, did a Ph.D. in Tabla, the North Indian drums, at Wesleyan, while also playing African and Indonesian music; Cheryl Bensman, a soprano, sang with Waverly Consort and other early music groups; Ben Harms, still another percussionist, plays with Calliope—a Renaissance music band; Jay Clayton, an alto, is primarily a jazz singer; Nurit Tilles, a pianist, studied Sundanese Gamelan in 1973.

Why are non-Western music, early music, and jazz good playing experiences for musicians in this ensemble? One reason is rhythm. I need musicians who have, and enjoy using, a strong rhythmic sense. Most early music shares with jazz, and most non-Western music, a fixed pulse. For a player to master such music and to find satisfaction in performing it, he or she must have a markedly firm sense of regular time and enjoy exercising it, in contrast to the player who prefers, for example, the more gestural rhythm found in German romantic music.

Another reason early music and jazz are valuable backgrounds for musicians in this ensemble is vocal style. In early music the vocal style generally calls for a lighter, more "natural" voice, with less vibrato than that found in bel canto or Wagnerian opera. It is this style that I find well-suited to my own music. Why? The operatic voice was developed, among other things, to be heard above an orchestra in a fairly large hall well before the invention of the microphone. The invention of the microphone and its ubiquitous use in popular music in the twentieth century has made it possible for a much smaller voice with little or no vibrato to be easily heard in great detail over even a very loud band or orchestra. This has created a climate in which I find most operatic voices to be somewhat artificial, loud and abrasive to listen to. Since we have microphones, I choose to use them with singers who are at ease with them. These singers can then be heard in great detail, even over an ensemble with considerable percussion, while singing with a smaller voice and little or no vibrato: altogether, a voice well suited to the kind of contrapuntal music that I write. Singers who have this kind of voice can be found in the worlds of early music and jazz, and in my ensemble that is where they have come from.

The musicians in this ensemble also have what I would call a chamber musician's mentality. As a music student, I remember one attitude from those students who planned to enter an orchestra and another from those who planned to make chamber music their life. The difference could be traced to some obvious facts. The orchestral player could be hired by an ongoing organization and hope to stay there, or move to a better one, while for the chamber musician, with the exception of a rare vacancy in a small number of name chamber groups, they had to form their own groups or play in several ensembles in order to survive. In other words, a chamber musician has to create his or her own livelihood.

In my own ensemble, the musicians continue to be involved with several other performing groups, since we play only a limited number of concerts, here and abroad, each year. Being of an independent turn of mind, many of the musicians in this ensemble have formed their own groups, for example: Russ Hartenberger and Bob Becker are founding members of the percussion ensemble Nexus; Nurit Tilles and Edmund Niemann began the duo keyboard team Double Edge; James Preiss is the founder of the Manhattan Marimba Quartet. These players are committed to these groups as well as to my own ensemble, so when we schedule concerts, my manager must take their schedules with these ensembles into account.

These facts about livelihood are important, but the basic reality is a musical one. My music is often structured with the use of multiple unison canons with different rhythmic positions going on in three, four, or more voices. The difficulties in playing this music, at least the pieces of the 1960s and '70s, are generally not in the individual parts but in fitting these parts into precise and sometimes unusual rhythmic positions in an overall contrapuntal web. This is often not so easy as a cursory glance at the part itself would suggest.

My music presents a challenge to the kind of musician who enjoys being part of a finely tuned ensemble where all the details can be heard. The virtuosity lies in their ensemble relationship to each other. This is the kind of musician I seek, and it is in the world of "expanded chamber music" that they are found.

After telling you that I write music for unusual ensembles with a great deal of percussion, I must now tell you that I also write for string quartet, but not quite what you might expect. *Different Trains,* completed in 1988, was commissioned by Betty Freeman for the Kronos Quartet. The piece is for string quartet and tape and begins a new way of composing that has its roots in my early tape speech pieces *It's Gonna Rain* (1965) and *Come Out* (1966). The basic idea is that speech recordings generate the musical material for musical instruments.

The piece presents both a documentary and a musical reality and begins a new musical direction by introducing a kind of theatrical element into a traditional chamber music form. In this particular piece the theater is, so to speak, in the mind, since there is nothing visual beyond the musicians. *Different Trains* points in a direction, however, that may very well lead to a new kind of documentary music video theater.

From all this, I conclude that the history of chamber music is very much in progress.

40 QUESTIONNAIRE (1989)

Musiques en Création, Festival d'Automne, Paris, 1989—accompanying booklet to celebrate the Bicentenary of the French Revolution, with responses to the same questions also from Boulez, Anthony Braxton, Ornette Coleman, Ligeti, Nono, Kagel, Busotti, and Takemitsu. The booklet also includes a fragment of musical notation by Steve Reich, which is in fact a short passage from *The Cave* at the words "his hand against all and the hand of all against him."

The Composer and the Concept of Pure Music

As a composer I have become interested, once again, in speech melody as a source for music. Back in 1965 and '66 I made *It's Gonna Rain* and *Come Out,* which were tape pieces using a speaking voice as their sole source.[1] Thereafter, from 1967 until 1982, I was concerned with purely instrumental music, and my use of the singing voice was exclusively vocalise with syllables chosen to imitate specific instruments within an ensemble. Starting with *Tehillim* and then *The Desert Music,* I became involved with setting text for singers. What I found was that once I had chosen the text, the text then *forced* me to do things musically I would not otherwise have done. This I found to be extremely stimulating. For example, I found myself writing constantly shifting meters to accomodate the shifting stress of syllables. Harmonically, I found myself using more chromatically altered chords to accom-

---

1. Plus small elements of ambient sound in the background of *It's Gonna Rain.*

modate problematic aspects of the text. In 1988, with *Different Trains,* a totally new situation evolved that combined my earliest interest in using recorded speech as source material, with my ongoing instrumental writing—in this case, the string quartet. The recorded voices were chosen for their melodic content, then written out in musical notation; and, finally, in the finished piece, each time a woman speaks she is doubled by the viola, and each time a man speaks he is doubled by the cello. All the melodic musical material comes out of the speech melodies used, harmonically supported for much of the time by the pulsed paradiddle patterns that suggest the constant motion of the trains. The result makes me want to spend considerable time in the future investigating the use of documentary material—both speech and other sounds—as the generating source of instrumental/vocal music.

Serialism

Perhaps one can see an influence between "serial thinking" and my early pieces like *Piano Phase.* No serial technique is used, but the degree or organization (albeit a totally different one) may remind one of the "total organization" in serial music. Of course, my early works are usually understood as a complete turning away from the general lack of pulse and tonal center in serial music, and certainly this is true. I sometimes see both serial music and Cage as influencing my music, however, by suggesting that any radical kind of organization is possible, on the one hand, and, on the other, forcing me back on my own rhythmic and tonal inclinations that received no satisfaction whatever from either of these musics. Serialism and Cage gave me something to push *against.*

The Function of Today's Music

I can do no better than paraphrase J. S. Bach: The function of music is to refresh the spirit and stimulate the mind.[2]

Technique and Musical Thinking

Perhaps serial and 12-tone music were a kind of break with natural principles of resonance and with human musical perception. This might explain why this music has remained so extremely unpopular, and why, after considerably more than 50 years, the postman does not whistle Schönberg. For myself, natural principles of resonance and human musical perception are not limitations; they are facts of life.

As to electronic technology, it has become part of our folk music. Look in the window of any popular music store and you will see what I mean. Personally, I find two technological tools of particular interest—the computer and the sampling machine. (In fact they are both computers, but the sampler is dedicated ex-

---

2. SR is referring to the title page of Bach's *Clavierübung,* Third Part, Leipzig, 1739. "For Music Lovers / and especially for Connoisseurs / of such Works, to refresh their Spirits."

clusively to making digital recordings.) I use the computer to generate publication quality musical notation for scores and parts. I use the sampler to record and integrate speech and other real sounds into a piece of instrumental/vocal music. Obviously, new instruments make new music.

Contemporary Music and Institutions

From about 1979, with the writing of *Variations,* until 1987 and the writing of *The Four Sections,* I was genuinely interested in writing for the orchestra. I was concerned with using multiples of strings and winds much as I had used multiple percussion and keyboards (and sometimes strings and winds) in my earlier pieces. In *The Desert Music,* in particular, I was able to create my own orchestra not only through composition but also through reseating the strings into three groups in an arc around the centrally positioned percussion (see the *Desert Music* performance placement diagram in no. 41, p. 164). This kind of orchestral thinking was later extended in *The Four Sections* so that each of the four movements was devoted in turn to strings alone, then to percussion, then to winds, and finally to full orchestra. Immediately on finishing *The Four Sections,* I felt very clearly that I had no further interest in writing for the symphony orchestra in the foreseeable future. I felt that, finally, most of the clichés about the orchestra are true: It was designed to play the music of Haydn through Schönberg, and does not reflect at all the impact of microphones, non-Western music, jazz, rock, computers, electric instruments, and so on. That is to say, in its bones the orchestra reflects eighteenth- and nineteenth-century Europe . . . but it is almost the twenty-first century, and I live in America.

There is also the "sociology" of the orchestra, undoubtedly connected to the music it plays, which also means that somewhere from 20 to 80 percent of the players would rather not play my music nor the music of my contemporaries. In contrast to this, the Ensemble Intercontemporain in France, the Schönberg Ensemble in Holland, the Ensemble Modern in Germany, the London Sinfonietta in England, and the Group 180 in Hungary, among others, are a new generation of musicians whose basic repertory begins with Schönberg, Stravinsky, and Bartók. These players can give definitive performances of my music and that of my contemporaries because: (1) they are usually no more than 15 to 30 in number, with each player taking sole responsibility for his or her part since there is generally no doubling; (2) they are utterly at ease with electronics of all sorts; and (3) they know this kind of music in their bones. It is with these kinds of musicians all over the world (of which my own ensemble is a part) that I cast my lot for the future.

Music of Today and Traditions

My connections to Western classical music have little or nothing to do with music from Haydn to Wagner. The influences I *would* mention include Debussy, Ravel, Satie, Stravinsky, Bartók, and Weill in the twentieth century, as well as Perotin, and much other music from before 1750. From French impressionism, I unconsciously began working with harmonies where the bass was coloristic, while the middle register was structural. I say "unconciously," because all Americans of my generation were surrounded by music influenced by Impressionism in movies, popular music, Gershwin, jazz, and so on. Debussy a little, Bartók more, and most of all jazz, aroused my interest in non-Western music. From Weill, I received, first, confirmation that popular sources are to be taken seriously and, second, that one must create one's own instrumental ensemble and vocal style.[3] From Perotin, I received the suggestion that augmentation could be taken to great extremes and not just in simple multiples of two. From other medieval, Renaissance, and baroque sources (as well as Bartók and Webern), I learned that canon is a powerful compositional tool that can be applied to *any sound* whatsoever.

Early influences other than Western classical music include jazz, particularly the be-bop of Miles Davis and Kenny Clarke, and the so-called modal jazz of John Coltrane. From Davis, I learned that fewer notes could be more effective than many, while from Clarke I learned similarly that a buoyant, floating, rather simple pulse was more effective than a cluttered, "filled" one. Coltrane taught me that a lot of music can be made with few changes of harmony.

Slightly later influences, during the 1960s and early '70s, were West African drumming, Balinese gamelan, and Hebrew chant. From West African music, I learned that repeating patterns superimposed so that their downbeats do not coincide occurred not just in tape loops but in other musical traditions as well. Balinese music taught me about music moving in different speeds simultaneously, and, in Gamelan Gambang, suggested much longer patterns. Hebrew chant historically showed the roots of Gregorian chant, and technically showed how shorter motifs can be combined to form longer monophonic lines, all in the service of a sacred text. From all these non-Western sources I learned about oral tradition as a way of passing on music without notation—this also clarified my need to work with my own ensemble (or ensembles like it) who were not only traditionally well trained but also well aware of, equipped for, and disposed toward my own music.

The Oeuvre

My pieces begin in basically two ways: whether I first think of the form, or I first hear the content. In pieces as disparate as *Four Organs* and *Different Trains*, I thought first of the form or compositional techniques, without having the slightest idea of what the piece would sound like. In *Four Organs*, I thought, "short chord gets long via augmentation." In *Different Trains*, I thought, "sampled speech and other sounds generate melodic lines for strings." In neither case did I have any idea how the music would sound until I actually began to work on it. In contrast to this, I dreamed the basic pattern to the early (1966) tape piece *Melodica*, and in many pieces, starting with *Music for 18 Musicians*, I started with a cycle of chords as the basis for the entire composition.

---

3. See *Kurt Weill, the Orchestra, and Vocal Style*, no. 44, p. 166.

The means for composing has also varied. Most pieces I have written at the piano or electric keyboard. Usually I have used multitrack tape to hear and test contrapuntal details. Recently I used a sampling keyboard loaded with guitar sound when writing *Electric Counterpoint*, since using a piano gave a mistaken impression of how the guitar would sound, especially with many guitars superimposed on each other. In *Different Trains*, I used both the sampling keyboard (this time loaded with speech and train sounds), together with a sequencer on my computer, in order to prepare the first few tracks of the multitrack tape in the studio. Then the Kronos Quartet began adding their four superimposed string quartet recordings.

The final stage for all pieces is rehearsal, during which small changes in instrumental parts are usually made so as to improve ease of execution. Any composer who does not take the suggestions of good players in order to improve individual parts is foolish indeed.

My approach is therefore a practical one. I begin with the original conception—form or content—and use whatever tools are appropriate to complete the work.

41 ON THE SIZE AND SEATING OF AN ORCHESTRA (1990)

First printed in *Contemporary Music Review*, Vol. 7, Part 1—an issue devoted to "Contemporary Percussion—the Performer's Perspective," guest editor Bob Becker. (The issue also includes a reprint of "Some Optimistic Predictions" and "Notes on the Ensemble," both from *Writings*, 1974.)

In 1979, after more than 15 years of composing for my own ensemble, I gradually became interested in composing for the orchestra. One of my main interests was to transfer certain techniques I was developing in smaller ensembles to the orchestra. In particular, I was interested in interlocking unison canons for instruments of identical timbre. For instance, three flutes in unison canon simultaneous with three clarinets, three oboes, and all the first violins divided in three equal groups also playing harmonically related unison canons. These ideas found orchestral form in 1984 in *The Desert Music*, for chorus and orchestra, and in 1987 in *The Four Sections*, for orchestra. In both pieces I found questions of orchestral size and seating to be essential for performance.

In 1984 in Cologne, during the rehearsals and first performance of *The Desert Music* by the West German Radio Orchestra, chorus, and members of my own ensemble conducted by Peter Eötvös, I became aware of certain ensemble difficulties within the orchestra that were related to its size and seating arrangement. Later that same year, during the rehearsals for the American premiere of the piece at the Brooklyn Academy of Music with the Brooklyn Philharmonic, chorus, and members of my own ensemble conducted by Michael Tilson Thomas, I was able to implement changes both in the size and seating of the orchestra that proved to make a significant improvement in performance, not only for *The Desert Music* but also for my 1987 work for orchestra, *The Four Sections*.

Most major orchestras employ about 18 or more first violins. This gargantuan string section may be appropriate for Sibelius, Mahler and Bruckner (and several neoromantic composers today), but I have found that it is much too overblown for me. By trial and error, I have come to the conclusion that when I write for orchestra, I generally need no more than 12 first violins and an overall string force of about 48 players—the size of a full classical as opposed to romantic orchestra.[1] As a general principle, I find that the fewer players there are on stage, the more intense the concentration.

The desire for a clear contrapuntal texture has also led me to reseat members of the orchestra. Specifically I have put the mallet players (marimbas, xylophones, and vibraphones), who often play continuously in my orchestral pieces, directly in front of the conductor. This is done not merely to enact the "percussionists revenge" (although this may be of merit), but because if they are in their customary place—40 to 60 feet from the conductor—and are playing continuously in a brisk tempo, then, as a result of the acoustical delay in sound traveling, the rest of the orchestra will see one beat from the conductor and hear another from the mallet instruments. By putting the mallet players directly in front of the conductor, and placing the other sections of the orchestra around them, one tempo is seen and heard simultaneously by the whole orchestra.

I also found it necessary in *The Desert Music* to reseat the strings, since they are playing divisi in three parts with each part playing the same repeating patterns but in different rhythmic positions (see the *Desert Music* performance placement diagram on page 164). As you may know, orchestral string players like to follow the leader in front of them, and if he or she is playing in a conflicting rhythm you can count on confusion. By seating the strings in three separate smaller groups—similar to the two groups in Bartók's *Music for Strings, Percussion, and Celeste*—each string group can both follow its own section leader and simultaneously contribute its own individual contrapuntal voice.

I would encourage all composers to rethink the orchestra in terms of forces and placement in order to best realize their musical ideas. Whether such rethinking, along with the added need for considerably greater rehearsal time and electronics, will be welcomed by orchestras is clearly another and thornier issue.

---

1. In addition, I made a chamber version of *The Desert Music* for two reasons. One is that this arrangement *sounds*—and one could argue as to whether or not it is better than the full orchestral original. Another is that large flexible chamber ensembles, particularly European groups like the the Schönberg Ensemble in Holland, the Ensemble Modern in Germany, Ensemble Intercontemporain in France, the Group 180 in Budapest, and the London Sinfonietta in England are interested in playing my music but need this version in order to play *The Desert Music*.

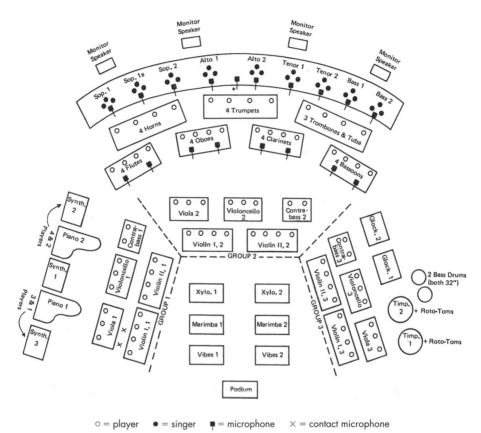

o = player   • = singer   ▮ = microphone   × = contact microphone

Performance placement diagram.

42 AARON COPLAND (1990)

Written at the request of *Newsday*, but not published until now.

I remember listening to recordings of Aaron Copland's ballets as a teenager and the romance of America they conjured up—clearly a more innocent America than the one we have come to live in. Later, at Cornell I heard his Clarinet Concerto written for jazz clarinetist Benny Goodman, and the Piano Quartet that began his encounter with 12-tone music. A more somber Copland here. Through William Austin of the Cornell music department I also became aware of the two works that have remained my favorites, his Piano Variations and Sextet, both from the 1930s. "Abstract" was a word used to describe those pieces, although the vital rhythmic element (American and jazz influenced) kept them very much alive. Like Charles

Ives and George Gershwin, Aaron Copland stayed in touch with the popular music of his time. And, like them, he represents American composition at its best.

First published (in German) in *MusikTexte*, Heft 46/47, Cologne, December 1992.

In the early 1960s, when I was a young composer working in a new way, my reaction to John Cage was that his direction was clearly not my own. Nevertheless, Cage's ideas about chance procedures were very much in the air and it seemed necessary to deal with them, one way or the other. In 1968, after I had composed *It's Gonna Rain, Come Out, Piano Phase* (which Cage included in his anthology "Notations"), *Violin Phase,* and other pieces, I wrote about Cage's use of process and the use of the row in serial music, and pointed out that I, by way of contrast, was interested in "a compositional process and a sounding music that are one and the same thing."[1]

In order to clarify in words what I had done musically, it was necessary to distinguish it from the dominant musical directions of that time: the European serialism of Stockhausen, Boulez, and Berio (with whom I had studied), and the chance procedures of John Cage.

During the late 1960s and early '70s, I had occasional contacts with Cage. We were both in a series of small classes on the computer language Fortran taught by James Tenney.[2] After one of these classes Cage played a preview of his then new *Cheap Imitation.* Later, he came to a private preview performance of my *Drumming.* During this time, I began to appreciate the integrity and consistency of Cage as a person.

My impression of his contribution is basically that his early percussion and prepared piano pieces will survive best.

It is sometimes suggested that these early works of his laid the groundwork for the kind of music I wrote in the 1960s and early '70s. In that Cage's early works were structured rhythmically rather than harmonically, there is clearly some technical affinity between his early work and my own. Since I never studied Cage's early works, however, they had no conscious influence on my music.

Over the years I have come to value those composers who have a distinct voice of their own. Talent and technique alone, without a distinct vision, seem increasingly irrelevant. John Cage had a vision and followed it with remarkable purity.

1. *Music as a Gradual Process,* no. 2, p. 33.
2. See *Tenney,* no. 33, p. 37.

44 KURT WEILL, THE ORCHESTRA, AND VOCAL STYLE — AN INTERVIEW WITH K. ROBERT SCHWARZ (1992)

Originally printed in the Kurt Weill Newsletter, volume 10, no. 2, Fall 1992. K. Robert Schwarz, author of *Minimalists* (New York, 1996) died in 1999. He was the son of the Russian emigré Boris Schwarz, violinist, conductor, and author of *Music and Music Life in Soviet Russia, 1917–1970* (New York, 1972).

KRS: Why didn't you write a music theater piece before *The Cave?*

SR: Actually, I was asked to write operas during the 1980s first by the Holland Festival and then by the Frankfurt Opera. Both times I said "no." At the time I knew I didn't want to spend several years writing a conventional opera, since I had misgivings about the form itself. What really opened the door to opera for me was *Different Trains*. I began to realize that if you could see people speaking on videotape and at the same time see and hear live musicians literally playing their speech melodies that would be a perfect place for me to begin a new kind of opera or music theater.

KRS: Did you have any model from the history of opera or music theater?

SR: The most useful historical model for me turns out to be Kurt Weill. What I learned from him is that if you're going to write a piece of music theater there are two basic questions you are obliged to ask yourself: What (and where) is the orchestra, and what is the vocal style?

Weill, as a student of Busoni and as a working composer, could have chosen a standard orchestra in the pit when he did the *Threepenny Opera*, but no, he chose a banjo, saxophone, trap drums—a cabaret ensemble. As to vocal style, again, given his background, it would have been natural to assume that he wanted bel canto operatic voices. Again he said no and chose a woman with a rough cabaret voice. The result is a masterpiece that completely captures its historical time. Not the time of Mozart or Verdi or Wagner—it captures the Weimar Republic—and the reason it does this is precisely because of his choice of orchestra and vocal style.

Since 1987, I have felt that the standard symphony orchestra is not my orchestra, it's the orchestra of Wagner and Mahler and the rest of the German romantics. My own orchestra is usually less than 20 musicians. I only need one player to a part, with amplification making possible balances between, say, solo strings and percussion. If you add more strings, they lose their rhythmic agility and develop a kind of overweight timbre that is inappropriate to my music. The amplification is not there as a kind of Band-Aid to poor orchestration. It's there because that is the one and only way to get the sound I need for the kind of music I write.

Similarly with vocal style. Historically, the bel canto voice in a Mozart opera had to be heard over an orchestra of something like 30 to 40 musicians, and we think of that now as a light operatic voice even though it has to be heard over all those musicians and often in a large hall. By the time we get to Wagner, he has expanded the brass section enormously and has necessarily to make a corresponding expansion in the number of strings to balance the brass. Hence, in Wagner opera the singer needs a huge voice just in order to be heard. In both cases, the vocal style is linked with the basic acoustic realities of sound volume coming from the orchestra. Well, about 100 years ago the microphone was invented and it then became possible to sing in a more intimate way with a small, more natural voice and still be heard over a very loud ensemble of woodwinds, brass, and percussion. This is in fact the kind of voice that I grew up hearing in popular music, jazz, and, later, rock. The acoustical realities changed with the microphone and the vocal style changed with it.

KRS: Are you saying that composers should avoid using the orchestra and bel canto voices if they write an opera?

SR: Certainly not, *if* they have a reason to use them. For instance, Stravinsky in *The Rake's Progress* is making his comment on Mozart opera and even Auden's libretto based on Hogarth is eighteenth century in subject and tone. Stravinsky needed a classical orchestra and so he specifies only double winds and brass with no trombones or tuba and with a cembalo part to be played by piano. This was the necessary orchestra for him to recreate his kind of eighteenth-century opera. Similarly, the vocal style in *The Rake's Progress* is usually sung by the kinds of singers who sing Mozart opera. A totally different example would be John Cage's *Europera*. Here Cage was manipulating, through chance procedures, material drawn directly from the standard operatic literature. He obviously needed the orchestra and vocal style of the standard repertoire to achieve this.

What I am objecting to is the automatic assumption on the part of composers today that opera equals bel canto voices on stage and orchestra in the pit. If it makes sense for what you are trying to achieve, fine, but if your opera is about characters who lived anywhere from the 1930s to the present, and then you unquestioningly have your singers sing as if they stepped out of eighteenth- or nineteenth-century Germany or Italy, you create a superficial and inadvertently foolish and amusing situation. If you were writing an opera about, say, General Eisenhower, and he appeared singing as if he stepped out of *The Marriage of Figaro*, that could well be seen as a joke. It would be altogether more serious—and genuinely more engaging, as well—to have him sing like Frank Sinatra. Instead of an orchestra in the pit, why not a complete Glenn Miller–style band on stage?

KRS: So you see Kurt Weill as pointing the way to the future?

SR: Definitely. Look at his musical context. Berg composed *Wozzeck* in 1921 with a huge orchestra and large vocal style and one can certainly see his work as done under the shadow of the death of German romanticism. Weill was aware of that death as well, but his reaction in 1928 is the *Threepenny Opera*. While Berg is looking backward, Weill instead does an about-face and looks to contemporary popular forms as material for music theater.

KRS: One of Weill's concerns throughout his life was in combining materials from popular culture with those from European high culture. In effect, he blurred the supposed divide between the two. Does that have special meaning for you?

SR: We are living at a time now when the worlds of concert music and popular music have resumed their dialogue. Perhaps I have had a hand in this restoration myself, but certainly Kurt Weill began it long before I was born. This dialogue is, of course, the normal way of the musical world. The popular French folk song of the fifteenth century, *L'Homme Armé,* served as the cantus firmus of more than 30 masses composed by the likes of Dufay, Ockeghem, Josquin des Prez, and Palestrina. Later, from about 1600 through the death of J. S. Bach, the instrumental suite was based on stylizations of actual dances of a somewhat earlier period often including allemande, courante, saraband, and gigue among others. The use of folk song by later composers includes, among others, Beethoven in the *Sixth Symphony,* Bartók and Kodály in many of their compositions, and (arguably) Stravinsky in *The Firebird, The Rite of Spring,* and *Les Noces.* It seems that the wall between serious and popular music was erected primarily by Schönberg and his followers. Since the late 1960s, this wall has gradually crumbled and we are more or less back to the normal situation where concert musicians and popular musicians take a healthy interest in what their counterparts have done and are doing. Kurt Weill pointed the way back in the 1920s.

45 THE CAVE

A New Type of Music Theater (1993)

Steve Reich and Beryl Korot

Throughout the work, five large video projection screens (each approximately 6 ft. × 8 ft.) present interviews, landscapes, and architectural footage in sequences timed with live music. In addition, in the first and last acts, texts from biblical sources are rhythmically typed out, and sung. The languages used include the original Hebrew, English, German, and French. We have developed a computer "typ-

In addition to her various art works, Beryl Korot's publications include: *Radical Software,* coeditor with Ira Schneider (first artists' video magazine), volumes 1 and 2 1970–74—very much in the style of the Whole Earth Catalogue; *Video Art* (see Korot, 1976) from which essays 17a and 17b are repinted in this book; and *Dachau 1974,* Studio international, May/June 1976.

ing instrument" with the help of
our technical consultant, Ben Ru-
bin, from the MIT Media Lab.

This work uses as its points of
departure not only the early tape-
speech pieces of Steve Reich *It's
Gonna Rain* and *Come Out* but
also, in particular, the more recent
Different Trains, and integrates
these with the techniques developed
by Beryl Korot in her multimoni-
tor video installations *Dachau 1974*
and *Text and Commentary* (1977)
and in her paintings.

Figure 45-1. Left to right: Beryl Korot, Steve Reich in Vienna, 1993. PHOTO BY DIDI SATTMAN.

All the musical and visual materials are drawn directly from the original documentary interviews. Musically, significant portions of the piece are based on the
speech melody of the interviewees. Visually the video uses details grabbed by
computer from the interview itself.

What this means on stage, for example, is that when an interviewee speaks on
one or more of the five large video projection screens, his or her speech melody is
exactly doubled and harmonized by live musicians on stage. In addition, with the
creation of computer-grabbed images from the video, details of the setting in
which the interviews were made are enlarged and abstracted to form individual
sets for each person.

There are 17 musicians, including four singers, and a conductor. The role of
the singers varies. In Act I, they act as a sort of chorus singing the biblical text; in
Act II, they sing what has actually been said by the interviewees; and, in the third
act, they do both.

The result is a new type of music theater, with aspects of both opera and
movies, all of which documents an ancient reality.

The Cave—Synopsis

In the Bible, Abraham buys a cave from Ephron the Hittite as a burial place for
his wife Sarah. The Cave of the Patriarchs, as it has come to be known, became
the final resting place not only for Sarah but also for Abraham and their descendants as well. In Jewish mystical sources the cave is also a passageway back to the
Garden of Eden. It is said that Adam and Eve are buried there.

The cave is of great religious significance for Muslims as well. While the Jews are
descendants of Abraham and Sarah through their son Isaac, the Muslims trace their
lineage to Abraham through his son Ishmael born to Hagar, Sarah's handmaid.

Today, the cave, located in the largely Arab town of Hebron, in the West Bank,
is completely built over and inaccessible. The ancient structures built above it reveal a long history of conflicting claims. One discovers not only the wall Herod

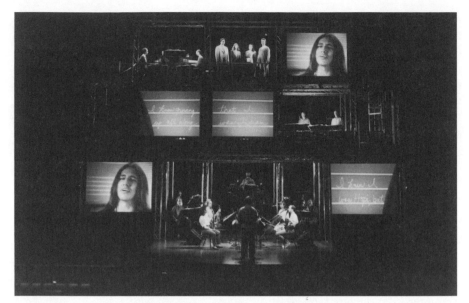

Figure 45-2. *The Cave,* performed by the Steve Reich Ensemble conducted by Paul Hillier at Royal Festival Hall, London, 1993. Left to right: Thad Wheeler, Edmund Niemann, Kenneth Dybisz, Phillip Bush, Elizabeth Lim, Todd Reynolds, James Bassi, Marion Beckenstein, Cheryl Bensman-Rowe, Garry Kvistad (bass drums), Paul Hillier, Hugo Munday, Jeanne LeBlanc, Scott Rawls, Bob Becker, Nurit Tilles, Leslie Scott, Russell Hartenberger. COURTESY OF NONESUCH. PHOTO BY ANDREW POTHECARY.

erected around the cave but also the remains of a Byzantine church, and finally the mosque built in the twelfth century, which has dominated the site ever since. Since 1967, the mosque built above the cave remains under Muslim jurisdiction, while the Israeli army maintains a presence at the site. Although tensions run particularly high, the site remains unique as the only place on earth where Jews and Muslims both worship.

The Cave is in three acts. In each act, we asked the same basic questions to a different group of people. The basic five questions were: Who for you is Abraham? Who for you is Sarah? Who for you is Hagar? Who for you is Ishmael? Who for you is Isaac? In the first act, we asked Israelis, in the second we asked Palestinians, and in the third we asked Americans.

Act 1:

West Jerusalem/Hebron
May/June 1989
56 minutes

Short pause

Act 2:

> East Jerusalem/Hebron June 1989 and June 1991
> 40 minutes

> Intermission

Act 3:

> New York/Austin April/May 1992
> 32 minutes

JONATHAN COTT INTERVIEWS BERYL KOROT 46
AND STEVE REICH ON THE CAVE (1993)

This interview was specially commissioned for inclusion in the program booklet at the first European performances and for the Nonesuch CD. All rights reserved. Used by permission.

JC: How did the idea for *The Cave* originate?

BK: We had a meeting at Ellen's Coffee Shop around the corner, because we'd been talking about collaborating, and we felt we had to be on neutral territory to continue our discussions. Steve came with the story about Abraham as the idol breaker, the iconoclast. In my reading, I had been struck by the story in the Bible of the three strangers (actually angels) who come to visit Abraham while he recovers from his circumcision, and who foretell the birth of his son Isaac and the destruction of Sodom and Gomorrah (over which he later argues with G-d). Not knowing who they are, but always showing hospitality toward strangers, we are told he runs to fetch a calf. At this point, the text leaves off and the oral tradition kicks in. He chases a calf into a cave and there he sees shadows. He knows intuitively that they are the shadows of Adam and Eve, as he also senses something verdant and lush, and again he intuits: This is the Garden of Eden. At that moment, he knows that this is the place where he and his family will be buried, and he takes the calf and returns to feed his guests.

Jonathan Cott is a contributing editor of *Rolling Stone* magazine. He is the author of numerous books, including *Stockhausen* and *Conversations with Glenn Gould.*

That story was magical to me because that simple act of fetching a calf to perform an act of hospitality for strangers connects Abraham with the prehistorical mother and father of all humanity. And the cave still exists, although underneath a partly Herodian, Byzantine, and mostly Islamic structure today in Hebron. And that was important, that there was actually a place that existed now that was connected to events that took place so long ago, that I could actually travel to with my camera.

SR: Over a year before the meeting, Beryl and I decided to collaborate based on the true underpinnings of the piece, which had nothing to do with the cave or any particular content. I was coming out of *Different Trains* and Beryl was coming out of *Text and Commentary* and *Dachau 1974*. The true underpinnings were our interest in making a new kind of musical theater based on videotaped documentary sources. The idea was that you would be able to see and hear people as they spoke on the videotape and simultaneously you would see and hear onstage musicians doubling them, actually playing their speech melodies as they spoke.

JC: And the visual style?

BK: There are no precedents in video as there are for a composer. It's basically a new medium with a developing vocabulary. But in the early '70s when I made my first multiple channel installation, *Dachau 1974*, I was quite concerned about precedents, and I looked both to the film medium and to the ancient technology of the loom to determine how to work in multiples. And it is the thoughts I had then that I drew on to create my work in *The Cave*. For one, the work, even though you are viewing multiples, remains fiercely frontal, and is to be read as one. That is my allegiance to film. But to create techniques in this new format to relate a narrative I turned to the ancient programming tool of the loom, and conceived of each channel as representing a thread. I then proceeded to make nonverbal narrative works by carefully timing and juxtaposing interrelated images, and by creating individual rhythms for each channel by alternating image and gray leader pause. Those techniques became the underpinnings for the visualization of Steve's score. He gave me the audio for the talking heads channel. It was up to me to provide the rest and make it work with the score. I chose five screens because of the variety of possibilities you have for interrelating the different threads, so to speak, and because you can still perceive five as one, thus maintaining a tight visual focus.

JC: Why this family? Why Abraham?

SR: Abraham is about as radical and visionary a person as we've ever had. He lived in a world where people saw the forces of nature as the highest value. The sun, the moon, the stars, trees, various statues—they worshiped these things. Abraham said, "None of the above."[1] There is a story in both the

---

1. See no. 28 (*The Desert Music—Steve Reich in Conversation with Jonathan Cott*), p. 127.

Midrash in Judaism and in the Koran in Islam about Abraham breaking the idols in his father's idol factory. He puts his life on the line by doing that and in both traditions is miraculously saved from the fiery furnace that King Nimrod throws him into. Here is a man who has a totally different conceptual take on the true focus for human worship—one that is unified, invisible, and ultimately ethical. And that view ultimately prevails, and we are still living with that view.

JC: So the iconoclasm works on several levels: One is the story of Abraham, the idea of completely new belief systems, and another is how you deal with traditionally bel canto opera—iconoclastic in terms of how "opera" has been practiced.

SR: I'm not saying other composers shouldn't write bel canto operas, but I've pursued something that interests me now, here in America in the 1990s, which naturally doesn't sound like something from eighteenth- or nineteenth-century Italy or Germany. We are living with musical realities that didn't exist during Mozart's or Wagner's time. The bel canto voice had to be loud enough to be heard over Mozart's orchestra and when Wagner later much enlarged the brass section of his orchestra, the Wagnerian voice had to be still louder in order to be heard—even a particular hall was built to facilitate this. But today—actually for many years now—microphones easily allow a singer with a pure nonvibrato voice to be heard over an ensemble even with much percussion in it. It seems to me that anyone writing for music theater today should at least try to decide for themselves (1) What is my orchestra?—And where is it placed in the theater?—and (2) What is my vocal style? The orchestra for *The Cave* is: two woodwind players doubling flutes, oboe, English horn, clarinet, and bass clarinet; four percussionists playing vibraphones, bass drums, kick drums, claves, and clapping; three keyboard players playing pianos, sampler, and computer keyboards; and string quartet. All the instruments are amplified except the bass drums and claves. The vocal style for the interview sections of the piece is speech with the inherent speech melody doubled and harmonized by the instruments. Then there are four singers (two lyric sopranos, a tenor, and a baritone) who sing in a natural nonvibrato voice that you would find in my earlier pieces and in earlier eras, medieval and Renaissance.

JC: Something combines the music and the visuals so that when you see it and hear it, it's like one thing.

BK: In visual terms, it's this commitment to the documentary material we gathered in the interviews. All the visual material had to come from the frame of the interviewee's image. Thanks to some pretty sophisticated computer graphics programs made for the home computer, I was able to grab the interviewees' image from the video into the computer, select details from these, rearrange them, and transfer them back to the video to become the setting for each of the talking heads. I then timed these stills to the music and to the talking heads so that the person speaking became embedded in a musical and visual portrait of him or herself.

SR: The speech melody of each person really is, as Beryl says, a kind of musical portrait of that person. It's *their* melody and I begin by writing it down as dictation. I have to find out the exact notes, rhythm, and tempo of what they say. Then there is the orchestration; it's one thing to double a speech melody with clarinet and quite another to punctuate it with bass drums. *The Cave* really comes out of the documentary footage. Whenever there was a musical or visual question about the piece, the solution was to be found by a still more careful examination of the source material itself. To give an example, Acts 1 and 2 end in A minor, because I found that inside the cave—or, rather, the mosque that sits on top of the cave—the acoustical resonance of the space with several prayers being said simultaneously was a drone in A minor. This was what I recorded there. Then I began looking for significant phrases spoken by the interviewees that were also in A minor, so that both acts would cadence there.

JC: To what extent does MTV affect your kind of work now?

BK: Our independent interests preceded MTV, but it definitely reflects on that phenomenon. And it makes our work more relevant because it relates to that type of folk art, although in a very different way. In the early years of video, late '60s, early '70s, when I edited *Radical Software,* we talked about the fact that video was then a one-way communication from the networks to the home but, with the advent of portable equipment, and the proliferation of video equipment in general, people could begin to write in the medium as well as read it. The possibilities for visual literacy increased, but this whole area of creating with such tools and developing new forms for presenting visual information is still so new. And the idea of creating something that was both rich in information and formally adventurous is a challenge the medium seems to offer, and yet is not often explored.

SR: We're living in a culture where music videos are a kind of urban folk art. People make them not only in professional studios but on home desktop computers. You can get a good hit on what folk music is today by simply looking in the window of any music store. What do you see? Samplers, amplifiers, electric guitars, and keyboards—all kinds of electronics. These are street instruments. That's what kids use to play rock.

Historically, composers have always been interested in folk music and the popular music of their day as well. You have dance forms used in Bach's suites, before him you have popular tunes like *L'Homme Armé* being used as the basis for large mass settings in the Renaissance, and more recently you have Bartók using Hungarian folktunes in many of his compositions, and Kurt Weill actually writing popular tunes and modeling much of his music theater on the cabaret style of the Weimar Republic. It seems to me when composers look down on all the popular music around them, they are generally suffering from some sort of emotional disorder. Personally, for me, it would have been unthinkable to compose any of the music I have if I hadn't heard jazz when I was growing up. Much later, in 1988, in order to compose *Different Trains,* I became involved with the sampling keyboard, which is an essential piece of technology in *The Cave* as well.

JC: I gather you didn't use a libretto.

SR: Instead of writing a libretto or having one written, we started out with a story from two holy texts, the Bible and the Koran, and some of their associated literature. Then we began asking, "Who for you is Abraham?" "Who for you is Sarah?" Hagar? Ishmael? and Isaac? to Israelis, Palestinians, and Americans. From their answers, we edited out the rest of our libretto. I don't really feel comfortable with the idea of singers acting biblical roles—that tenor is Abraham . . . hmm. We really have no idea how these 4,000-year-old characters looked, and it's always awkward when someone portrays them. The reality is that Abraham and the others only live in the words and thoughts of the living. In our piece, *The Cave,* they live in the words of the people we interviewed. I remember trying to explain this back in 1989 to an opera set designer we thought might work on the piece, and he just couldn't get it. He kept insisting that he couldn't begin his work until he had a finished libretto. That was how he worked, click, click, and no other way.

Of course, a few weeks later, our set designer, John Arnone, got the idea immediately, as did Richard Nelson, our lighting director, and Carey Perloff, our stage director. Anyway, the fact is that the libretto was finished in January 1993, when the piece was completed.

As it turned out, the work is a narrative told three times from the points of view of three different cultures. We had a general outline as we began, then a general working procedure, and the libretto evolved as the music and video evolved.

JC: What are the politics of this work?

BK: In framing the questions in terms of the biblical characters of Abraham, Sarah, Hagar, Ishmael, and Isaac, we attempted to steer away from the politics of the Middle East and the Arab/Israeli conflict. We feel that the underpinnings to that conflict relate beyond politics to the culture and religion of these peoples, so that is the focus of our work. Insofar as the main actors of this work are the interviewees speaking today, however, politics inevitably seeps in around the edges. An Israeli settler answers the question of "Who, for you, is Ishmael?" by saying "You can see him in the street," while a Palestinian woman answers a question about Hagar by saying "She was a refugee, I think." What to us was most revealing, however, was how familiar all those we interviewed, Israeli and Arab, were with these ancient biblical and koranic figures. When the chief curator of the Shrine of the Dead Sea Scrolls said of Abraham, "a legendary figure, we know nothing about Abraham," it was not with academic indifference. The "cave" for people living in this part of the world has significance and physical reality. Whether from a secular or religious or historical perspective, they knew who these characters were.

In America, however, the story is different. We are much farther away from the cave here, many people never hearing of it, even among the religious. Abraham to some is Abraham Lincoln. Ishmael is the lonesome cowboy riding off into the sunset, the archetype of the individual going it alone. To a black woman living in Texas: "When I think of Hagar, as a black female, I really think of myself." In Act 3, the "cave" comes home, and the audience, mostly Western, is asked to reflect on itself.

SR: Abraham and the others aren't here anymore. As I said, they only live in the minds of the living. For some, particularly in the Middle East, they're very much alive and for others—particularly in America—they become forgotten or turned to other purposes. When I asked the sculptor Richard Serra, he said, "Abraham Lincoln High School, high on the hill top midst sand and sea— that's about as far as I trace Abram." When I got to Ishmael he said, "Call me Ishmael—Moby Dick." Mary MacArthur says, "The man we all identify with." "He's the James Dean of the Old Testament," says Ann Druyan.

BK: We often joked that it's like a Rorschach.

JC: You're both Jewish with roots in this country. Did you learn anything new or gain a different perspective on the Muslim tradition concerning Abraham?

SR: Yes, absolutely. It was a chance to meet Arabs and talk with them about something we both shared and respected. So it was a very positive experience there, and also here in America, where we got advice from Dr. Assad Busool of the American Islamic College in Chicago, Dr. Mahmoud Ayoub of the Temple University Department of Religion, and from Imam Talal Eid, the religious leader of the Islamic Center of New England in Boston. It was a pleasure to meet and work with them, as it was to work with Rabbi Shlomo Riskin of Efrat outside Jerusalem, and with Rabbis Ephraim Buchwald and Hershel Cohen of Lincoln Square Synagogue in New York, who advised us about Jewish law and tradition. In a more peaceful world, we would have interviewed not only Palestinians but also Egyptians, Syrians, Iraqis, Jordanians, and so on, because they all view themselves as children of Abraham and Ishmael.

JC: What about the American response?

BK: In the first two acts, the people that we interviewed felt very connected to that story and to the cave. They were living with the cave. In the third act, most of the interviewees had never heard of the cave. There really is no cave in America—there is no umbilical cord, the connections are very thin.

JC: Do you find that sad?

BK: There's a kind of sadness, but sometimes the answers were so fresh and alive and contemporary and questioning. Perhaps we're very long on commentary here and shorter on text. At the end of the third act, the borders to the stills become more and more dominant until the slow final downward pans of the visual are all borders, or one could say, all commentary.

SR: There were several Americans who were very conversant with the Bible. But mostly what we found were people who could barely remember Abraham, Sarah, Hagar, Ishmael, and Isaac—they gave us either cultural or personal psychological responses to these characters. The young Hopi Indian we interviewed said he had no idea who Abraham was. Later on he said, "When I was growing up, my father never stressed the Indian either. They say you can always go back to the Hopi rez—no matter what." That's *his* cave.

For many Jews and Arabs in the Middle East, there's a sense of living with the cave—a defined, accepted spiritual universe.They aren't looking for something—they have something. They know where they're from and they're happy still being there and living that, whereas for the Western Odyssean person it's the searching that counts. In the American section of our piece, you can see some people shedding the spiritual concern: "Drop it, forget it, it's irrelevant."

JC: Let me turn the tables on you both. Who are Abraham and Sarah to you?

SR: Abraham, for me, was one of the most radical thinkers that ever lived. He had a basically new and different spiritual insight that challenged all the accepted views of his day; the complete absorption in, the worship of, any thing or any one including yourself, is putting blinders on the mind and heart—very risky saying that to Nimrod. He put his life on the line.

BK: Sarah left Ur, too, and traditionally she is viewed as a partner on a new path. Some feminists have suggested that she was a priestess from a matrilineal culture that existed in ancient Iraq and she is trying to assert her dominance in a growing patriarchy. She makes the decision to have her line become the new nation that leads eventually to Moses and David and in the Christian tradition to Jesus Christ. Alice Shalvi, the Israeli feminist whom we interviewed, suggested that it was because of the nature of Isaac's personality that she chose him and not Ishmael to receive the inheritance. He is very different from the heroes of other myths or traditions. He is neither hunter or warrior, but a herdsman and meditator in the fields. But still, the tension and strife in the story is traced to her (although Abraham is not at his best here either, insofar as he lets Hagar and Ishmael leave with no provisions except water). Unlike Sarah, however, Abraham comes down to us as the man who offers hospitality to strangers, and as a true universalist.

JC: And Hagar?

BK: She was an Egyptian princess in the court of Pharaoh, and supposedly she left with Abraham and Sarah voluntarily. Remember, the Bible is very laconic and many years pass when we hear of no dissension between these two women. Surrogate mothering, as we know today, is a very complicated role to play. She was placed in a difficult situation, and then banished into the wilderness. In the Islamic tradition she goes to Mecca, but remember, too, that in the Bible she is also highly esteemed. After all, she is the first woman whom G-d speaks to. So what appears to be a simple story of banishment is not simple at all. Her son Ishmael is destined to become father of a great nation. It is just not the nation the Bible focuses on. The story of a particular people, the Jewish people, coexists within its own sacred text with the information that family members go off in other directions and become important figures in other traditions.

JC: So, the seed for peace is already in the book of Genesis itself, isn't it?

SR: Yes—Isaac and Ishmael come together to bury Abraham. The traditional Jewish view is that Ishmael's and Isaac's presence at their father's burial was a sign of their reconciliation. And if they could do it, perhaps it suggests Arabs and

Israelis can, too. But it requires real generosity of spirit and a genuine willingness to accept difference. As the Israeli Uri Simone in our piece says of Ishmael: "He's our relative—he's different."

JC: The story of Abraham has a lot to do with the themes of separation and repair.

BK: In our interview with Uri Simone, an Israeli biblical scholar, he talks about how Abraham's life is characterized by constant separations, first from his home, his land, his culture, then from Ishmael, and potentially, in the nonsacrifice of Isaac, from him, too.

SR: He has to give up Ishmael, whom he dearly loves, and then he has to be ready to give up Isaac too. In the story when Hagar is cast out, she finds herself and Ishmael at the well of Be'er lehai roi. Much later, when Isaac is about to meet his future wife Rebecca, he's meditating in the field by Be'er lehai roi. What is he meditating about? Some in Jewish tradition say he's thinking about his half-brother Ishmael whom he misses. Ishmael is on his mind.

JC: What should be on our minds as we experience *The Cave?*

SR: Well, on the one hand, that perhaps this is your story. Maybe you've dismissed it—or ignored it for a long time. But you're free to return to it. You came from here. Do you wish to keep your distance or do you want to reacquaint yourself?

On the other hand, just in terms of the music, you may find the many speech melodies an unusual musical guide to personality. As Janáček said, "speech melodies are windows into people's souls . . . for dramatic music they are of great importance"—important because it's impossible to separate the music from the person speaking.

---

47 THOUGHTS ABOUT THE MADNESS IN ABRAHAM'S CAVE (1994)
STEVE REICH AND BERYL KOROT

Written at the invitation of and published in the *New York Times*, Sunday, March 13, 1994.

Unknown to most Westerners before the terrible massacre of February 25, the Cave of the Patriarchs in Hebron on the West Bank is sacred to both Jews and Muslims. Since 1968, it has been the only place on earth where they both actually pray in the same building. Traditionally, it is the site that Abraham/Ibrahim bought from Ephron the Hittite about 4,000 years ago to bury his wife Sarah, and where he and some of their descendants are buried. It also represents the central metaphor of *The Cave.*

We knew when we set out to make this work that the place resonated not only with the events of the ancient past but with the present Israeli-Arab conflict as well. We chose, however, to steer away from the overtly political and to focus instead on the response of Israeli Jews, Palestinian Muslims, and Americans to questions about the ancient biblical and koranic characters associated with this site. In this way, current events emerged indirectly into a dialogue with the ancient past.

Hebron is one of the most ancient towns in this part of the world. An Israeli cabalist and teacher we interviewed remarked: "Hebron means in Hebrew 'to unite.' It comes from the same root as 'a friend,' 'a link.' The link between what? Between Abraham and the country, between his sons Ishmael and Isaac. It may be the place of war, but it is also the place of the link."

In Arabic, the town is called El Khalil, a name based again on the root word for 'friend.' A Palestinian journalist from Hebron told us, "We call Ibrahim 'khalil-Alah,' which means in Arabic 'the friend of God.' "

Over the centuries, different groups have laid claim to the site of this cave. In the first century, King Herod built the huge stone walls that surround it. The Byzantines later built a church, which was partly destroyed and replaced by the Muslims in the twelfth century with the mosque we see today.

Two stories of Abraham/Ibrahim were in our minds when we began our work. One is of Abraham, who greets three strangers coming out of the desert, washes their feet, and offers them food, which he fetches himself. The calf he seeks runs away into a cave, *the* cave, and when he follows it there, he has a momentary vision of Adam and Eve resting on their biers. Rather than remain in the realm of the mystical, he attends to the task at hand and returns to feed his guests. This attribute of hospitality, of returning to the task at hand, of serving food to strangers as a holy act, makes him beloved to both Jew and Muslim.

In both traditions, there is an almost identical story of Abraham/Ibrahim as the destroyer of idols who puts his own life at risk. He argues first with his father and then with King Nimrod against the worship of natural objects or persons. Abraham makes a complete break with the accepted, constricting views of his time.

Most Americans we interviewed had little or no knowledge of or attachment to Abraham or Sarah or Hagar or Ishmael or Isaac, and still less to this distant and mostly forgotten cave from which their own mythology is, in part, derived. In contrast, the Jews and Muslims, although caught in a terrible conflict, reveal their commonality through their knowledge of the cave and the figures associated with it religiously, historically, and culturally.

While we were making and presenting *The Cave*, two major news events occurred: the Gulf War and the signing of the Israeli Palestinian declaration of principles. People who saw the work in process in our studio during the war wished we could show the work then, since Abraham is from the ancient city of Ur, now in Iraq. We were relieved when the war ended and happy that the work was first seen at a time of relative peace, but we knew that because of the depth of its metaphor, the work was not tied to a particular event. In time, there would always be another.

The recent massacre of Muslim worshipers by a fanatic religious Jewish settler in a mosque, *this* mosque, was not only an act of hideous mass murder but an attempt to deny all forces for reconciliation. It was also an attack on the legacy of Abraham, who fed strangers, was not ensnared by the idols of his day, and deeply loved both of his sons, Ishmael and Isaac.

With the aid of Muslim and Jewish advisers, we rooted *The Cave* in the biblical and koranic figures of Abraham/Ibrahim and his family, not only because they formed a classic story for music theater but also because we feel that without a spiritual rapprochement there can never be real peace in a land where these traditions run so deep.

We do not think that *The Cave* or any other artwork can directly affect peace in the Middle East. Pablo Picasso's *Guernica* had no effect on the aerial bombing of civilians, nor did the works of Kurt Weill, Bertolt Brecht, and many other artists stop the rise of Hitler. These works live because of their quality as works of art. Their message survives through the quality of their artistry, and some individuals who see or hear them can be changed by the experience, as if a fire in the mind of one lighted a fire in the mind of another. William Carlos Williams wrote in *Paterson,* Book V, "through this hole / at the bottom of the cavern / of death, the imagination / escapes intact."

The current cycle of political events leaves too little room to maneuver. Peace as a religious value is cast aside to settle old scores, and all citizens of this area are denied what they seek. In the Bible, Ishmael and Isaac come together to bury Abrahim/Ibrahim. Peace in this part of the world could create a great flowering of culture throughout the region, and offer something culturally distinct that we believe the West may have forfeited in its embrace of the secular as religion. But peace will never come at the expense of either Ishmael or Isaac—or in the absence of their memory.

---

48 ANSWERS TO QUESTIONS ABOUT DIFFERENT TRAINS (1994)

SR interviewed by Wolfgang Gratzner. First published in *Nähe und Distanz—Nachgedachte Musik der Gegenwart,* Salzburg, 1995.

WG: *Different Trains* seems to be based on the musical concept that all the musical motives are transcribed from human speech melodies. How did you discover this principle and why did you insist on it?

SR: Although I personally became aware of speech melody in my early tape pieces *It's Gonna Rain* (1965) and *Come Out* (1966), it is something I believe musicians have been aware of for centuries.

Not so long ago, Janáček wrote down the speech melodies of his fellow Czech citizens in his notebook and used them in his operas. Bartók noted that while collecting folk songs in (what used to be) Yugoslavia, the music would change when the language changed. It is no accident that rock and roll is strong in English and German and less so in French and Italian. It is also no accident that the bel canto voice arose in Italy. Some African languages are tonal—the speech melody is part of the meaning. In our Western languages, speech melody hovers over all our conversations, giving them their fine emotional meaning—"It's not what she said, it's how she said it." We are, with speech melody, in an area of human behavior where music, meaning, and feelings are completely fused.

Recently, the digital sampling keyboard was invented, which allows myself and other musicians to play any sound we find in the world around us at the precisely right musical time. This has the potential of introducing a kind of theatrical element into an instrumental piece (as in *Different Trains*) as well as opening up new areas of audio and video for opera (as in *The Cave*).

WG: You chose 45 small parts from different statements concerning the times before, during, and after World War II. How did you choose which voices to use?

SR: The voices that you hear in the first movement of *Different Trains* belong to Virginia, then age 77, my governess from age 1 to 10 who accompanied me on my many four-day train trips between my father in New York and my mother in Los Angeles in the years 1938 to 1941; and to Lawrence Davis, a retired Pullman porter 85 years old, who used to ride those same trains in those same years. In the second movement, you hear the voices of three Holocaust survivors who later came to America: Rachella, born in Rotterdam, living in Seattle; Paul, born in Budapest, living in Boston; and Rachel, born in Brussels and recently died in Florida. In the third movement, you hear a mixture of these voices.

Different Trains is, among other things, an autobiographical piece. Traveling back and forth twice a year for four years, on a train for four days at a time with my governess, between two divorced parents, between the ages of two and five, made a strong impression on me. Virginia's voice recalls this time quite precisely as does Mr. Davis'. Their voices—particularly the phrases chosen—are also extremely melodic. Since my trips between New York and Los Angeles (with a stop in Chicago) happened in the years 1938–41, I began reflecting on the fact that if I had been in Europe at that time, as a Jew, my train trips would have been quite different. This suggested searching out the voices of Holocaust survivors now living in America which I found at an archive at Yale University. What they say is chosen both for the meaning of the words and the speech melody simultaneously. All these people were chosen as witnesses to a time now passed in my life and in the life of the world.

WG: You selected and ordered the text fragments. The progression from the neutral beginning "from Chicago to New York" up to the remembrance of the Nazi horror in Germany represents a dramaturgy of increasing intensity in movements 1 and 2. Comment on the function of movement 3, please.

SR: In the third movement, the Holocaust survivors tell of the war ending and coming to America—"to Los Angeles," "to New York." They follow a geographical path in the United States similar to the one that I took as a child—but in a totally different human context. At the end Rachella, who ends up in Seattle, tells a brief story: "There was one girl who had a beautiful voice. And they loved to listen to the singing—the Germans. And when she stopped singing they said 'More, more' and they applauded."

Musically, the third movement is in contrast to the first two. In the first two, the drumming hand alternation "paradiddle" pattern (left-right-left-left/right-left-right-right) in the strings never ceases until the end of the second movement when the train finally arrives in Auschwitz. Also, the texture is homophonic—short melodies presented over broken chords in the "paradiddle" rhythm. In the third movement, the texture becomes completely contrapuntal, with all the melodic material coming from the speech melodies. The third movement is, in my musical and human estimation, the finest of the three. It brings us to the present, long after the war. It is also the least obvious.

WG: The turn to Europe in movement 2 is indicated by sirens. Are there any other musical changes between movement 1 and 2?

SR: Besides the sirens you will note that the harmonies are generally more chromatic and "darker" in the second movement. You may also note the difference between American (first movement) and European (second movement) train whistles. American trains whistles of this period in the '30s and '40s are mostly long held perfect intervals of fourths and fifths. European train whistles of this same period are mostly in short triadic shrieks.

WG: In comparison, movement 2 includes the most text fragments. Neverthless, it is the shortest movement. Why?

SR: In movement 2, in contrast to movement 1 and some of movement 3, it seemed appropriate *not* to repeat what was said. If you don't hear what one of the Holocaust survivors says, you miss it. The speakers move more rapidly from one phrase to the next. More things are said in a shorter period of time. These phrases cannot be "played" with in the same manner as those in the first movement.

WG: Two texts heard in movement 1 return in movement 3: "from New York to Los Angeles" and "One of the fastest trains." Why?

SR: The phrase "from New York to Los Angeles" is said by Mr. Davis both in movement 1, when he is describing his and my own trips, and in movement 3 when Rachella takes this same trip after the war on her way to Seattle. At the same time, it brings back musical material from the first to the last movement and begins to tie the piece together. This is continued with the return of the phrase "one of the fastest trains," which is repeated and now reharmonized. Both phrases bring back the paradiddle rhythm of the first movement and the homophonic texture as well into what has been, up to that point, a purely contrapuntal movement. The words "fastest trains" seem now to imply that the "train of events" moves quickly as well—especially in the voice of an old woman looking back on her life, now almost over.

WG: At the beginning of the third movement, the statement "and the war was over" is followed by the question "Are you sure?" Generalizing the Nazi horror as fascism, was it your aim to keep the quoted skeptical question in mind as a question about present forms of fascism?

SR: In all honesty, I had no such question in mind. It is rather the tentative quality of voice and feeling that "Are you sure?" gives, along with its purely musical content (b, b, f♯) that made me choose it. I find it interesting that you feel such a question is relevant today in Germany. I can only tell if such is the case from reading newspapers here in the United States and during my occasional visits to Germany. I would say that that during a visit to Berlin for performances of *The Cave* during 1993 I felt that fascism might not be completely dead in the streets of Germany.

WG: Did the topicality of *Different Trains* change since 1988 from your point of view?

SR: I don't think the topicality of *Different Trains* has changed since 1988 so far as I can see. It was clear to me when composing the piece that while the subject matter was important to me, for listeners the music must stand on its own. I think that topicality will remain for several years but then will unfortunately fade. However, if the drama of the "topic" is well preserved in the music, then it can survive as long as there are musicians to play it.

WG: Do you think it is possible to understand your idea of this piece without a comment, and without understanding the texts?

SR: This is a question for all music with a text and for music theater as well. I would say that one can have no interest whatsoever in Nordic mythology and still enjoy Wagner and one can also enjoy rock songs without understanding any words whatsoever. On the other hand, if you understand the words of the song, you will get more out of it, and if you know a bit about Nordic mythology (and its twentieth-century manifestations), you will get a greater understanding of Wagner. With *Different Trains* (and any piece with a text), it must work for listeners who don't read any comments about it and who perhaps can't even understand the words—or the composer has failed.

DUET (1994) 49

Duet was composed in 1994 and is dedicated to Yehudi Menuhin and to those ideals of international understanding which Menuhin has practiced throughout his life. The piece is approximately five minutes in length. It is scored for two solo violins and a small group of violas, celli, and bass. Beginning and ending in F, the music is built around simple unison canons between the two violins who, from time to time, slightly vary the rhythmic distance between their two voices.

50 NAGOYA MARIMBAS (1994)

A short program note written for the Nonesuch recording.

Nagoya Marimbas (1994) is somewhat similar to my pieces from the 1960s and '70s in that there are repeating patterns played on both marimbas, one or more beats out of phase, creating a series of two-part unison canons. These patterns, however, are more melodically developed, change frequently and each is usually repeated no more than three times, similar to my more recent work. The piece is also considerably more difficult to play than my earlier ones and requires two virtuosic performers. Fortunately, Bob Becker and James Preiss, both members of my ensemble for over 20 years, are the amazing performers on this recording.

Nagoya Marimbas was commissioned by the Conservatory in Nagoya, Japan to mark the opening of their new Shirakawa Hall in 1994. It is about five minutes in duration.

51 THE FUTURE OF MUSIC FOR THE NEXT 150 YEARS (1994)

Written in answer to a question about the next 150 years posed by *The Musical Times* as part of its 150th anniversary issue in February 1994.

While it is obviously impossible to say what will be the case 150 years from now in terms of classical music, clearly present tendencies and problems will lead to a very different situation than the one we find today.

In terms of tendencies, composers have historically had an ear out for the folk and popular music of their day and in our time that means rock and roll. Elements of that music have already found their way into the concert hall (amplification, synthesizers, electric guitars, etc.) and this will undoubtedly continue. I for one am particularly interested in how digital sampling will be developed by composers, since that allows the use of literally any sound played by keyboard, percussion pad, or other instrument within a musical ensemble. The combination of sounds from our everyday world—particularly the human speaking voice—together with traditional musical instruments is an area that I believe will continue to be fruitful in the future.

Video sampling will be introduced as well and it will become possible to play a keyboard and trigger one or more video images. The use of this, as well as pro-jected video, will find an increased role in opera and musical theater. The intro-duction of contemporary or historical video or film footage will prove of great dramatic value integrating the "news of the day," captured on video or film, into live musical theater. This will tend to bring more of the world around us into the opera house, and will certainly not mean the end of "serious music" but, rather, new means of making it.

In terms of problems, orchestras are having their share here in America. Audi-ences are diminishing and getting older. I for one would like to see the kind of change suggested earlier by Ernest Fleischmann and others, namely, that we have fewer but larger musical organizations performing in larger geographic areas and with a repertoire ranging from Perotin to the present rather than much narrower one presently in place. Basically this would involve combining an early music en-semble along with a full classic/romantic orchestra and a new music ensemble, each with their own music directors, into one large musical organization that could then present concerts of medieval, Renaissance, classical, romantic, and modern music in a wide geographic area. It would, particularly in America, offer musicians the opportunity to play, and audiences to hear, a wider range of music than is the case now. Whether this would attract a larger audience here in Amer-ica remains to be seen, but it would certainly make for a more lively musical life.

BEAUTIFUL/UGLY (1994) 52

Written for and first published in the *Neue Zeitschrift für Musik*, Mainz, 1994.

To evaluate the expression, "That's beautiful" you have to know something about the person speaking.

Wittgenstein said, "If you ask yourself how a child learns 'beautiful,' 'fine,' etc., you find it learns them roughly as interjections. . . . The word is taught as a sub-stitute for a facial expression or a gesture."

Ligeti's *Atmosphères* is beautiful to my ear, but perhaps others outside the new music field might disagree. They might say, "It's ugly but good movie music."

One could say of some of Schönberg's music that it was ugly but that it was great.

One could say of Adorno, he invents meaningless intellectual jargon to justify the simple fact that he likes Schönberg and doesn't like Stravinsky.

One could also say, with some justification, that frequently "beautiful" and "ugly" are political words.

To evaluate the expression, "That's ugly," you have to know something about the person speaking.

If a musician I respect says of a piece that it is incredibly beautiful, that carries considerable weight. A music critic saying the same piece is ugly usually carries very little weight (although it may carry political weight). A child saying that same piece is ugly is definitely worth serious consideration.

53 SCHÖNBERG (1995)

> A season of Schönberg concerts was held at the Chatelet—Théatre Musical de Paris during the period November 1995–May 1996. The accompanying booklet also contains various essays on the composer, and reprints some letters of Schönberg and several black and white reproductions of his paintings. Reich was no doubt invited to contribute somewhat in the role of devil's advocate.

Arnold Schönberg's influence in America was quite pronounced during the 1950s and '60s. It was, of course, due to the activities of Stockhausen, Boulez, and Berio at this time that brought renewed interest in serial music. Even John Cage was, in many ways, a follower of his teacher Schönberg (with whom he studied at UCLA) most especially in Cage's rejection of any sort of harmonic organization of musical form. This brought about the situation in the late 1950s and early '60s (during which time I was a music student at Juilliard and then at Mills College, with Berio), that anyone writing music that was not either serial or aleatoric was simply not worthy of the slightest consideration.

Now, about 35 years later, what remains musically? Well, of serial music, some works of Boulez, Stockhausen, and Berio, and a few others. Their imitators, particularly in America, appear more and more exactly as what they always were: Americans once again aping their European betters. Even in terms of John Cage, it seems that while his books and essays of the '60s and beyond remain of theoretical interest, his music that is most played and admired seems to be the percussion and prepared piano works of the 1930s and '40s.

There are, it seems, some fundamental problems in Schönberg's musical thinking. The main problem is this: The reality of cadence to a key or modal center is basic in all the music of the world (Western *and* non-Western). This reality is also related to the primacy of the intervals of the fifth, fourth, and octave in all the world's music as well as in the physical acoustics of sound. Similarly for the regular rhythmic pulse. Any theory of music that eliminates these realities is doomed to a *marginal* role in the music of the world. The postman will *never* whistle Schönberg. (It has been almost 100 years but even 200 or more will bring no improvement in this respect.)

This doesn't mean Schönberg was not a great composer—clearly he was. It does mean that his music (and all the music like his) will always inhabit a sort of "dark little corner" off by itself in the history of all the world's musics. It is thus no accident that his (quite understandably) most popular works all predate his invention of the 12-tone system. The piano pieces Opus 11 and 19, and the *Five Pieces for Orchestra* Opus 16 (particularly the third movement, *Farben*, or "Changing Colors on a Lake"[1]) as well as *Verklärte Nacht, Pierrot Lunaire,* and so on, will, it seems, remain as his most performed and listened to works. This is not due to a limitation in the intelligence of listeners, it is due to a limitation of Schönberg's later music.

After Schönberg, Berg, and Webern came a pause followed by Stockhausen, Boulez, and Berio and after them came myself, Riley, Glass, Young, and later, others. This most recent group of composers, of whom I am a part, have been involved in something, on the one hand, quite new in terms of the musical structure of repetition and slow harmonic change and, on the other hand, in a process of restoration. That is, the restoring of melody, counterpoint and harmony in a recognizable but completely new context. That this music has been listened to with interest worldwide, particularly among the young, should come as no surprise. That this music arose in part as a complete turning away from Schönberg and his ideas comes as no surprise either.

CITY LIFE (1995) 54

The idea that any sound may be used as part of a piece of music has been in the air during much of the twentieth century. From the use of taxi horns in Gershwin's *An American in Paris* through Varese's sirens, Antheil's airplane propeller, Cage's radio, and rock 'n' roll's use of all of the above and more starting at least in the 1970s, and more recently in rap music, the desire to include everyday sounds in music has been growing. The sampling keyboard now makes this a practical reality. In *City Life,* not only samples of speech but also car horns, door slams, air brakes, subway chimes, pile drivers, car alarms, heartbeats, boat horns, buoys, and fire and police sirens are part of the fabric of the piece (see ex. 54-1).

1. See no. 31, *Three Movements*, p. 136.

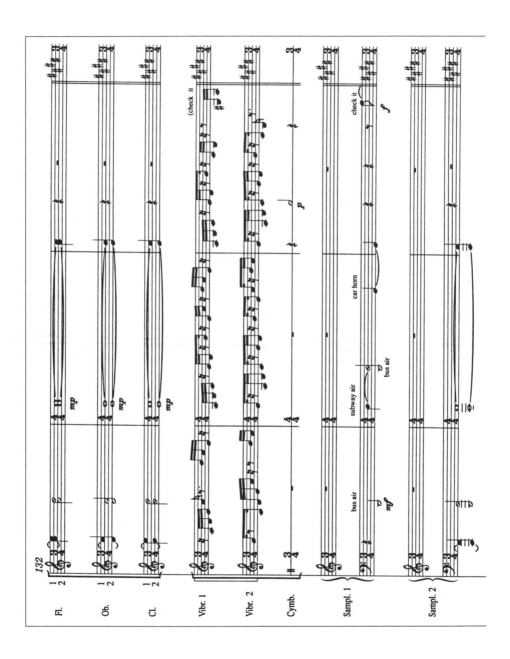

188

Example 54-1. *City Life*, first movement, mm. 132–34. COPYRIGHT © BY HENDON MUSIC, INC., A BOOSEY & HAWKES COMPANY. REPRINTED BY PERMISSION

In contrast to my earlier *Different Trains* (1988) and *The Cave* (1993), the prerecorded sounds here are played live in performance on two sampling keyboards. There is no tape used in performance. This brings back the usual small flexibility of tempo that is a hallmark of live performance. It also extends the idea of prepared piano since the sampling keyboards are "loaded" with sounds, many recorded by myself in New York City. These different nonmusical sounds also suggest certain instrumental couplings. Thus, woodwinds for car horns, bass drums for door slams, cymbal for air brakes, clarinets for boat horns, and several different instrumental doublings for speech melodies.

City Life is scored for two flutes, two oboes, two clarinets, two pianos, two samplers, three (or four) percussion, string quartet, and bass. Like several earlier works, it is an arch form A–B–C–B–A. The first and last movements use speech samples as part of the musical fabric and both feel like "fast" movements, although the actual tempo of the first is moderate and the fairly rapid tempo of the last movement is harder to perceive because of the many sustained sounds. The harmonies leading to E♭ or C minor in the chorale that opens and closes the first movement reappear in the fifth movement in a more dissonant voicing and finally resolve to C minor, which then ambiguously ends as either a C dominant or C minor chord. The second and fourth movements do not use any speech whatsoever. Instead, each uses a rhythmic sample that determines the tempo. In the second, it is a pile driver, in the fourth, heartbeats. Both start slow and increase speed. In the second this is only because the pile driver moves from quarter-notes to eighths and then to triplets. In the fourth movement, the heartbeats gradually get faster in each of the four sections of the movement. Both movements are harmonically based on the same cycle of four dominant chords. The third and central movement begins with only speech samples played by the two sampler players. When this duet has been fully built up, the rest of the strings, winds, and percussion enter to double the pitches and rhythms of the interlocking speech samples. This central movement may well remind listeners of my early tape pieces *It's Gonna Rain* (1965) and *Come Out* (1966).

City Life (1995) is a tripartite commission from the Ensemble Modern, the London Sinfonietta, and the Ensemble Intercontemporain. The world premiere was performed by David Robertson conducting the Ensemble Intercontemporaine in Metz on March 7, 1995. The German premiere was given by the Ensemble Modern conducted by Sian Edwards at the West German Radio in Cologne on March 11, 1995, and the British premiere performance was given by the London Sinfonietta at Queen Elizabeth Hall on May 10, 1995, Markus Stenz conducting. The American premiere was with Bradley Lubman conducting my own ensemble at Alice Tully Hall in New York City on February 10, 1996. The piece is approximately 24 minutes in duration. The five movements are as follows:

1. Check it out

2. Pile driver/alarms

3. It's been a honeymoon—can't take no mo'

4. Heartbeats/boats & buoys

5. Heavy smoke

For the first movement, a street vendor in lower Manhattan was recorded saying "check it out." The source of the third movement's "It's been a honeymoon— can't take no mo'" was recorded at a mostly African American political rally near City Hall. Most of the speech samples in the fifth movement are from actual field communications of the New York City Fire Department on the day the World Trade Center was first bombed in 1993.

PROVERB (1995) 55

The idea for *Proverb* was originally suggested to me by Paul Hillier, who thought of a primarily vocal piece with six voices and two percussion. What resulted was a piece for three sopranos, two tenors, two vibraphones, and two electric organs, with a short text from Ludwig Wittgenstein. Since Paul Hillier is well known as a conductor and singer of early music and since I share an interest in this period of Western music, I looked once again at the works of Perotin for guidance and inspiration.

The three sopranos sing the original melody of the text in canons that gradually augment or get longer. The two tenors sing duets in shorter rhythmic values against held tones from the sopranos. The two electric organs double the singers throughout (except at the very beginning when they sing a capella) and fill in the harmonies. The piece is in constantly changing meter groupings of twos and threes, giving a rhythmically free quality to the voices. After about three minutes of voices and organ only, the vibraphones enter enunciating these interlocking shifting groups of two and three beats.

The original theme in the voices is then inverted and moves from B minor to E♭ minor. In this contrasting section, the original descending melodic line becomes a rising one. The last part of the piece is one large augmentation canon for the sopranos returning to the original key of B minor with the tenors singing their melismatic duets continuously as the canon slowly unfolds around them. This is concluded by a short coda that ends, as the piece began, with a single soprano.

Although the sopranos sing syllabically with one note for each word (and every word of the text is monosyllabic), the tenors sing long melismas on a single syllable. Perotin's influence may be heard most clearly in these tenor duets against soprano, which clearly resemble three-part organum. That same influence plays a more indirect role in the soprano augmentation canons which are suggested by the augmentation of held tenor notes in Perotin's organum (see ex. 55-1).

The short text, "How small a thought it takes to fill a whole life!" comes from a collection of Wittgenstein's writings entitled *Culture and Value*. Much of Wittgenstein's work is "proverbial" in tone and in its brevity. This particular text was

Example 55-1. *Proverb*, mm. 495–501. Copyright © 1987 by Hendon Music, Inc., a Boosey & Hawkes company. Reprinted by permission.

written in 1946. In the same paragraph from which it was taken, Wittgenstein continues, "If you want to go down deep you do not need to travel far."

As an undergraduate, what originally drew me to Wittgenstein was his idea that philosophical problems could be understood by looking at how we normally use language. For instance, the philosophical question, "How can a mind (or soul) be inside a material body?" is using the noun "mind" or "soul" as "spoon" or "stone." Wittgenstein asks how we would teach a word like "mind" or "soul" to a child. In what language games would we use these words? This kind of close, subtle examination of everyday speech had a strong appeal to me. As to his text that I used in *Proverb,* I was trying to embody it in the piece. That is, the "small thought" is the idea of canon or round.

Proverb was cocommissioned by the BBC Proms as part of their 100th Anniversary season in 1995 and by the Early Music Festival of Utrecht. It was first performed as a partial work in progress by the BBC Singers with members of the Ensemble Modern conducted by Peter Eötvös on September 7, 1995, in The Royal Albert Hall, London. During the following two months, the original seven minutes were thoroughly revised and the piece was completed in December 1995. The duration is approximately 14 minutes. The premiere of the finished work was performed by Paul Hillier conducting the Theatre of Voices and members of the Steve Reich Ensemble at Alice Tully Hall, Lincoln Center, in New York City on February 10, 1996. The European premiere was at the Musik Centrum Vredenburg, in Utrecht, September 1, 1996, with Paul Hillier conducting the Theatre of Voices and members of the Slagwerk den Haag.

MUSIC AND LANGUAGE (1996) 56

Reich was interviewed by Barbara Basting for the Zurich magazine *du,* and the result is a fascinating exposition of his views on speech-melody. The "interview" appeared originally (in German) in *du,* vol. 5, May 1996, under the title *Sprechmelodien.* (The original prints exactly the same very few questions.)

DU: In a recent film on *City Life* (by Manfred Waffender) you said that the music of each culture is rooted in the language of that very culture. Could you try to describe that link more exactly?

SR: Your question is a good one, and I'm afraid it would take a lifetime of careful work to really answer it in detail. My remark in the film was based on an intuitive feeling I have, but there certainly is evidence of the connection between a nation's music and it's spoken language. I will try and give you a number of examples from a number of sources, beginning with myself, that begin to show some of these connections.

Since the early 1960s I have been interested in speech melody. That is, the melody that all of us unconsciously create while speaking. Sometimes this speech melody is quite pronounced (as in children) and sometimes it is almost nonexistent (as in those speaking in a monotone). Since English is the only language I speak and understand with fluency, all of my compositions using prerecorded speaking voices have been in English.

In *The Cave* (1993), the audience sees and hears Israeli, Palestinian, and American interviewees speaking about the biblical characters Abraham, Sarah, Hagar, Ishmael, and Isaac. For the Israeli and Palestinian acts of the piece, I only used interviewees who spoke English fairly well so that I could fully understand not only the literal meaning of what they said but all its possible nuances. What I found was that in terms of the different speech-melodies of these three groups of speakers, the English language proved to be the great equalizer. There was no characteristic Israeli or Palestinian speech-melody distinct from that of Americans. In general, *it was speaking English that dominated the rhythm and cadence of the speakers.* The syllables, with their rhythms and accents, dominated the speech melody of all the speakers. My guess is that if I had been able to understand either Hebrew or Arabic, and recorded the Israelis and Palestinians in their native language, there would have been a large shift in general speech melody based on a wholly different spoken language. I would imagine that even working with British English (as opposed to American) would produce a small shift in the general speech melody but nowhere near as great as the change created by, for instance, French or Italian.

Clearly what language you speak will largely determine the rhythmic aspect of the melody of your speech. The question you ask is how does this effect the entire nation's music? I would answer that all *vocal* music using a particular language will in general be strongly affected by the rhythm and cadence of that language. The model here would be folk music where there tends to be a very direct setting of the language in its common vernacular form. The art music of a nation or culture normally tends to reflect its folk music. When that ceases to happen you have the musically unhealthy situation that pertained in American art music in the 1950s and '60s when it lost all connections to American folk music (read jazz and rock and roll) and instead self-consciously modeled itself on European serial models instead. As you will see later, the music and writings of Bela Bartók and Leoš Janáček were also in part a kind of corrective to a similar problem in their own countries at an earlier date.

The relationship between folk music and language can be appreciated in our own time by observing how successful rock and roll is in English and often in German as well. But do you really want to hear Italian or French rock? This is, I believe, based on the rhythm of English and German in contrast to the more fluid rhythms of the romance languages. Similarly, it is no accident that bel canto arose in Italy and, at least to my ear, sounds artificial as a vocal style in English.

This relationship between spoken language and folk music and the relationship between folk music and art music has been written about in some detail by the composers Bartók and Janáček and also by the ethnomusicologists A. M. Jones and Simha Arom in their studies of African music.

Bartók, known primarily as a composer was, of course, also an important ethnomusicologist who collected hundreds of Hungarian and Eastern European folk songs using an Edison wind-up cylinder recorder in the early part of the twentieth century. In one of his essays from 1942 on the investigation of musical folklore, he writes about the relationship between language and folk song:

> When a folk melody passes the language frontier of a people, sooner or later it will be subjected to certain changes determined by the environment, and especially by the differences of language. The greater the dissimilarity between the accents, inflections, metrical conditions, syllabic structure and so on, of the two languages, the greater the changes . . . in the "emigrated" melody. . . . Indeed, the life of folk music and the life of languages have many traits in common.[1]

In another essay, "Hungarian Folk Music" from 1933, he gave a linguistic reason for a musical practice in Hungarian and English music:

> In the Hungarian language every word has the accent on the first syllable. The following syllabic sequence is impossible in German: short & accented + long & unaccented. (The English language is indeed more flexible, owing to the existence of the so-called Scottish rhythm, which corresponds exactly to the Hungarian dotted one.)[2]

As early as 1920, in an essay entitled "Hungarian Peasant Music," he wrote about folk music as a basis for art music:

> We had no traditions whatever in the Hungarian art music to serve as a basis on which we could have advanced further. The declamatory attempts in vocal works of our predecessors were nothing else but imitations of Western European patterns which were inconsistent with the rhythm of the Hungarian language. Debussy, in order to get rid of Wagnerian declamatory style, had the facility to reach back to the declamation of the ancient French language. We Hungarians have nothing but our *parlando* peasant melodies as the means of enabling us to solve this question.[3]

The composer Leoš Janáček was the first to speak of speech melody and to use it in his operas (see ex. 56-1). In 1918 he wrote:

> I envision a Czech name in its Czech version next to its German one. That was how the guard called out the name of the railway station on 18 August 1917.
> How the different spirit of both languages shone through here. Our version is ranged in notes of a warm triad Db–F–Ab. The German version cut harshly and

---

1. Bartok,1992, p. 30.
2. Ibid, p. 76.
3. Ibid, p. 306.

Example 56-1. "Moravany! Morawaan!"
by Janáček.

roughly in the same triad, with a dissonance of a seventh; it has crushed the third syllable and torn off the last one; it has ground into grumbling the sweetness of the first two. In the Czech version, you hear a song that winds along in equal lengths within a rainbow of colors; o-a-a-y . . .

The melodic sweetness of the Czech word has disappeared in the German version, the musical union of speech melody has thinned down . . .

It is what has not been translated from the Czech that has triumphed: speech melody, the seat of the emotional furnace . . .

This melody, its surface and edges, are of one metal: this is how speech melody is joined together with the contents of our consciousness. This is how it is molded together with the reflection of the speaker's inner life, and the reflection of the environment in which it is spoken. . . . If speech melody is the flower of a water lily, it nevertheless buds and blossoms and drinks from the roots, which wander in the waters of the mind.[4]

Like Bartók, Janáček was a firm believer that folk music was a solid basis for art music. In 1927 he wrote:

If I grow at all, it is only out of folk music, out of human speech. . . . Once an educated German said to me: 'What, you grow out of folk song? That is a sign of a lack of culture!' As if a man on whom the sun shines, on whom the moon pours out its light, as if all that surrounds us was not a part of our culture. I turned away and let the German be.[5]

If the folk music of a given country is tied closely to at least the rhythm of everyday speech, and the art music is in turn tied to the folk music, then we can begin to see the connections between a nation's language and its music.

In Africa, these connections are much more pronounced and built not only on the rhythm of speech but also on its pitch as well. This is the case because in many African countries they speak tonal languages. In a tonal language, the speech melody is not only a kind of emotional aura surrounding what is said but *is also part of the literal meaning of the words*. If the speech melody is different, the words have a different meaning.

4. Janáček, 1989, pp. 40-43.
5. Ibid. p. 61.

The ethnomusicologist A. M. Jones was the first great pioneer in the transcription and analysis of African music. He was keenly aware that the Ewe tribe in Ghana, whose music he analyzed, spoke a tonal language. He also noted how difficult it is to be sure of the exact pitches in ordinary speech without some objective device to record them. He wrote of this problem of comparing speech melody to song melody as follows:

> It is obvious that we cannot start to evaluate the problem unless we can be sure of the reliability of the data we use. In the case of the song melody this is fairly straightforward. . . . In the realm of speech we are presented with a very much more difficult problem involving considerable finesse. As contrasted with the relatively sustained and stable sounds produced in singing, speech does not to our ears present a series of defined musical notes. . . . Clearly the subjective method of listening is totally inadequate. What we need is an apparatus which will give an objective and measurable reading of the tones used in speaking. The tonometer we invented for the purpose . . . consists of three units—a microphone, an amplifier, and the tonometer itself. The latter indicates the speech tones by means of a row of 66 metal reeds tuned between the limits of 70 and 287 vibrations per second, which is what is needed in dealing with adult male voices.[6]

After recording the speech pitches and then an Ewe song using the same words, Jones put the results on graph paper with one line for the speech and another for the song. From this he concluded:

> There is an obvious trend of agreement in the direction of the two graphs . . . To a surprising extent, in spite of the musical dictates inherent in creating a good tune, the range of semitones covered by the song and by the speaking voice is by and large remarkably similar.[7]

More recently, the ethnomusicologist Simha Arom published a large study of Central African music. He, like Jones, also notes the tonal nature of the languages he encountered:

> Indeed, almost all the Central African vernacular languages are tonal. In a tonal language, each vowel can be inflected; the same syllable, when uttered at different vocal pitches or registers, may carry quite different meanings. The Ngbaka language, for instance, has three *level* tones (low, medium, high), to which are added four *gliding* tones. . . . It is easy enough to imagine the number of melodic cells that such combinations could generate. . . . It follows, if the words of a song are to keep their meaning and remain intelligible, that its melody must necessarily remain subservient to them and reproduce their tonal schema. Every change in words of a given melody, inevitably entails a modification in the melodic line.[8]

6. Jones, 1959, vol. 1, pp. 233–34.
7. Ibid. p. 236.
8. Arom, 1991, pp. 11–12.

In Africa, both the rhythm and pitch of languages are directly mirrored in vocal music, while in the West it is primarily the rhythm of languages that affects folk music and art music drawn directly or indirectly from it. In terms of recent Western musical history, it is precisely the "nationalist" composers like Janáček, Debussy, Bartók, Stravinsky (from the early Russian ballets at least through *Les Noces*), Ives, Copland, and, in our own time, me, Adams, and others who show the effect of spoken language (via folk music, hymn tunes, or other more recent popular sources) in their compositions.

DU: Why has language become interesting for you as a basis for your compositions since a certain time, especially in your most recent work?

SR: My interest in using spoken language as a basis for music began as the indirect result of reading the poetry of William Carlos Williams in the 1950s. I tried to set his poetry to music and found I only "froze" its flexible American speech-derived rhythms. Later, in the early 1960s, it occurred to me that using actual tape recordings of Americans speaking might serve as a basis for a musical piece that would utilize the same sources as Williams's poetry. This led to my two early speech tape pieces, *It's Gonna Rain* (1965) and *Come Out* (1966). Both of these tape pieces presented the voices of black Americans whose speaking voices were extremely melodic. Through the use of repetition and phase shifting the speech melody of their voices became intensified.

Years later, in the 1980s, I became interested in constantly changing meters to capture what I heard in setting the classical Hebrew of the Psalms in *Tehillim* (1981). This technique of constant meter change led to *The Desert Music* (1984) where I was finally able to successfully set Dr. Williams's poetry to music for chorus and orchestra. Eventually all this came full circle in 1988 when I used recorded speaking voices together with a string quartet in *Different Trains* (1988). In this piece, the recorded speech melody formed the basis for melodic material to be played by the strings. The unity between the speech melody and the music became complete. More recently, in *The Cave* (1993), it is seeing and hearing the Israeli, Palestinian, and American interviewees speaking about the biblical characters Abraham, Sarah, Hagar, Ishmael, and Isaac that forms the theatrical basis for the piece. As each interviewee speaks on one of five large video screens, their speech melody is exactly doubled by some or all of the musicians who are themselves on stage next to, above or below the video screens.

What particularly interests me in using spoken language, as opposed to setting a text to music for voices to sing, is what could be called the "documentary" aspect of recorded voices. The particular voices of my governess, the porter, and the Holocaust survivors in *Different Trains* tell the actual story of a period in history from just before to just after World War II. There is no singer's "interpretation" but, rather, this: people bearing witness to their own lives. Their speech melody is the unpremeditated organic expression of the events they lived through. The same can be said of the Pentecostal street preacher in *It's Gonna Rain,* the boy accused of murder in *Come Out,* as well

as all the Israelis, Palestinians, and Americans in *The Cave*. As Janáček said;
"speech melodies are windows into peoples' souls."[9]

DU: Could you try to describe how you are working with language?

SR: As I have indicated, there are basically two different areas. The first is using
actual speech recordings as source material, which may then be combined with
musical instruments, and sometimes singers. In this case, the musical material
for the instruments and singers comes from the speech melody of the recorded
voices.

The second area is the traditional one; setting a text to music to be sung by
singers accompanied by instruments. Within this area there is also a more unusual case where singers will not sing words but, rather, imitate the sound of
some of the musical instruments playing in the ensemble. This kind of "vocalise" singing is found in my early works *Drumming* (1971), *Music for Mallet
Instruments, Voices, and Organ* (1973) and *Music for 18 Musicians* (1976). In
this case, the singers become another "instrumental" sound in the ensemble. In
The Desert Music (1984), the singers sometimes sing William Carlos Williams's poetry and at other times they sing just the syllable "dee" and become
part of the overall orchestral sound.

My most recent piece, *Proverb* (1995), returns to setting a text. In this case,
it is a short one from the philosopher Ludwig Wittgenstein: "How small a
thought it takes to fill a whole life!" This text is set for three sopranos, who
sing it in canons of ever augmenting durations. In contrast to their singing of
these words, two tenors take just the first syllable of a word from the sopranos and sing long melismas (that may well remind the listener of Perotin) on
that single syllable for an extended period.

DU: In your music, do you appreciate the referential, semantic aspects of language
or rather its structural, syntactic features—and why?

SR: The most interesting thing about your question is that you leave out the most
important musical aspect of language; its sound. As a composer, if I don't care
for the *speech melody* of someone speaking, then the meaning of their words
is of no consequence. On the other hand, once the speech melody has caught
my ear, the meaning of the words can never be overlooked. Even in my earliest tape speech piece, *It's Gonna Rain,* both the speech melody *and* the meaning of the words are inextricably bound together. How could it be otherwise?
When people speak, the semantic, structural, and melodic issues from them in
one breath. The phrase "It's gonna rain" as said by the black Pentecostal
preacher in my tape piece from 1965 is at once a common everyday American
idiom, a reference to the biblical flood—and, therefore, the end of the world
(which in the 1960s clearly had nuclear overtones)—and the pitches E–D–D–
F♯. How do you propose to separate these elements? The beauty (and terror)
is that they are all one.

9. Ibid., pp. 121–22.

In the case of setting a text to music, as in *Tehillim, The Desert Music,* and *Proverb,* then I would say that again the meaning or semantic aspect is inextricably linked with the rhythm of the poetry or prose, which I believe you would call its "structural features." If the meaning is expressed in different words, we no longer have the same poem. How do you propose to separate the meaning from the structure of, "Western wind, when wilt thou blow? The small rain down can rain"? How will you separate them in simple prose like, "It's gonna rain"? (Even "It's going to rain" is a phrase of a different nature with different implications about the speaker.) How can one separate them in the example from *The Desert Music* (see ex. 56-2)?

Musically speaking one could, of course, set this text with different notes and one could also set it in a rhythm that went against its accents and syllabic structure, but its linguistic rhythm as a line of poetry remains in either case. And the meaning of that line of poetry is locked into the precise arrangement of the words that make it up. Change one word—or the order of existing words—and you change the meaning. I have set this line with its American English accents intact, which intensifies the original rhythm of the poetry itself. In the music that follows, the above example becomes the subject of a three-part canon in the women's voices that is repeated several times. Thus, the subject of the words (repetition in music) and the music itself become one and the same thing. I have set the words not "poetically" but literally. I have done what they say.

Thus, the answer to your question is that the meaning and rhythm of words interests me in equal measure. Why?—Because they cannot be separated.

DU: How do the possibilities of electronics influence your use of language in your work?

SR: Since I began working in this way in the 1960s, tape recorders were already a reality in music for several years. I became interested in using recordings for the reasons I mentioned earlier, having to do with the poetry of William Carlos Williams. The technology not only was there, it was inexpensive enough so that I could work with it at home. I found that it was not a question of having professional quality equipment or not being able to work with tape. Rather, it depends on one's musical ideas. If those ideas incorporate the "graininess" of street recordings, like those used in *It's Gonna Rain* and *Come Out,* then it will be the excellence of those musical ideas and their working out that will determine if the finished piece is a successful piece of music or not.

Another aspect of technology and language is my use of the microphone to amplify a "natural" nonvibrato singing voice similar to that used in singing folk or jazz as well as medieval and Renaissance music. I am drawn to this kind of singing because it has the rhythmic agility needed to perform my music. It was then necessary to amplify it in order to it to be heard over many percussion instruments, as in *Drumming* and *Music for 18 Musicians.* As I said earlier, the bel canto voice seems quite inappropriate both to American English and to this time in history. The use of the microphone by popular, jazz, and rock singers for over 90 years has made a certain type of nonvibrato amplified

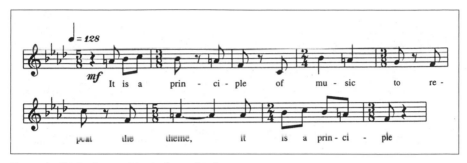

Example 56-2. *Desert Music,* from third movement.

voice very much the norm for our period in history. Since this is our folk music and since my music does have ties to this folk music, I was drawn to this type of voice rather than to an operatic one modeled on an earlier historical period in Europe when there was no such thing as amplification.

More recently in the late 1980s I began using the sampling keyboard, another device created for use in popular music. In essence, this is a digital recorder with a piano style keyboard attached to it. You can record any sound you want into it and it will play that sound back when you press certain notes you have assigned that sound to. I view the sampling keyboard, as well as the synthesizer, electric guitar, electric bass, and so on as contemporary electric folk instruments.

Yet another technological development has made an impact on my music and that is the computer. Like many other composers today, I use a software program to write music just as writers use a word processing program. The music is then printed out in a fully engraved form, ready for publication. Such a piece of technology not only saves a great deal of money for composers since they no longer have to pay copyists; it, like any other tool or instrument, has an effect on the music itself. Specifically, it would have been just about impossible for me to have composed *Different Trains, The Cave,* and *City Life* without using a computer and sampling keyboard. In the first two pieces, the prerecorded tape was made using both the sampler and the computer and, in *City Life,* all the sounds I recorded in New York City were then fed into two sampling keyboards that are played live on stage along with the rest of the instrumental ensemble. When a street merchant says "Check it out," that prerecorded voice is played back at precisely the right musical moment by the sampler players and at that same time the vibraphones and pianos and woodwinds all double the speakers speech-melody with no use of tape recorders during the performance. This allows all the musicians to make the small changes in tempo that naturally occur in performance but that are eliminated when following a prerecorded tape. This kind of technology will undoubtedly find its way into other pieces of mine and many other composers in the future.

Written for this book.

I didn't hear any of Feldman's music until 1962, when I heard a piece of Stockhausen's called *Refrain*. I only realized later that this was Stockhausen's "Feldman piece" just as *Stimmung* was his "LaMonte Young piece." In 1963, I wrote *For Three or More Pianos or Piano and Tape,* which was influenced by *Refrain*—which is to say that it was influenced by Feldman without me even knowing it at the time.

When I moved back to New York from San Francisco in September 1965, I didn't pay much attention to Morton Feldman. I knew he was there, that he was part of the group around John Cage, that his music was quiet. But at the time it was important for me to get away from all of it—from Feldman and Cage just as from Stockhausen, Berio, and Boulez.

In 1971, Feldman and Cage attended a private loft performance of *Drumming*. Later, at a party, Feldman and I had a chance to talk and from 1971 on we met from time to time. He was, as everyone knows who ever met him, an absolutely unforgettable human being. During that time he generously told me that my *Four Organs* had made a strong impression on him. Gradually I became aware of his *Piece for Four Pianos* from 1957 (eight years before my own *It's Gonna Rain*), which utilized a rhythmically free form of changing phase relationships. All four players play from the same score but are free to pass through the chords at their own pace.

By the '80s, when Feldman started writing longer pieces, I foolishly didn't take the time to listen to them and Feldman drifted out of my musical consciousness. Then, in 1987, Morty died.

Within the next few years I began to listen to some of his late works. Two of them, *Piano and String Quartet* (1985) and the *Turfan Fragments,* particularly struck me. *Piano and String Quartet* is the most beautiful work of his that I know, and on examining the score I began to see that many of its quiet mysterious chords were actually inversions of themselves. Repetitions of material were never exact repetitions. In the *Turfan Fragments,* there is again a play of rhythmic phase relationships within the music. Feldman was able to combine extremely chromatic harmony, soft dynamics, and generally slow flexible tempos with "minimal" phase and variation techniques. I felt like I was getting a composition lesson from the grave. I wanted to call him, to tell him, that I had missed the boat with his late pieces, to ask how he made them—but that was no longer possible.

I miss Morton Feldman, and I love and admire his music.

Written for this book.

Figure 58-1. Steve Reich and Luciano Berio, Torino, 1994. Photo by Garry Kvistad.

Before I studied with Berio at Mills College in California I heard his *Circles,* a setting of the American poet e e cummings for voice, harp, and percussion. It was sung by Cathy Berberian and conducted by Berio at the New School in New York in about 1960. It was an ear and mind opener. I can remember what seemed like numberless sentimental settings of cummings in the 1950s by American composers whose names I can't remember. In contrast, here was an Italian who clearly understood that cummings's poetry was largely "about" the individual syllables of which it was made. The first syllable of the first word "stinging" was separated into a very long held "ssss" followed by "ting" and finally "ing" by the soprano whose sibilance on "ssss" was answered by two sandpaper blocks rubbed together by a percussionist. The marriage of instrumental timbre with syllabic timbre went exactly to the heart of cummings's poetry. It was a lesson in text setting without need of a classroom.

When I studied with Berio from 1961 to 1963 at Mills, he early on played a tape piece of his, *Omaggio a Joyce,* which showed again how speech—often broken down into the syllables of *Finnegan's Wake*—could be a riveting source for tape music as well. It was more interesting to me by far than tape pieces made with electronically generated tones and it encouraged me later in 1965–66 with my own speech tape pieces.

As a composition student with Berio I continued to use 12-tone rows as I had done since 1960 while still at Juilliard. My procedure was not to transpose, invert, or retrograde the row but to repeat it over and over again. Berio saw a three-minute string orchestra piece I had written while still a student at Juilliard that used a repeated row throughout. He said, "If you want to write tonal music, why don't you write tonal music?" I said, "That's what I'm trying to do." Berio's straight-to-the-point response helped me on my way. I thank him for that and for his music.

Three Tales recalls three well-known events from the early, middle, and late twentieth century—Hindenburg, Bikini, Dolly. Each of these reflects on the growth and implications of technology during the twentieth century from early air transport to the current ethical debate on the future of our species. This debate, about the physical, ethical, and religious nature of the expanding technological environment, has continued and grown pervasive since 1945.

The first tale, *Hindenburg* (see ex. 59-1), utilizes historical footage, photographs, specially constructed stills, and a videotaped interview, which provide a setting for the archival material and text about the zeppelin. Starting with the final explosion in Lakehurst, New Jersey, in 1937 it includes material about the zeppelin's construction in Germany in 1935 and its final Atlantic crossing. The unambiguously positive attitude toward technology in this era is presented through newscasters of the era.

The second, *Bikini,* is based on footage, photographs, and text from the atom bomb test at Bikini atoll in 1946–1954. It also tells of the dislocation and relocation of the Bikini people, living totally outside the Western world, which determined their fate. While *Hindenburg* is presented more or less chronologically in four discreet scenes with silence and black leader separating them, *Bikini* is arranged in three image/music blocks that recur in a nonstop cycle repeated three times, forming a kind of cyclical meditation on the documentary events. A coda briefly explores the period of time after the explosions and ends the tale. Interspersed throughout are the two stories of the creation of human beings from Genesis. Not sung but, rather, "drummed out" by the percussion and pianos, as if they existed (as indeed they do) in another dimension.

The third tale, *Dolly,* shows footage, text, and interview comments about the cloning of an adult sheep in Scotland in 1997. It then deals extensively with the idea of the human body as a machine, genetic engineering, technological evolution, and robotics. While *Hindenburg* uses only one "cameo" interview from the present to comment on the past and *Bikini* uses none, *Dolly* is filled with interview fragments from members of the scientific and religious communities. Interviewees include Dr. James D. Watson, Richard Dawkins, Stephen Jay Gould, Rodney Brooks, Marvin Minsky, Steven Pinker, Sherry Turkle, Bill Joy, Jaron Lanier, and Rabbi Adin Steinsaltz, among others. Although similar to the earlier *The Cave* in the use of interviews, new formal treatments of the interview fragments lead to very different results. Specifically, "slow motion sound" (an idea I had in the 1960s, but which is only now technically possible; see no. 1, page 26)

Figure 59-1. *Three Tales*, Act 1, "Hindenburg," performed at Brooklyn Academy of Music Next Wave Festival, 1998. Performed by the Steve Reich Ensemble conducted by Bradley Lubman. Left to right, back row: Micaela Haslam, Russell Hartenberger, Edmund Niemann, Steve Trowell, Gerard O'Beirne, Robert Kearley, Nurit Tilles, Bob Becker, Olive Simpson; front row: Garry Kvistad, Elizabeth Lim, Todd Reynolds, conductor Bradley Lubman, Scott Rawls, Jeanne Le Blanc, James Preiss. COURTESY OF BROOKLYN ACADEMY OF MUSIC. PHOTO BY DAN REST.

allows one to see and hear people speaking in slow motion without changing the pitch of what they say. Another new technique, "freeze frame sound," is the sound equivalent of a film freeze frame in that a single vowel or consonant is extended for a long time leaving a kind of audible vapor trail behind each speaker that becomes part of the overall harmony. In addition, a talking robot has an important role. The two versions of the creation of human beings, the Tree of Knowledge, and other biblical material are presented in various ways. Different attitudes toward the science and technology we so avidly embrace are embedded in the interview fragments, including a religious perspective not heard in public discussion.

Three Tales is a new kind of musical theater in which historical film and video footage, videotaped interviews, photographs, text, and specially constructed stills are created on the computer, transferred to videotape, and projected on one large 32-foot screen. Sixteen musicians and singers take their place onstage below the screen. The completed work runs about 65 minutes.

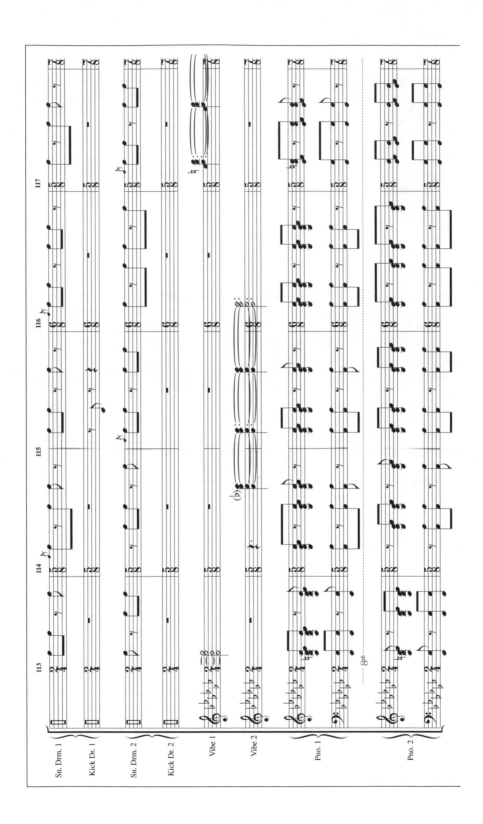

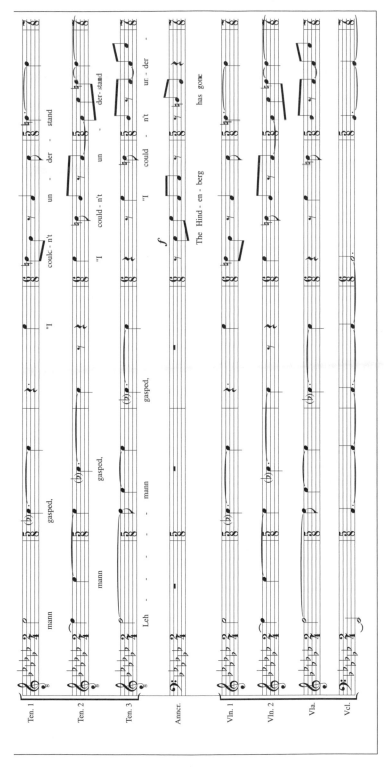

Example 59-1. *Three Tales*: Act 1, "Hindenberg," Scene 4, mm. 113–17. Copyright by Hendon Music, Inc., a Boosey & Hawkes Company. Reprinted by permission.

Three Tales is co-commissioned by the Vienna Festival, Barbican Centre—London, Festival d'Automne a Paris, Hebbel Theater—Berlin, the Holland Festival, Settembre Musica—Torino, Centre Belém—Lisbon, Brooklyn Academy of Music Next Wave Festival, and the Spoleto Festival—USA. The completed *Three Tales* has its world premiere performances at the Vienna Festival May 12–15, 2002, and then at all the cocommissioning venues. A version for television broadcast has been commissioned by the BBC for transmission in September 2002.

60 TRIPLE QUARTET (1999)

Triple Quartet exists in three versions: one for string quartet and pre-recorded tape, another for three string quartets (12 players), and a third for part of an orchestral string section (36 players).

Triple Quartet is in three movements, fast-slow-fast, and is organized harmonically on four dominant chords in minor keys a minor third apart: E minor, G minor, B♭ minor, C♯ minor, and then returning to E minor to form a cycle. The first movement goes through this harmonic cycle twice with a section about one minute long on each of the four dominant chords. The result is a kind of variation form. Rhythmically the first movement has the second and third quartet playing interlocking chords (see ex. 60-1) while the first quartet plays longer melodies in canon between the first violin and viola against the second violin and cello.

The slow movement is more completely contrapuntal with a long slow melody in canon eventually in all 12 voices. It stays in E minor throughout.

The third movement resumes the original fast tempo, maintains the harmonic chord cycle, but modulates back and forth between keys more rapidly. The final section of the movement ends in the original key of E minor.

The initial inspiration for the piece comes from the last movement of Bartók's Fourth Quartet. While no musical material is taken from the Bartók, its energy was my starting point. While I was working on *Triple Quartet,* two other composers found their way into my consciousness. As I was beginning the piece my friend Betty Freeman sent me a CD of the complete Schnittke string quartets performed by the Kronos Quartet. I had never heard a note of his music. In listening to his quartets I was struck by his virtuosity, and moved by the incredible mesto of his Second Quartet. Listening to the "density" of his music goaded me to thicken my own plot harmonically and melodically. Rhythmically, the second and third quartets play in conflicting rhythmic values partly inspired by Michael Gordon's *Yo Shakespeare.* The result, all in all, is a piece considerably more dissonant and expressionistic than expected.

Triple Quartet was commissioned by and is dedicated to the Kronos Quartet. It is approximately 15 minutes in duration.

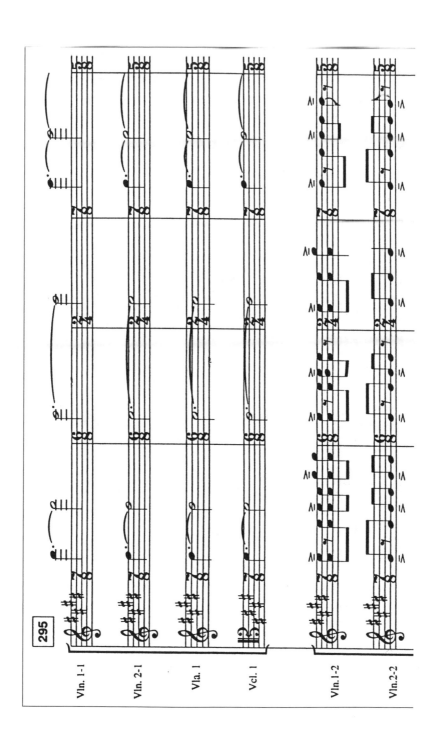

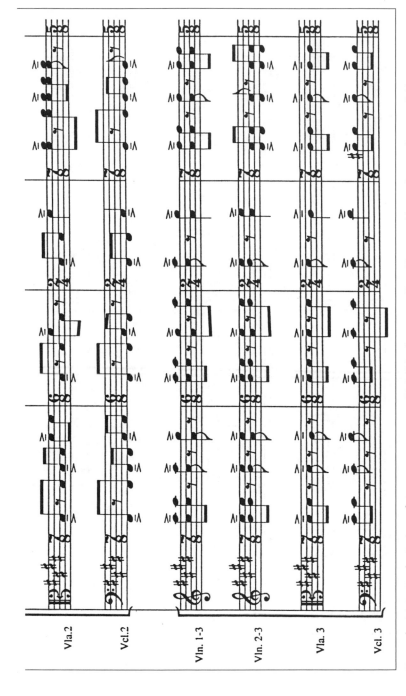

Example 60-1. *Triple Quartet*, first movement, mm. 295–98. COPYRIGHT © BY HENDON MUSIC, INC., A BOOSEY & HAWKES COMPANY. REPRINTED BY PERMISSION

Pirke Avot 2:1

Know what is above you.
An eye that sees,
an ear that hears
and all your deeds recorded in a book.

Know What is Above You was written in a little over a week in April 1999. It was commissioned by WNYC in New York City for the early music vocal group Anonymous 4. Scored for three sopranos and one alto, it is three minutes in duration. First the melody is sung by sopranos 1 and 3, and then goes immediately into canon with sopranos 1 and 3 singing against soprano 2 and alto. The canon is repeated again in somewhat longer rhythmic values and is repeated a third time in still longer values coming to a cadence in G minor where it began. The singing is accompanied by three small tuned drums similar to the drums used in my earlier *Tehillim*.

The text is an excerpt from Pirke Avot, a small tractate of the Mishna (the earliest part of the Talmud, edited into final form in the second century C.E.), which deals with ethics. It became so popular in traditional Judaism that it is reprinted in all prayer books. The excerpt may seem "judgmental" to our contemporary American sensibility. For much of the twentieth century, the scientific worldview has increasingly described us only as molecules of various substances electrically charged for a longer or shorter lifetime. In contrast, this text suggests that we are not alone, that an Eternal Being cares about us, that our every thought, word, and deed has its effect on our character, our soul, and on the souls of those around us—and that it all really matters.

Written for *Opera Magazine* on its fiftieth anniversary; the questions are from the magazine's editor, Andrew Clements.

Why should composers still write operas today?

How will the form evolve in the twenty-first century, and will it survive?

When composers want to take something that seizes their attention from the world around them and bring it into their music, the result is usually opera or a more recent form of music theater. Whether it be the opening of the Suez Canal, Nordic mythology, Hogarth etchings, or Abraham's burial place, anything of compelling interest to the composer will serve as material for a music theater work. It is therefore difficult to imagine composers ever tiring of composing operas.

That said, the only way music theater will remain of interest is if its form is constantly changing to honestly reflect its time and place. While there may be reasons to summon up an earlier form (Stravinsky evoking Mozart for the eighteenth-century tale of *The Rake's Progress*), in most cases the composer will consciously or unconsciously reflect his or her time and place. Weill's *Threepenny Opera* drastically alters conventional operatic vocal style and orchestration to suit Weimar Germany, yet the result is both timeless and universal. At the end of the twentieth century, I find collaborating with a digital video artist like Beryl Korot, to create music theater works with one or several video projection screens creating both the mise-en-scène and dramatic content of the work, to be perfectly natural in a world awash in computers and television. Instead of an orchestra created over 100 years ago, when balance between strings, wind, brass, and hardly any percussion was achieved by multiplying strings to huge numbers, I find it idiomatic to use a small ensemble of solo strings, winds, and lots of percussion, with amplification particularly on the strings to create a balance while maintaining great rhythmic agility. Likewise, a huge vocal apparatus with wide vibrato will not work in such an ensemble and needs to be replaced by amplified lighter nonvibrato voices as found in early music or jazz. The possibility of using sampling keyboards that can record and then play back documentary sound as part of the musical ensemble is another powerful tool for future music theater.

The prognosis is for long life. Eyes and ears open to the world we live in. All good opera is ethnic opera.

63 LIGETI (2000)

Reich was invited to contribute to a collection of short pieces about György Ligeti for the program of a concert of Ligeti's music given by the Ensemble Sospeso in New York City, on March 25, 2000, Bartók's birthday.

I first met György Ligeti in Berlin in 1973 at the Akademie der Kunst where I was performing *Drumming* with my ensemble. He was warm, friendly, and complimentary, and I remember making some gently kidding remark about how much money he must have made when his *Atmosphères* was used as film music by Stanley Kubrick in *2001*. Ligeti immediately made it clear to me in no uncertain terms that he had been, in essence, ripped off by Kubrick. A few months later, I asked if he would write on my behalf to the DAAD in Berlin. He did and, as a result, I was an artist in residence there, briefly, in 1974. Many years later we spent an evening together at a Kronos Quartet concert at the Brooklyn Academy of Music when they performed Terry Riley's *Salome Dances for Peace*.

I, like almost everyone else, have always had a high regard for Ligeti's music. *Atmosphères* is an amazing piece, which defines huge clusters as a compositional technique. It is not an experiment but a superbly realized masterpiece. He was immediately his own man—not "another European serialist." He has remained unique. His piece for 100 metronomes may or may not owe something to my *Pendulum Music,* but I had the pleasure of enjoying his highly amusing piece as choreographed by the superb Belgian choreographer Anne Teresa de Keersmaeker.

Ligeti has also proved to be the European composer who has best understood both American and non-Western music. Not only my own music but also that of Riley and, more recently, Nancarrow has benefited from his perceptive interest. He has been able to absorb what interests him from our styles and make it his own in such a way that he remains totally himself. Ligeti has also, with the help of the great ethnomusicologist Simha Arom, become familiar with Central African polyphony. This music has been similarly "well digested." That Ligeti mentions both Riley and myself in the title of his *Self Portrait* is an honor that means a great deal to me.

It is fitting to honor György Ligeti on Bartók's birthday in 2000. He is clearly the greatest Hungarian composer of the second half of the twentieth century. May he continue well into the twenty-first.

DE KEERSMAEKER, KYLIAN, AND EUROPEAN DANCE (2000)   64

Written especially for this book.

In 1981 or 1982, I received a letter from a young Belgian choreographer and dancer asking if it was all right for three musicians in my ensemble to perform *Piano Phase*, *Violin Phase*, and *Clapping Music* live for her new choreography, which would also include the tape piece *Come Out*. I replied that it would be fine. It didn't strike me at the time, but her name was Anne Teresa de Keersmaeker. She was to become one of the most important choreographers in the world. It was not until 1998 that I finally saw *Fase,* the hour-long masterpiece she was working on then. I had never seen such a revelatory choreography done to my music. She knew precisely what my early pieces were about.

The performers to date have always been de Keersmaeker and Michele Anne de Mey. The carefully detailed use of lighting right at the start in *Piano Phase* creates overlapping shadows that accentuate the repetitive motions that slowly move in and out of phase (see fig. 64-1). The second section, *Come Out,* is done on a darkened stage with two small hanging lamps directly over the dancer's heads while they sit on stools. It suggests a police station. The movements, all done while sitting, serve to intensify the feelings of interrogation, brutality, anger, and sexuality that are all implicit in the tape: implicit but never understood or mentioned by music critics, until de Keersmaeker captured both the technique and the audible theater in *Come Out.* The third dance, to *Violin Phase,* is de Keersmaeker's solo. Again, she not only captures the formal aspect of the piece but, during the extended resulting melodies near the end, goes to the heart of its underlying lyricism. The final section, done as a kind of "vaudeville step" unison duet to *Clapping Music,* is a light touch at the end, yet when the two dancers work their way from upstage left to downstage right, directly under the two "police" lamps still in place, the whole piece snaps together.

I actually saw other pieces of de Keersmaeker's before I finally saw *Fase* in 1998. The first was *Rosas danst Rosas,* which made clear beyond any doubt that here was an amazing new choreographer at work. Her combination of highly systematic organization filled with intensely passionate movement was something I had never seen before. She had taken the formal structure in American art, music, and dance of the 1970s and coupled it with a powerful emotional expressionism coming out of European art, music, and dance in the 1980s to create an absolutely riveting work.

In the years that followed, I saw *Stella,* danced to live performances of Ligeti's *Piano Preludes* and his piece for 100 metronomes. A few years later, I saw *Woud* choreographed to Wagner, Schönberg, and Berg. It became clear that de Keersmaeker was expanding her vocabulary both in movement and in her choices of music. Most recently, I saw her 1998 choreography to my *Drumming* where the relation between music and movement, so explicit in *Fase,* is now much more complex.

Of the many other choreographies that have been made to my music, undoubtedly the most remarkable is Jiri Kylian's *Falling Angels* done to *Drumming—Part One* (1971). I was fortunately able to attend a performance of this work at the Brooklyn Academy of Music in 1994 when the Netherlands Dance Ensemble performed there. As a basic mark of his serious approach to the piece, Kylian had the music played live by four drummers (in a loge next to the stage in full view of the audience) under the direction of Michael de Roo, who was already familiar with my music.

Figure 64-1. *Fase*, four dances to music by Steve Reich, choreographed by Anne Teresa de Keersmaeker and performed by, left to right: Anne Teresa de Keersmaeker, Michèle Anne de Mey. PHOTO BY ROSAS.

Many choreographers (and also a few music critics early on) focused on the formal organization of my early pieces to the unfortunate exclusion of all the interpretive and expressive nuances that make my, and indeed all, music, come alive. Kylian, on the other hand, saw both aspects at once and fused them perfectly in his choreography. While the dancers often form straight lines and work in unison, there are sudden, frequent, and surprising "microvariations" of personal nuance and psychological expression—often extremely amusing—that perfectly compliment all the small accents, stick noises, and interpretive irregularities that happen in any performance of *Drumming—Part One*. The effect of his brilliant choreography was to capture in dance just the fusion of intellectual rigor, rhythmic accuracy, and unpredictable interpretive individuality that is at the heart of any successful performance of this music.

De Keersmaeker in Brussels, Kylian in Amsterdam, and Pina Bausch, the source of contemporary European dance theater, in Wuppertal, along with younger dance artists like Wim Van de Keybus, also in Brussels, have created a large and varied body of work that American choreographers would do well to study and contemplate.

The following interview is based on various meetings with the composer in his New York apartment during 1998–99.

PH: How do you begin a composition? I think some people have the impression that the melodic and rhythmic details of your works are sometimes just by-products of the process of composition, and that the genesis of the works themselves tends to lie elsewhere. Can you say how a work forms itself in your mind, and if you ever develop a simple melodic or rhythmic idea and then work that up into a piece?

SR: In the early pieces, in the '60s and up to *Drumming* in 1971, I almost always began with a melodic pattern. I'd play it on piano or marimba or synthesizer and record it and then make a tape loop of the pattern so it would play over and over. I went back to the instrument and while the loop played I began in unison with it and ever so gradually increased my tempo so that I was finally one beat ahead of the tape and then two beats and so on. This was how *Piano Phase* was done. With *Violin Phase,* I became interested in stopping after I was four beats ahead, holding that canonic relationship and listening to all the melodic patterns that resulted from that two voice relationship. This introduced what I called "resulting patterns" into the work that became so particularly pronounced in *Drumming,* where they were sung by women's voices over the marimbas and then whistled or played by piccolo over the glockenspiels. The only early piece that didn't start that way was *Four Organs,* which began with a sentence on paper: "Short chord gets long"! People have often asked me about *Four Organs:* "What system did you use for the augmentation," and I replied "my ears," because if you look at it carefully there is no mathematical system. It's entirely developed by ear as to how long the duration of each little incremental increase in the durations should be.

PH: So you didn't construct the basic pattern for *Piano Phase,* it was a musical idea that just happens to be a very interesting mix of six and four?

SR: Yes, it was a spontaneous musical idea, but when I analyzed it there were two groups of three in the left hand and three groups of two in the right; the overlapping hands just naturally fell into those two separate patterns. Earlier in '65 and '66, *It's Gonna Rain* and *Come Out* are both driven by the engine of very melodic speech. That was the inspiration and the basic material of those pieces, both built around the way the words were actually spoken—and not just the melodic aspect of the speech but the meaning as well. *It's Gonna Rain* is really about the end of the world and *Come Out* is a civil rights piece. The last tape piece, *Melodica* in 1967, was a piece that I dreamed and then realized the following day with that toy instrument and tape.

PH: But what about the later larger works ? There must have been a certain amount of precomposition going on?

SR: In *Music for 18 Musicians* in 1976, I started by composing a harmonic cycle that was the basis of the piece. That was the first time but certainly not the last: *Sextet, The Desert Music, New York Counterpoint, The Four Sections, Electric Counterpoint, City Life, Triple Quartet,* and *Three Tales* all began by composing either a single harmonic cycle, or several—one for each movement.

PH: In some of those works where you develop a cycle, at some point did you walk into the room with a rhythm?

SR: In the text pieces, I always begin with the words. In *The Desert Music,* I went to William Carlos Williams's poetry. No music in mind. I knew it was going to be built on the text. I went through all his poetry and finally got those selections and then I printed them out on pieces of paper, and I started arranging the pieces of paper on my marimba. Then I realized I had to make copies of a couple of them and finally the layout of these sheets of paper was in an arch form, ABCBA. I then sat down and started composing harmonic cycles that seemed to match the tone and meaning of each text/movement. The first cycle would also be the fifth, the second cycle would be the fourth, and the third would stand alone. And what happens is that the first and last are the clearest tonally, although there's some ambiguity, it then gets more ambiguous in the second and fourth. Finally, in the third, the bass is wandering in thirds so you never can pin it down harmonically. The nature of the harmony reflected the meaning of the words. That was the precomposition.

Earlier, when I wrote *Tehillim,* I asked myself: "What part of the psalms can I say to anybody, Jewish or non-Jewish?" So, in making that choice, again the text came first, including the order of the individual psalm fragments. Then, with the text on the piano, I was looking at the Hebrew, just saying it and improvising with this little drum, and out came the melody, just the way it has for composers for centuries. A melody pops into one's head (or sometimes emerges gradually) as one says the words.

What was interesting was that, not only did the words come out with a melody, but the 12–123–12–123 rhythmic groups of two and three . . . where did that come from? I never did anything like that before! And that became a new for me way to make music, without short canonic repeating patterns, because this constant metrical shifting between groups of two and three (usually interlocking in two drums) was propelling the music, which could now be much more melody and accompaniment in a complex but extremely appealing new rhythmic context.

Later on, when I got to *The Desert Music* and found myself doing the same kind of thing, I said to myself: "But that's how I set Classical Hebrew—interesting." And then I thought: "That's how I can set William Carlos Williams, who wrote in what he called 'the flexible foot' "—the flexible syllabic lengths we find in American speech. It's now become part of my vocabulary. It began purely intuitively, but I later realized that it opened up a whole new kind of rhythm; constant pulse with ever-shifting groupings. Certainly I heard changing meters first in Bartók and Stravinsky, but this was carrying that idea a step further so that the piece *constantly* changed meter based on shifting groupings of twos and threes. As to how to exactly group them, the text and its syllables gave me the answer.

From *Tehillim* and then *The Desert Music,* the constant shifts of groups of threes and twos led to a number of works with that same kind of rhythmic underpinning. It wasn't an intellectual process in its birth, it was an intuitive musical response to the Hebrew Psalm text.

PH: And the purely instrumental pieces?

SR: I usually began the early pieces with a melodic pattern and, starting in 1976, I began using harmonic cycles to outline the structure of the piece.

The first thing in *Drumming* was the rhythmic pattern, which I started playing spontaneously on the two sets of tuned bongos that I had set up in my studio. The drums were tuned to G♯, A♯, B, C♯, and later came the idea of gradually changing timbre to marimbas while using the same pitches. The piece begins in the tenor range and works its way up from the bottom of my three-octave small marimbas to their top and then to the bottom of the glockenspiels and to their top. At that point, the pitches almost begin to disappear. At the end of the glock section, there's this high noise—actually the highest pitches we can still barely hear as pitch—which then descends again to the entire ensemble of drums, marimbas, glockenspiels, women's voices, and piccolo. That came out of very process-oriented thinking. But again it was driven by that rhythmic pattern. The rhythmic module supplied the energy that led to everything else.

As I said, with the exception of *Four Organs,* all the early pieces began with a repeating pattern—a pattern that suggested it might spin itself out in a musically interesting way. There were additional parts of *Piano Phase* that I rejected. Very early on, I realized repeating patterns are only interesting in an ambiguous metric context. *Piano Phase, Violin Phase, Drumming,* and even *Music for 18 Musicians* all work in a kind of ambiguous $\frac{3}{2} = \frac{6}{4} = \frac{12}{8}$ meter where there is ambiguity between three groups of four or four groups of three or six groups of two.

PH: Have you finished writing for orchestra now?

SR: Basically, yes. I've turned down a number of proposed commissions. The truth is that "the" orchestra is not my orchestra. It's clearly the orchestra formed at the end of the nineteenth century by Wagner, Brahms, and the other late romantics. My music's life's blood is rhythmic vitality and clarity which is best orchestrated by having one player to a part. To make the strings, for instance, as loud as they need to be to balance the percussion, I amplify the strings. In the orchestra in the nineteenth century, microphones did not exist and loudness was a function of the number of players. Hence, 18 first violins, 16 seconds, and so on. Gargantuan. It works for German romantic music, but it's acoustic foolishness with mine. I use amplification for balance and to keep rhythmic agility. No other way to do it.

This became really clear to me after *The Four Sections* in 1987 and I decided at that point to face the acoustic facts. On another level, I would say that my "assignment" in life was not to write orchestra pieces—that seems to be John Adams's "assignment." Mine seemed to be indicated, at least in part, by my early interest in speech as a source of musical sound and meaning. *Different Trains* in 1988 was an extremely important piece for me, because it made clear, once again, after a few orchestral experiments, what it is I'm supposed to be doing with my life.

Different Trains began as an idea: string instruments imitate the speech melody of a speaking voice. First, I thought the speaker would be Bartók, but there were problems with rights and I began to realize that I didn't need Bela Bartók looking over my shoulder as I wrote for string quartet—I mean, it's hard enough to compose as it is! Then I got interested in using recordings of Wittgenstein, but they don't seem to exist. Finally, I began thinking about my own life and the early train rides I used to take as a child between my divorced parents in New York and Los Angeles. Musically speaking, once I had the spoken words and saw they worked beautifully with the strings, what I then needed was a locomotive, which turned out to be the drumming rudiment where you alternate hands L–R–L–L, R–L–R–R. That pattern served well and "pulls the trains" continuously in the first two movements.

PH: What are the tools of your trade as a composer?

SR: Between 1965 and 1986, they were the various mallet percussion instruments, a piano, and some kind of synthesizer to sound like strings, winds, and brass, if they were needed, and an eight-track tape recorder. Occasionally, musicians would come over to try things. For instance, does the oboe go above the clarinet or clarinet above oboe? And brass players came over to try out different voicings of brass chords. When I was writing the guitar piece *Electric Counterpoint,* Pat Metheny suggested (as I didn't know anything about the guitar) that I just write single lines; and since there were so many of them, the chords were taken care of. When I was trying things on piano, they sounded very muddy. I had just been given a sampling keyboard and tried an electric guitar sample. The same material that sounded muddy on the piano sounded much brighter and clearer on guitar samples. That led me to try a sequencing program in my new computer that would actually play the piece back with the sound of multiple guitars. From that point on (1986/7), I began using the computer and samplers in place of the eight-track recorder.

PH: But you still use music manuscript paper?

SR: Oh yes, and I have music notebooks from 1965 to the present. Whereas before I would spend a month or so in one notebook, now (after about 1987) I can spend a year in the same notebook, because it's just little jottings in shorthand and then I work out the details on the computer. Basically I solve all questions of pitch at the piano and work out rhythm and orchestration on the computer. I do a lot of "Save-As" on the computer so I can trace how the piece grows and changes. I am a composer who lived first in the age of pencil and paper and now in the age of hard disks.

PH: I notice that your working space is quite small.

SR: If I didn't have the percussion in the middle of it, which I don't use as much now while composing, it wouldn't be so crowded. I'll move those instruments one of these days.

PH: Do you find the noise of New York disturbing?

SR: There are double windows in this apartment. When I'm hard at work and playing things back it's not so bad, but really the noise in New York is insufferable and when I go out I wear ear plugs at all times here.

PH: In Vermont, do you have other instruments?

SR: In Vermont, there are basically the same things in my studio. But the silence where we live there is incredible. When we take a walk, the loudest sound is our footsteps.

PH: How do you structure your working day when you're composing? I've noticed you do tend to answer the phone.

SR: I answer the phone generally; occasionally I won't. Basically, I've found I can go straight back to what I was doing. I have written most of my music between 12 noon and 10 at night. Before 12, it's morning prayers, exercises, breakfast, and, since most of my business life is connected to London, that's the time I can speak to people there because of the five-hour time difference.

PH: What is your favorite reading and what over the years do you come back to?

SR: The Torah and centuries of commentary thereon. I now read about 70 percent Jewish religious books and 30 percent musical books or books about a topic in our *Three Tales* video opera. For instance, now I'm reading about genetic engineering, DNA, robotics, nanotechnology, technological evolution, the sociology of computer users, and the ethics of human cloning. As a young man I used to read books on non-Western religions, but since becoming involved in Judaism, in the mid-'70s, that's become by far the largest part of my reading.

PH: And poets?

SR: I was very involved in contemporary poetry during the '60s in San Francisco, and the early '70s back in New York. I was particularly interested in William Carlos Williams, and in Charles Olson, Robert Creeley, and others in what was called the "Black Mountain" school. I haven't read a great deal of poetry since *The Desert Music* in 1984, although recently a friend's daughter, Tessa Rumsey, sent me her first book and it's quite good.

PH: Your early career as a composer in New York was bound up with the visual arts and visual artists. Is that still the case? Do you go more often to art galleries or concerts?

SR: I go more often to concerts but I have maintained an interest in the visual arts. When I was first here in '65, back from San Francisco, a lot of the people I was friendly with lived right near here—Richard Serra, Sol Lewitt, Michael Snow. For instance, the first concert I gave of my own music in New York City was given at the Park Place Gallery, run by Paula Cooper—who now has become very well known as a gallery owner herself—and it was a cooperative gallery of minimal artists. Socially, I was more involved with painters and sculptors than I was with other composers. There were some other composers I knew, but most were involved with John Cage and others in that circle; and while I admired those people, that was not my direction.

It seemed only natural through the connection with these artists that the galleries and museums that displayed their work invited myself and other composers like Glass to give concerts there, because we were part and parcel of this group of artists.

PH: So first with Cage's generation and then yours, there seems to have been a very close relationship here in New York between modern music and modern art—more so than in any other city?

SR: There used to be lots of concerts in art galleries, but I think the reason it stopped is because there is no close relationship now between musicians and visual artists; and when there is, that will happen again. That's also why our kind of music became known as "minimal music," because painters and sculptors were exploring these kinds of things before composers did. But already by 1976, *Music for 18 Musicians* was premiered at Town Hall, at that time a rather distinguished concert hall. And then I was frequently invited to Europe by the radio stations and festivals and we performed at more or less normal concert venues. Even in London, the first concert we played was at the ICA and the second was the first ever given at the Hayward Gallery at an exhibition of Mark Rothko paintings. But generally, from that point on, the venues began to be more traditional music venues.

As for concerts: I used to go to every concert of new music that I knew about; now I go to hardly any, just the very few I really want to hear. I go to many of the Bang on a Can things. I'm very fond of them. They give concerts where they don't just perform their own music, but also whatever they feel is worth listening to—most of which isn't (which is normal), but some is, and so they are lively events.

PH: Bang on a Can is a New York group of composers and performers who seem very much influenced by what you have done. How well do you know them, and what do you think of their work? I'm thinking primarily of course of the three composers, Julia Wolfe, David Lang, and Michael Gordon.

SR: Beryl and I have become good friends with all of them. Michael Gordon has written one piece in particular that I think is a very good and important piece, called *Yo Shakespeare*, which basically consists of layered, contrasted rhythms (see ex. 65-1). He wrote it mostly in $\frac{4}{4}$, but there are all kinds of conflicting meters going against this. He also invented something that seems excruciatingly difficult, but people now have learned to play it—which is the split triplet: let's say you've got a bar of $\frac{4}{4}$ and for the first two beats you've got a quarter-note triplet; well, you get, let's say, two of the notes to the triplet then a group of four eighths, and the last quarter-note triplet at the end. Now, I would be stopped dead in my tracks, but I've seen a number of groups do it. And what's interesting is that a lot of melodic material emerges out of a basic hocketing technique.

Then there's David Lang, who has written what I think is a very successful,

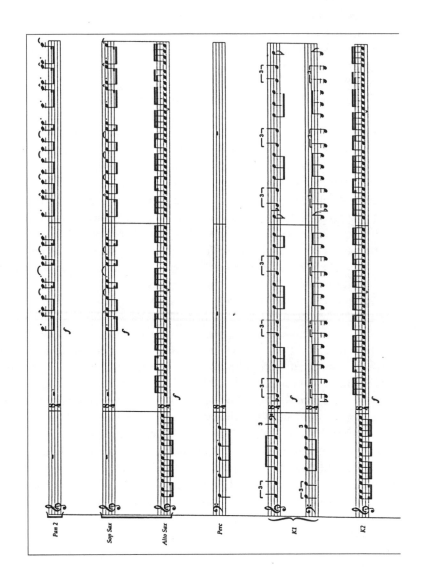

Example 65-1. From *Yo Shakespeare* by Michael Gordon. Reprinted by permission.

strong piece called *Cheating, Lying, Stealing* (see ex. 65-2). It's in an ABA form and basically what he's doing is to take a cadential figure where the notes really work, they're very strong, and he keeps varying the cadence rhythmically by an eighth note off each time. It keeps the material, which might be dull if you were just to repeat it, off-kilter in a way that keeps your attention. There's a long slow section in the middle with a very high register cello that is very edgy and very successful, and then goes back to the cadential material at the end.

Julia Wolfe did a piece called *Lick* (see ex. 65-3), which is heavily pop-oriented, as the title might suggest, and what's most interesting about the piece is really in the first three or four pages of the score where there's this remarkable use of time. You hear a very sharp attack and then utter silence. It's all counted—but you don't hear that. And then there will be another incredibly sharp attack, maybe two notes this time. And then there's nothing again, and you're just waiting until another one comes. And it works, your attention is riveted.

PH: Are there other American composers outside the Bang on a Can group whose work interests you?

SR: Yes, I've heard very good pieces from Michael Torke. He's an extremely gifted more traditional composer with a very fluent technique. He went through Eastman and then he went through Yale studying with Martin Bresnick—who also taught all the Bang on a Can people. He arrived in New York in his early twenties, and immediately got a lot of big performances—New York City Ballet and a lot of orchestral performances. At first, when I heard his music, I got the impression that he was one of these very talented kids who knew how to do everything but didn't have a voice of his own.

And then he wrote two pieces based on the Book of Proverbs. The first piece, *Four Proverbs* (see ex. 65-4), is for nonvibrato female voice, and chamber ensemble, and it had such a natural melodic flow that I was just swept away. It clearly was coming right out of him. It was the kind of music you simply can't argue with. I think it had to do with the text: direct and succinct. I mentioned that to him and he agreed. Additionally, there was a very interesting method he worked out for setting the text. He was attaching each word to a particular note, so that whenever that note appeared, then the word would appear—and as he made variations in the melody, the words would begin to shift around, too. But given the text of the Proverbs, this always worked, because it's so laconic. It's a lovely and intelligent piece. Then he went on and wrote a very emotionally charged piece for chorus and orchestra, *Book of Proverbs*.

Then there's Ingram Marshall, who is a very good example of precisely the kind of composer who has always had a very particular vision—somewhat subdued, somewhat, shall we say, Northern?—and very consistent. It carries through from piece to piece whether the piece is electronic or acoustic, whether it's chamber or orchestral. Ingram has an ongoing involvement with

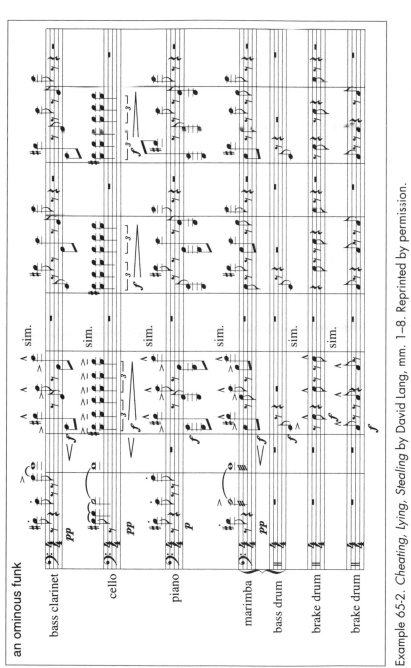

Example 65-2. *Cheating, Lying, Stealing* by David Lang, mm. 1–8. Reprinted by permission.

Example 65-3. *Lick* by Julia Wolfe, mm. 1–8. Reprinted by permission.

electronics, but it just seems to be part of achieving this kind of "wash" of sound that he can also achieve orchestrally. The orchestral piece *Kingdom Come* is particularly successful (see ex. 65-5), and so is the piece he was doing with you, *Hymnodic Delays*.

PH: One of the things that interests me about Bang on a Can, apart from the music, is the whole phenomenon . . .

SR: . . . banding together as a cooperative to do it yourself?

PH: Yes. First of all, the name is very "New York," but it also comments neatly on the attitudes it seems to stand for. And then it seems to be doing a little bit of what you and other composers were doing when you first came to New York—it's provided a point where things coalesce.

SR: Well, what happened when I began—and Glass and Riley, too—was that the composer was involved in the performance and there was an ensemble, at least in my case and Glass's case, which persists. That was unknown in twentieth-century America. In Bang on a Can, the composers are not involved in the performance primarily. But the "Bang On A Can All-Stars" are very accomplished performers who play all over the world, and who not only play Gordon, Lang, and Wolfe, but a whole lot of other composers as well.

PH: The other strong influence they acknowledge is Louis Andriessen.

SR: Michael Gordon and Julia Wolfe studied very informally with Andriessen in Amsterdam, and David Lang also listened to his music and looked at his scores. Louis is in the unusual position of being a European whose appeal is to the nonacademic strand in American music.

PH: And you hear Andriessen's influence a little bit in the choice of instrumentation as much as any musical technique.

SR: Right. They avoid the standard combinations and go heavily toward percussion and winds with amplification.

PH: And the Andriessen connection is something that in turn was strongly influenced by your work.

SR: Well. My ensemble first played in Holland in about '72 and I immediately met Louis and other people on the scene. Louis heard *Piano Phase, Drumming*, and *Four Organs* early on and was very enthusiastic and supportive. I think it inspired him to start his early group Hoketus. I had been talking about hockets in the late '60s, and he took the kind of things I was interested in, along with his own abiding love of Stravinsky, and put them together in his own way.[1]

PH: Also jazz bands.

SR: Yes, big bands, Stan Kenton–type things from the '50s.

Another person I had a lot of contact with as early as 1970 was Michael Nyman. I think Michael was so discouraged with the way things were musically in England in the late '60s that he simply was not composing. You know he worked with Thurston Dart and had a background in baroque music. He was interested in pop music, too. And given Maxwell Davies and Birtwistle and Sandy Goehr, there was just no place for anything like that. Performing with my ensemble and going through my music pretty closely encouraged him to form the Michael Nyman Band, which is where he really found his voice.

PH: And then the other English composers.

SR: I met all those people in 1972 when I went to England to perform *Drumming*. At that stage of the game, I couldn't afford to bring 12 musicians and singers with me from America, so I just brought over the hardcore and we joined up with Michael Nyman, Cornelius Cardew, Gavin Bryars, Michael Parsons, and Chris Hobbs, who rehearsed and then performed with us at the Hayward Gallery. Cornelius performed with us on the Deutsche Grammaphon recording (see fig. 65-1).

PH: Those composers formed what was then the English "experimental" school.

---

1. Reich quotes a definition of *hocket* at the beginning of No. 4.

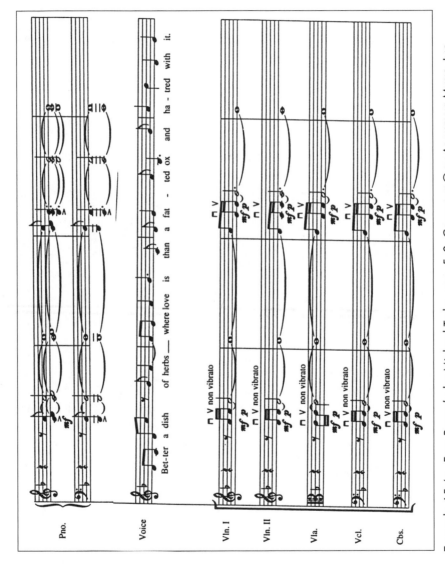

Example 65-4a. *Four Proverbs* by Michael Torke, mm. 5–8. Copyright © by Adjustable Music, Inc. Reprinted by permission of Hendon Music, Inc. a Boosey & Hawkes Company, Agent.

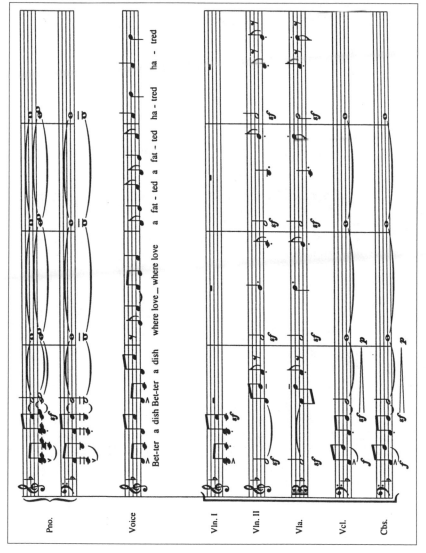

Example 65-4b. *Four Proverbs* by Michael Torke, mm. 51–54. Copyright © by Adjustable Music, Inc. Reprinted by permission of Hendon Music, Inc. a Boosey & Hawkes Company, Agent.

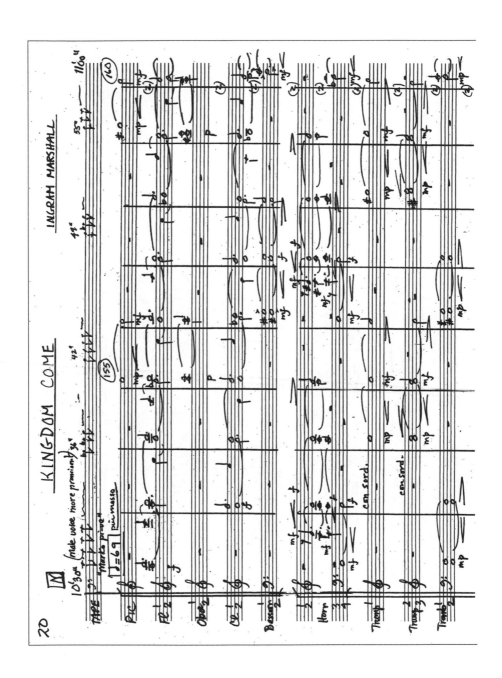

KINGDOM COME

INGRAM MARSHALL

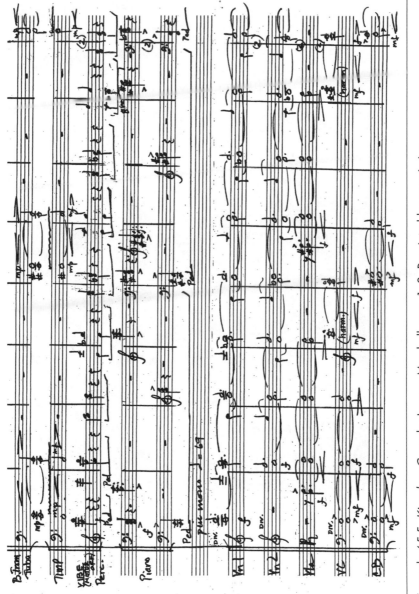

Example 65-5. *Kingdom Come* by Ingram Marshall, mm. 1–8. Reprinted by permission.

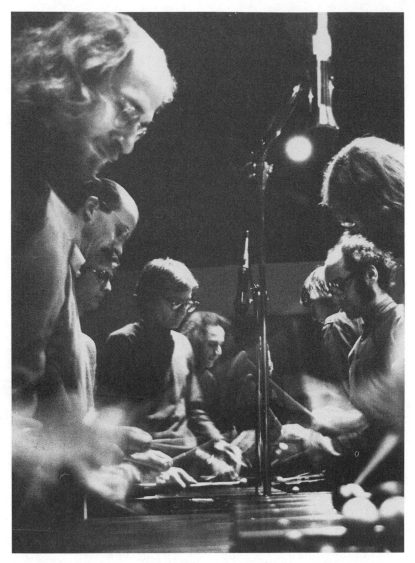

Figure 65-1. *Drumming* (part two) during rehearsal at Hayward Gallery, London, in 1972. Left to right: Russell Hartenberger, Gavin Bryars, Steve Chambers, Jon Gibson, Steve Reich, Christopher Hobbs, Michael Nyman, James Preiss, face just out of frame on extreme right, Cornelius Cardew. PHOTO BY CHRISTOPHER DAVIES.

SR: Exactly. And Howard Skempton was connected to all of them. I guess it was an influential experience for them—if you physically play a piece you take a lot home. But Cornelius, his thinking was quite different. I remember he couldn't accept *Clapping Music*—he said it was somehow against the audience. He had some leftist theory that we were "usurping the proletariat" or something.

PH: Because the performers get to clap?

SR: Yes, whereas I always thought of the piece as "music for the common man"; I mean you can do it without any instruments at all! But it's a real loss—he passed away so young.

PH: So your early appearances in England and in Holland definitely had a lasting effect?

SR: It appears so. But what is interesting is, where does it go? It always seemed to me that, starting from the very earliest days—when *In C* was around, and my early pieces and Glass's early pieces—that this was very fertile ground. And now, here we are with the likes of Arvo Pärt, John Adams, Louis Andriessen, and all the other people we're talking about, plus several others in Eastern Europe; so this has really become the dominant style today. And as a result of that, it's a very different and more open musical world now, compared to when I went to school in the late '50s when there was really just one way to write—à la Boulez, Stockhausen, Berio, or Cage.

PH: John Adams has acknowledged your music as an important influence on him; on some of his earlier recordings, his works were even paired with yours. What do you believe is the distinctive quality in his music, and in which of his works do you find this quality most strongly evident?

SR: John Adams is a composer with prodigious orchestral skill. I think it is that virtuosity, often coupled with strong emotional conviction, that really gets to people. He has been able to blend the kind of techniques that Riley, I, and Glass originated with a knowledge of and sympathy with late nineteenth-century romantic music that classical music listeners really connect with. The poet Ezra Pound talked about poets in terms of being "inventors" or "masters." I would put John in that second category and myself in the first. Obviously, there is some mastery needed to get your inventions across in a powerful way, and some invention is needed by every master. Nevertheless, there may be some truth in that distinction.

As you might imagine, I prefer his early work, like *Shaker Loops, Phrygian Gates,* and *Harmonium.* Actually, my ensemble presented the first performances of John's music in New York with him conducting *Shaker Loops* at the Guggenheim Museum in 1978. Since then, he has increasingly been involved with orchestral works and operas. I recently have come to admire his *Harmonielehre* for large orchestra, yet John is keenly aware that the present orchestra is a nineteenth-century creation trying to survive in the twenty-first century. I feel he is right to continue to write for it, since that seems clearly to be his "assignment"—his music is conceived for the orchestra. As to his operas, it seems that in *Nixon in China,* instead of orchestra and bel canto voices, he could have scored it for a big band of the period and pop-style singers. This could have been more evocative of the subject matter and more interesting in terms of orchestration. In other words, he could have learned from Weill in the *Threepenny Opera.* But this is a small point. John Adams is a great composer and I am proud to have had even a small influence on his music.

Figure 65-2. Left to Right: John Adams, Ezra Reich, Steve Reich in Vermont 1980. Photo by Beryl Korot.

PH: Still on the question of influence, you and Glass worked closely together for a while, then went your separate ways. Can you say anything about why that happened? And I would also be interested to know what aspects of his music you find the most significant—either from that earlier time or later.

SR: After Phil turned up at the second of my three concerts at the Park Place Gallery back in March 1967, he invited me to look at what he was writing. He showed me a string quartet that was certainly far from the prevailing dissonance of the time, but as yet, showed no clear alternative technique. Between March 1967 and November 1968, I looked at, played through, and criticized a number of the pieces he was writing. One was called *How Now* for piano and utilized modular material with a fixed order for playing the modules but no real addition to the techniques developed by Riley's *In C* or my Phase pieces. Then he wrote *In Again Out Again* for two pianos, which we played. Each part had repeating patterns of differing lengths so that they changed contrapuntal relationships so rapidly it didn't make much sense when listening. Finally, in November 1968 he composed *1+1* for one player and amplified table top. The player taps the table top with his or her fingers or knuckles. This little piece provided the basic technique for what I hear as his best works. Like most really good ideas, it was very simple. There were two rhythmic patterns and you could alternate them by addition or subtraction. For instance, if we call them A and B, you could have A, B, A, B, B, A, B, B, B, A, B, B, A, B. It was up to the player to do the addition or subtraction as they liked. Shortly afterward, in February 1969, he used this technique with pitches that could be played by any instrument. It was a single line of music that used the addition and subtraction he discovered in *1+1*. This new piece was called *Two Pages for Steve Reich* (see ex. 65-6). Later, it was shortened to *Two Pages*. I think that is the short story of why we "went our separate ways." Nevertheless, that piece is a remarkable work in that, as they say, he gets a lot from a little. It opened the door to quite a number of his works, including *Music in Fifths* and then the really beautiful *Music in Similar Motion*. He continued developing this technique up through *Einstein on the Beach* which is, of course, a great collaboration between him and Robert Wilson.

PH: What about European composers—I believe you've met Arvo Pärt on a couple of occasions. How did you first meet?

Example 65-6. *Two Pages* by Phillip Glass, mm. 1–3. Copyright © DUNVAGEN. REPRINTED BY PERMISSION.

SR: That was here in New York; he came to visit me in 1985 when he was here for a concert of his music in the Continuum series. I think I'd just finished *The Desert Music*, because I had it out on the piano and he looked at it and said, "You need a vacation!" Pärt said he had heard my music earlier on. But when you showed me the 1964 piece *Solfeggio*, I thought that it was an enormously striking and interesting thing to see that Pärt basically had the gist of the whole thing in '64—to have a completely serialized, tightly organized C Major scale. It's perfect! It's like squaring the circle.

PH: Some people seem to dismiss him as being just too simplistic.

SR: I find it amazing that certain music critics have nothing to say about him—as a matter of fact, he's a very good composer to analyze because he has such a strong technique—it's not just intuition.

PH: So you rate him . . .

SR: . . . of the living European composers, Arvo Pärt seems to me by far the composer I most want to hear more of, and to be the most important living European composer. In many ways he's working entirely against the grain of all the things we've talked about. The influence of popular music doesn't seem to have interested him at all, and the whole business of opera and theater seem to be of no interest either. So in terms of the zeitgeist, what's he doing? He's writing church music in the late '80s through the late '90s, and he's become enormously popular. What does this say? Obviously that he himself is a religious man who, because of his very compelling, very simple, and also very systematic musical style is able to reach people who seem to be thirsting for the very things his music gives them. And—because he sets religious texts—I think it is extremely positive and much needed in this ultra-secular, radically materialistic world we Westerners now inhabit.

PH: Most of the composers that we've been talking about don't write very much for the standard orchestra—they write for other combinations.

SR: Yes, I think that's a very juicy topic, on which there is already a bit in this book, but more could be said. The orchestra was never static until just after the time of Wagner—when it simply froze. The microphone—it's over a hundred years old now—immediately had a profound effect on popular music, particularly on vocal style, which could become more natural, smaller, intimate and yet be heard over a very raucous background. This apparently didn't make an impression on composers like Stravinsky, Bartók, and Schoenberg in the early part of the twentieth century. But after World War II, there was a huge shift. First of all, America became the dominant country on the planet and its culture began to affect Europe and even countries outside the Western world. And, in doing so, the orchestra begins to be seen, correctly, as a European period piece. Absolutely perfect for the period. But the period ceases to exist. And nowadays, most of the people we've been talking about are people who are looking for other kinds of ensembles. It seems to me that every historical period has its orchestra, which is not just a predilection of a particular composer but also embodies the culture that all these composers are living in. I would say the amplified ensemble is "the orchestra" of our time.

PH: So we almost have two "classical" music cultures living side by side.

SR: Well, now we're wondering what will become of the whole thing. Why such enormous plates full of Mozart and such skimpy servings of Perotin, Machaut, or Josquin? Certainly not musical quality. Rather, the orchestra is large and expensive and has to be fed with now rather doubtful income from several concerts a week of the same repertory of about 50 pieces. My preference would be to see the numbers of orchestras shrink into a more sustainable position. We would have a smaller number of very dedicated first-rate orchestras, so one could get excited about hearing the C minor symphony of Beethoven, done with such dedication because it wasn't done to death. And I get the feeling that that is the way it's going.

PH: But you still have people, probably far too many people, training to be members of the conventional symphony orchestra.

SR: When I was at Juilliard back in the '50s, there were orchestral types and soloists; and then there were the other people, primarily chamber musicians, who were going their own way. The people in the orchestral world auditioned for job openings in those large musical corporations, with medical benefits, guaranteed income, and a secure financial life. The others had to invent their lives, very much as some composers invent their lives. Even at that point, I found myself friendly with the jazz types, the percussionists, the pianists, and string players who were going toward chamber music, early music, and new music. They were dedicated to the idea that they were going to make a living playing the music they loved—and most of them have.

PH: And they are the ones who have been most involved in creating the kind of vibrant new music we've been discussing. It's hard to believe that in 30 years, the same people who are the force behind the orchestras—the fundraisers, the money givers—that they will still be there with the same philosophy.

SR: I don't see it—because it seems like that kind of culture is receding. The orchestras devour a huge amount of money, and their size and financial metabolism dictates almost everything else that follows. The sociology of most of those people is really remarkably consistent with the overblown proportions of the organization itself. Of course, there are always exceptions and the most striking and interesting by far is Michael Tilson Thomas and the way he is leading the San Francisco Symphony.

Thomas is certainly the greatest living American conductor. His performances and recordings of Ives and Gershwin, perhaps our greatest American composers, are the best on the planet. I've been fortunate in having him perform my music since back in 1971, when he had the audacity to perform *Four Organs* with me and three members of the Boston Symphony Orchestra. The performance at Carnegie Hall created a riot, because of the nature of my piece on an otherwise more or less normal orchestral concert presented to the usual conservative Boston Symphony Orchestra audience in New York. Now, what is interesting here is that *Four Organs* is obviously not an orchestral piece—only four keyboard players and one percussionist shaking maracas.

The orchestra has within it the possibility of being divided into all sorts of smaller traditional or highly unusual combinations. So, cut to 1996, and there is MTT in San Francisco opening his first June Festival with Ives's *Holiday Symphony* (preceded by Lou Harrison, who worked with Ives, reading Ives's text for each holiday), followed by Cage's *Renga with Apartment House,* with members of the Grateful Dead performing. The next day he had me performing *Clapping Music* with one other percussionist from the orchestra, Meredith Monk singing solo, piano music of Henry Cowell, Harrison's *Organ Concerto* for small ensemble, many other pieces for all sizes and combinations of instruments, and, finally, Thomas himself improvising with members of the Grateful Dead on a tone cluster of Henry Cowell. Now, how about that for a couple of orchestral concerts? Needless to say, Davies Hall was sold out. Orchestral administrators elsewhere seem to think programming movie music will save the day—can you believe it?

How about a Music Center with maybe 120 musicians and three music directors, one for medieval, Renaissance, and baroque music, a second for classical and romantic, and a third for twentieth- and twenty-first-century music? Ernest Fleishmann, when he ran the Los Angeles Philharmonic, also suggested this as a plan for the future. I believe it might be worthwhile both for musicians and listeners—for instance, a cellist who had studied gamba but then started playing romantic orchestral music might be able to join the early music specialists for a few concerts. A percussionist, tired of their limited role in classic and romantic music, might enjoy performing a number of twentieth-century concerts with an ensemble oriented heavily toward percussion and keyboards. Listeners like the kids who made *Chant,* a Gregorian chant CD, a best-seller, and who regularly buy early music recordings along with their rock and roll, might actually go to the music center to hear a concert of organum. Instead of 150 years of orchestral music, the music center could offer 1,000 years of music.

Figure 65-3. Left to Right: Steve Reich, Terry Riley, Phil Lesh, Michael Tilson Thomas in San Francisco, 1996. PHOTO BY JOSHUA ROBISON.

I don't know if the orchestral situation is as problematic in Europe, but I get the feeling they are experiencing some fall-off in interest and attendance.

PH: Your work certainly still receives a lot of support from European promoters in terms of commissions and first performances. I know that *The Cave* could only really have happened in the way it did because of the commitment from mostly European presenters, and I understand it's the same with the large piece you're currently working on, *Three Tales*. Both these works use prerecorded speech-melody and are collaborations with your wife, the video artist Beryl Korot. How do they differ from each other musically?

SR: The basic assumption in *The Cave*, and in *Different Trains*, too, was that the music would follow the speech melodies of the speakers exactly. As they spoke, so I wrote. This was completely in keeping with the subject matter; the Bible and the Koran in *The Cave* and the Holocaust in *Different Trains*. I felt it would be inappropriate to electronically manipulate the speakers in those pieces. But when I finished *The Cave*, I felt I had gone far enough in the direction of having the music determined by speech melodies of those interviewed— so many fast changes of tempo and key. I wanted to use documentary material again but make the music take the lead instead of following.

In *Three Tales*, I found the solution. Prima la musica! Quarter-note equals 144 and I'm in three flats and if the radio announcer describing the zeppelin's crash isn't speaking in three flats and quarter-note equals 144, well, he will be soon! The idea in *Three Tales* is to maintain the *musical* momentum of constant tempo that is such a basic part of my music as well as the slow changes of harmonic rhythm that give it its "specific gravity" and then digitally change the sampled sound of Zeppelin motors or B-29 bomber drones or speech samples so that they fit the music. The musicians keep on playing and the sampled material just "rains down."

In *Three Tales*, I was also finally able to realize an idea that had just been a concept piece, since it was impossible to realize back in the 1960s; *Slow Motion Sound*. It's the exact equivalent of slow motion in video or film. I slow the speech or other sound down to many times its original length *without changing its pitch or timbre*.

In the first movement of *Hindenburg*, for example, there's an augmentation canon (influenced by *Proverb*) sung by three tenors on the words, "It could not have been a technical matter"—which is what the German ambassador said to the *New York Times* back in 1937 when the Zeppelin went up in flames. As the tenors augment these words, longer and longer, you also hear the famous radio announcer Herb Morrison ("Oh the humanity!") first at normal speed, and then with his voice stretched out to many times its original length. When anyone speaks, their vowel sounds are not just a particular pitch, they're actually glissandi sliding up or down, depending on context. Normally, the vowels go by much too quickly for us to perceive that, but when Morrison's manic voice is enormously slowed down, you hear these glissandi in the vowels sort of smearing against the tonally stable voices of the tenors. The effect, when coupled with images of the explosion in slow motion, is definitely unsettling.

Later, once in *Bikini* and constantly in *Dolly*, I use another technique I imagined in the '60s, but couldn't realize until just now. It's the musical equivalent of "freeze frame" in films, when the action just stops—freezes to a still single frame. In terms of sound it can be the final vowel in the word "zero" just continuing as "oh" for several bars of music after the speaker has finished. The final sound of a spoken word is continued with no change of pitch or timbre. It's creating a new kind of "choral" texture in *Dolly*.

PH: Will each of the three separate tales be treated in a similar kind of way?

SR: It looks at this stage as though Beryl and I will end up with a kind of A, A1, B form.

PH: That's the same basic structure as *The Cave*.

SR: Yes, but arrived at in a totally different way with radically different results. The first two acts will be somewhat similar to each other, in that there is very little contemporary interview material added to the archive material of the period. In Act 1—*Hindenburg*—there is just one woman we interviewed in 1997 who appears only in scene three. A cameo role. In Act 2—*Bikini*—there are no interviews. There are voices we have used from archive material of the period, but no material that Beryl videotaped with her camera, and who then appear as "talking heads." And the archive material itself is far more radically transformed both in the video and the sound than in *The Cave*.

Then in Act 3—*Dolly*—the story is basically short. She was cloned and we'll see how she's doing—not too much to tell. What's interesting are the potentially useful and the undoubtedly terrifying genetic possibilities floating around now. For instance; are we going to continue to sexually reproduce or are we going to go to the baby store? This seems to be on the way. Would you like to live forever? Marvin Minsky,[2] and others like him, say something like, "We can get you spare parts as long as you'd like—and when your brain goes, we'll get you a new one and then you'll be your own 'mind child.' And if that doesn't satisfy you, we can put electrodes all over your body, download every thought and emotion you have onto a floppy disc, upload that floppy disc into a robot and then 'you' will live forever." Feel better? So *Dolly* will be mostly filled with excerpts from interviews we do with scientists and religious people.

Right now we're half way through *Bikini*, and the first story of the creation of human beings, from Genesis 1, is drummed out on screen by the whole ensemble from time to time. That's the story that ends with human beings being given "dominion" over all the other animals on earth. No one sings it, it's as though it's happening on another plane. The performers are playing and singing and the biblical text just flashes every few minutes. Later in *Bikini*, we introduce the second story of the creation of human beings from Genesis 2. That's the story where G-d forms a lump of earth and breathes a soul into its nostrils and a living human is created and then put into the Garden of Eden to "serve it and to keep it"—quite a different assignment. And those two stories shed enormous light on our situation here in the early twenty-first century.

PH: So when is the first performance of the next segment?

SR: We're not going to present it like that. It was a mistake to present Act 1, *Hindenburg*, by itself, but it began with a request from Dr. Klaus Peter Kehr, the first co-commissioner of *The Cave*, to have something ready for 1997 at the Bonn Opera. We had part of Act 1 ready then. Since the Ensemble Modern was performing, they were then asked to repeat that performance, and so *Hindenburg*, the complete first act, began to be performed as if it was a complete work—it was not. So, we'll finish *Bikini*, and then finish *Dolly* and then the completed work *Three Tales* will be premiered in 2002.

PH: What plans do you have for other new pieces, apart from *Three Tales*?

SR: Well, the Kronos Quartet would like a big piece. Anne Teresa de Keersmaeker wants a short piece, which I look forward to. Then there's plans for a *Counterpoint* piece for solo cello with many other cellos prerecorded for Maya Beiser, the cellist with Bang on a Can. It also could be performed live with mul-

2. Writer on artificial intelligence, Marvin L. Minsky is Toshiba Professor of Media Arts and Sciences and Professor of Electrical Engineering and Computer Science at the Massachusetts Institute of Technology. His books include *The Society of Mind* (New York, 1986), an d(with Seymour A. Papert) *Perceptrons: Introduction to Computational Geometry* (New York, 1972; expanded edition, 1988).

tiple cellos. The Master Chorale in Los Angeles want a piece for the opening of the new hall there designed by Frank Gehry in 2004. The Amadinda Percussion Quartet in Budapest would like a large piece.

Additionally, Michael Gordon, David Lang, Julia Wolfe, and I have been talking about a new ensemble that would be the only American equivalent to European groups like the Ensemble Modern, Ensemble Intercontemporain, Ictus Ensemble, and so on. The ensemble we are planning would be the only one in the world to specialize in commissioning new works for live musicians together with audio, video, computer, and other media. I would hope to write a big piece for them, working for the the third time with Beryl Korot doing the video. The tentative title for that piece is *The Mind Body Problem*.

TEXT CREDITS

Number 3, "Wavelength," was first printed *in Presence and Absence: The Films of Michael Snow 1965–1991,* edited by Jim Shedden and printed by the Art Gallery of Ontario in 1995. Copyright © 2001 Courtesy of the Art Gallery of Ontario.

Number 6, "First Interview with Michael Nyman," copyright © Michael Nyman 1971/2001, first printed in *The Musical Times* 102 (1971), reprinted with permission.

Number 19, "Second Interview with Michael Nyman," copyright © Michael Nyman 1976/2001, first printed in *Studio International* 1976.

Number 28, "The Desert Music—Steve Reich in Conversation with Jonathan Cott," by Steve Reich and Jonathan Cott, reprinted from the album *The Desert Music* (Nonesuch Records #79101). All rights reserved. Used by permission.

Number 33, "Tenney," by Steve Reich, first published in *Perspectives of New Music* 25, nos. 1–2 (Winter–Summer 1987), reprinted by permission.

Number 34, "Texture—Space—Survival," by Steve Reich, first published in *Perspectives of New Music* 26, no. 2 (Summer 1988), reprinted by permission.

Number 38, "Different Trains," by Steve Reich, reprinted from the album *Different Trains* (Nonesuch Records #79176). All rights reserved. Used by permission.

Number 41, "On the Size and Seating of an Orchestra," first printed in *Contemporary Music Review* 7 (Part 1, 1990); copyright © OPA (Overseas Publishers Association) N.V., reprinted with permission from Gordon and Breach Publishers.

Number 44, "Weill," copyright © 1992, Kurt Weill Foundation for Music Inc.

Number 45, "The Cave." *The Cave* (synopsis) by Steve Reich and Beryl Korot. copyright © 1993 by Hendon Music, Inc., a Boosey & Hawkes company. Reprinted by permission.

Number 46, "Jonathan Cott Interviews Beryl Korot and Steve Reich on *The Cave,*" by Jonathan Cott, reprinted from the album *The Cave* (Nonesuch Records #79327). All rights reserved. Used by permission.

Number 47, "Thoughts about the Madness in Abraham's Cave," copyright © 1994 by The New York Times Co. Reprinted by permission.

Number 48, "Answers to Questions about *Different Trains,*" first printed in *Naehe und Distanz— Nachgedachte Musik der Gegenwart*; Hofheim-Wolke, 1996. Reprinted with permission.

Number 51, "The Future of Music for the Next 150 Years," copyright © Steve Reich, first published in *The Musical Times,* June 1994.

Number 52, "Beautiful/Ugly," first published in *Neue Zeitschrift fürMusik* 6 (1994), copyright © *Neue Zeitschrift für Musik*, Postfach 3640, 55026 Mainz, Germany.

Number 56, "Music and Language—Answers to Some Questions," first published in *du* magazine, Switzerland, May 1996.

Number 62, "Two Questions about Opera," first published in *Opera Magazine,* February 2000.

Alburger, Mark. *A Conversation with Steve Reich* in *20th Century Music*, 4, no. 12 (December 1997), pp. 1–18.

Arom, Simha. *African Polyphony and Polyrhythm: Musical Structure and Methodology*. New York: Cambridge University Press, 1991.

Baker, Kenneth. *Minimalism: Art of Circumstance*. New York: Abbeville Press, 1988.

Bartók, Bela. *Essays*. Selected and ed. Benjamin Suchoff. New York: St. Martin's, 1976. Lincoln, NE: University of Nebraska Press, paperback edition, 1993.

Battcock, Gregory, ed. *Minimal Art: A Critical Anthology*. New York: Dutton, 1968.

Berger, Maurice. *Labyrinths: Robert Morris, Minimalism, and the 1960s*. New York: Harper & Row, 1989.

Bernard, Jonathan W. *The Minimalist Aesthetic in the Plastic Arts and Music*. In *Perspectives of New Music*, 31, no. 1 (Winter 1993), pp. 86–132.

———. *Theory, Analysis, and the "Problem" of Minimal Music*. In *Concert Music, Rock, and Jazz since 1945: Essays and Analytical Studies*, ed. Elizabeth W. Marvin and Richard Hermann. Rochester, NY: University of Rochester Press, 1995, pp. 259–84.

Cage, John. *Silence*. Middletown, CT: Wesleyan University Press, 1961.

Cohn, Richard. *Transpositional Combination of Beat-Class Sets in Steve Reich's Phase-Shifting Music* in *Perspectives of New Music*, 30 (Summer 1992), pp. 146–77.

Coyote, Peter. *Sleeping Where I Fall*. Washington, DC: Counterpoint, 1998.

Crawford, Richard, R. Allen Lott, and Carol J. Oja, eds. *A Celebration of American Music*. Ann Arbor: University of Michigan Press, 1990 (essay *James Tenney* by Peter Garland pp. 477–486).

Cumming, Naomi. *The Horrors of Identification: Reich's Different Trains*. In *Perspectives of New Music*, 35 (Winter 1997), pp. 129–152.

Davis, R. G. [Ronnie]. *The San Francisco Mime Troupe: The First Ten Years*. Palo Alto, CA: Ramparts Press, 1975.

DeLio, Thomas, ed. *Contiguous Lines: Issues and Ideas in the Music of the '60s and '70s*. Lanham, MD: University Press of America, 1985.

Dennis, Brian. *Repetitive and Systemic Music*. In *The Musical Times*, 115 (1974), pp. 1036–38.

Duckworth, William. *Talking Music.* New York: Schirmer Books, 1995.

Epstein, Paul. *Pattern Structure and Process in Steve Reich's* Piano Phase. In *The Musical Quarterly,* 72 (1986), pp. 494–502.

Feldman, Morton. *Essays.* Ed. Walter Zimmerman. Kerpen, Germany: Beginner Press, 1985.

Fox, Christopher. *Steve Reich's* Different Trains. In *Tempo,* 172 (1990), 8.

Gagne, Cole, and Caras, Tracy. *Soundpieces: Interviews with American Composers.* Metuchen, NJ: Scarecrow Press, 1982.

Heisinger, Brent. *American Minimalism in the 1990s:* In *American Music,* 7 (1989), pp. 430–47.

Herzog, Avigdor. *Masoretic Accents.* In *Encyclopedia Judaica.* New York: Macmillan, 1971–1972.

Hillier, Paul. *Arvo Pärt.* New York: Oxford University Press, 1997.

Idelsohn, Abraham. *Jewish Music in its Historical Development.* New York: Dover, 1929; reprinted 1967; reprinted as *Jewish Music: Its Historical Development,* with new introduction by Arbie Orenstein, New York: Dover, 1992.

Janáček, Leos. *Uncollected Essays on Music.* Selected, ed., and trans. by Mirka Zemanova. London: Marion Boyars, 1989.

Johnson, Timothy A. *Minimalism: Aesthetic, Style or Technique?* In *The Musical Quarterly,* 78 (1994), pp. 724–73.

Jones, A. M. *Studies in African Music.* Oxford: Oxford University Press, 1959.

Korot, Beryl. *Video Art—An Anthology.* Compiled and ed. by Ira Schneider and Beryl Korot. New York: Harcourt Brace Jovanovich, 1976.

Lewitt, Sol. *Sol Lewitt.* Ed. by Alicia Legg, designed by Sol Lewitt. New York: Museum of Modern Art, 1978.

McCutchan, Ann. *The Muse that Sings: Composers Speak about the Creative Process.* New York: Oxford University Press, 1999, pp. 11–21.

McPhee, Colin. *Music in Bali.* New Haven, CT: Yale University Press, 1966.

Mertens, Wim. *American Minimal Music.* London: Kahn & Averill, 1983.

Nyman, Michael. *Experimental Music: Cage and Beyond.* New York: Cambridge University Press, 1972; reprinted with new introduction by Brian Eno, Cambridge: Cambridge University Press, 1999.

———. *Steve Reich: An Interview with Michael Nyman."* In *The Musical Times.* 112 (March 1971), pp. 299–31.

Potter, Keith. *Four Musical Minimalists: La Monte Young, Terry Riley, Steve Reich, Philip Glass.* Cambridge: Cambridge University Press, 2000.

Reich, Steve. *Writings about Music.* Halifax: Nova Scotia College of Art and Design, 1974.

Restagno, Enzo. *Reich acura di Enzo Restagno con un Saggio su "La Svolta Americana."* Turin: Edizioni di Torino, 1994.

Reynaud, Bérénice, ed. *Steve Reich: Écrits et Entretiens sur la Musique.* Paris: Christian Bourgois, 1981.

Rich, Alan. *American Pioneers: Ives to Cage and Beyond.* London: Phaidon, 1995.

Rockwell, John. *All-American Music: Composition in the Late 20th Century.* New York: Knopf, 1983.

Rosowsky, Solomon. *The Cantillation of the Bible.* New York: Reconstructionist Press, 1957.

Schwartz, Robert K. *Minimalists.* London: Phaidon, 1996.

———. *Process vs. Intuition in the Recent Works of Steve Reich and John Adams*. In *American Music*, 8 (1990), pp. 245–73.

———. *Steve Reich: Music as a Gradual Process*. In *Perspectives of New Music*, 19 (1980/81), pp. 373–92; and 20 (1981/82), pp. 225–86.

Schwarz, David. *Listening Subjects: Semiotics, Psychoanalysis, and the Music of John Adams and Steve Reich*. In *Perspectives of New Music*, 31, no. 2 (Summer 1993), pp. 24–56.

Snow, Michael. *The Collected Writings of Michael Snow*. Waterloo, ON: Wilfrid Laurier University Press, 1994.

Spector, Johanna. *Jewish Songs from Cochin, India*. Ed. by Pinchas Peli. The Fifth World Congress of Jewish Studies, vol. 4. Jerusalem: World Union of Jewish Studies, 1973.

Strickland, Edward. *American Composers: Dialogues on Contemporary Music*. Bloomington: Indiana University Press, 1991.

———. *Minimalism: Origins*. Bloomington: Indiana University Press, 1993.

Warburton, Dan. *Aspects of Organization in the* Sextet *of Steve Reich*. Ph.D. dissertation, University of Rochester, 1987.

———. *A Working Terminology for Minimal Music*. In *Intégral*, 2 (1988), pp. 135–59.

Wasserman, Emily. *An Interview with Composer Steve Reich*. In *Artforum*, 10/9 (1972), pp. 44–48.

Werner, Eric. *The Sacred Bridge*. New York: Columbia University Press, 1959.

Wickes, William. *Treatise on the Accentuation of Psalms, Proverbs, and Job*. 1881, republished New York: KTAV Publishing, 1970.

Wittgenstein, Ludwig. *Philosophical Investigations*. London: Macmillan, 1958.

In preparing the index for a book so full of names—people, institutions, concert venues—we felt it necessary to choose between those who are simply cited once or twice and those who have played a significant role in Reich's works and writings as represented in the text. This index is therefore somewhat selective.

The reader's attention is drawn to the following list of categories, under which may be found consideration of various aspects of Reich's compositional style and technique: augmentation, canon, cantillation, drumming (African drumming and talking drums), ethnic music, gamelan, harmony, jazz, melodic construction, metric modulation, phasing, process, resultant patterns, rhythmic construction, sampling, tape (including tape loops), speech melody, text setting, and video.

Steve Reich's name is sometimes abbreviated to SR. **Bold** print denotes a chapter or dedicated portion thereof.